LIBRARY OF HEBREW BIBLE/
OLD TESTAMENT STUDIES

481

Formerly Journal for the Study of the Old Testament Supplement Series

CONSTRUCTIONS OF SPACE I

Theory, Geography, and Narrative

edited by

Jon L. Berquist
and
Claudia V. Camp

t&t clark

NEW YORK • LONDON

T & T Clark International, 80 Maiden Lane, New York, NY 10038

T & T Clark International, The Tower Building, 11 York Road, London SE1 7NX

T & T Clark International is a Continuum imprint.

Library of Congress Cataloging-in-Publication Data
Constructions of space I : theory, geography, and narrative / edited by Jon L. Berquist and Claudia V. Camp.
    p. cm. -- (The library of Hebrew Bible/Old Testament studies ; # 481)
  Includes bibliographical references and index.
  ISBN-13: 978-0-567-02707-8 (hardcover : alk. paper)
  ISBN-10: 0-567-02707-4 (hardcover : alk. paper) 1. Bible--Geography--Congresses. 2. Space perception in the Bible--Congresses. 3. Space perception--Congresses. I. Berquist, Jon L. II. Camp, Claudia V., 1951- III. Title. IV. Series.

  BS630.C64 2007
  220.9'1--dc22   2007034509

Printed and bound in Great Britain by Biddles Ltd., King's Lynn, Norfolk

For James W. Flanagan,
co-chair of the Constructions of Ancient Space
Seminar in the American Academy of Religion and
the Society of Biblical Literature, 2000-2005,
whose scholarship and mentoring in critical spatiality
made this volume possible

CONTENTS

Part III
SPACE IN BIBLICAL NARRATIVE

PREFACE

From 2000–2005, the Constructions of Ancient Space Seminar met as a jointly sponsored program unit within the American Academy of Religion and the Society of Biblical Literature, following upon the work of the Constructs of the Social and Cultural Worlds of Biblical Antiquity Group (originally titled Constructs of Ancient History and Religion, with additional sponsorship from the American Schools of Oriental Research). The Seminar represented the first formal and prolonged consideration of critical spatiality within these guilds of religious scholarship. When James W. Flanagan called the Constructions of Ancient Space Seminar together (and invited me to co-chair the Seminar with him), few of us had done any work in spatial theory. Few even realized that Flanagan had been publishing on this topic for some time (1987; 1999). The scholars who undertook Jim's challenge did so more out of a conviction regarding his insights into the future of biblical scholarship than out of a previously held notion that this particular direction would prove as fruitful as it has.

The Seminar began to examine some of scholarship's assumptions about space, endeavoring to bring those assumptions under critical analysis. To do so, members of the Seminar turned to a number of different theorists in critical spatiality and human geography. One of the Seminar's goals was to search for helpful theoretical perspectives, exploring them to see what biblical studies (and religious studies in general) could learn from this work. Another desire was to bring into conversation different orientations within the academic guilds, especially across the divide that sometimes separates historical, sociological, and archaeological work from literary and cultural study. Also, the Seminar intentionally invited a mix of specialties within biblical studies (Hebrew Bible and Early Christianity), as well as philosophers of religion and scholars of contemporary religions. This produced a rich discussion. The Seminar's members produced a number of early works that began the critical study of space within religion, beginning with additional work by Flanagan (2000; 2001). Soon, a number of papers and ideas that began in the Seminar were published in a festschrift for James W. Flanagan (Gunn and McNutt 2002). The present volume (and a forthcoming volume in this same series) offers many of the other results from the Seminar, as well as from discussions that took place during meetings of the Catholic Biblical Association. Conversations on spatiality now occur in several dedicated groups not only within the American Academy of Religion and the Society of Biblical Literature, but also in other groups such as the American Society of Church History and the European Association of Biblical Studies.

Throughout these chapters, readers will find a number of definitions of space and theories of critical spatiality. In this still-new endeavor, there is no attempt to synthesize the various perspectives or to reach a conclusive agreement of terminology or method. Rather, these investigations point to a diversity of fascinating directions in which critical spatiality can embolden and enliven biblical studies. We hope that the conversation begun in the Constructions of Ancient Space Seminar and continued within these pages can take place more widely in the field of biblical studies.

Jon L. Berquist, for the editors

Works Cited

Flanagan, James W. 1987. Beyond Space–Time Systemics. *JSOT* 39:22–29.

_____. 1999. Ancient Perceptions of Space/Perceptions of Ancient Space. *Semeia* 87:15–43.

_____. 2000. Space. Pages 232–37 in *Handbook of Postmodern Biblical Interpretation*. Edited by A. K. M. Adam. St. Louis: Chalice.

_____. 2001. Mapping the Biblical World: Perceptions of Space in Ancient Southwestern Asia. Pages 1–18 in *Mappa Mundi: Mapping Culture/Mapping the World*. Edited by Jacqueline Murray. Working Papers in the Humanities 9. Windsor, Ont.: Humanities Research Group, University of Windsor.

Gunn, David M., and Paula M. McNutt, eds. 2002. *"Imagining" Biblical Worlds: Studies in Spatial, Social and Historical Constructs in Honor of James W. Flanagan.* JSOTSup 359. London: Sheffield Academic Press.

ABBREVIATIONS

ABD	*Anchor Bible Dictionary*. Edited by D. N. Freedman. 6 vols. New York, 1992
BR	*Bible Review*
FRLANT	Forschungen zur Religion und Literatur des Alten und Neuen Testaments
JBL	*Journal of Biblical Literature*
JJS	*Journal of Jewish Studies*
JNSL	*Journal of Northwest Semitic Languages*
JSNTSup	Journal for the Study of the New Testament: Supplement Series
JSOT	*Journal for the Study of the Old Testament*
JSOTSup	Journal for the Study of the Old Testament: Supplement Series
LHBOTS	Library of Hebrew Bible/Old Testament Studies
LXX	Septuagint
MT	Masoretic text
OTL	Old Testament Library
SBL	Society of Biblical Literature
SNTSMS	Society for New Testament Studies Monograph Series
ZAW	*Zeitschrift für die alttestamentliche Wissenschaft*

LIST OF CONTRIBUTORS

Jon L. Berquist
  Westminster John Knox Press

Claudia V. Camp
  Texas Christian University

Thomas B. Dozeman
  United Theological Seminary

Mark K. George
  Illif School of Theology

Mary Huie-Jolly
  Presbyterian Homes of Georgia

Wesley A. Kort
  Duke University

Burke O. Long
  Bowdoin College

William R. Millar
  Linfield College

Steven James Schweitzer
  Associated Mennonite Biblical Seminary

INTRODUCTION:
CRITICAL SPATIALITY AND THE USES OF THEORY

Jon L. Berquist

An Overview of Human Geography

For nearly two centuries, philosophers have been commenting that we have been witnessing time's annihilation of space. Karl Marx argued in this direction as early as his manifesto. In so doing, he reflected the early nineteenth century's preoccupation with changes in communications and transportation technology. Much attention was given to the cultural implications of these technology shifts, but Marx's interest was in the effects of such technology on capital accumulation (Harvey 2001, 378). By lowering the human and economics costs of transportation, trade made possible the accumulation of capital over a wider space. Spatial difference mattered less as a result of this temporal compression (Crang 2001). Thus, human geography suffered in the wake of this disregard for spatiality.

Through the first half of the twentieth century, geography's chief concerns included areal differentiation and locational analysis. In order to resist Marx's critique, geography attempted to show the differences between regions and to demonstrate how locality affected the production of meaning and culture. In the 1960s, the "new geography" arose in an attempt to combine geography with quantitative techniques in economics. The goal was to turn geography into an empirical science that could persuade through its numerical data. However, by the 1970s, geographers grew more insistent in their questioning of this approach's positivist assumptions (Gregory, Martin, and Smith 1994b, 3). Through the 1980s, this postpositivist human geography interacted with Marxism and the various post-Marxisms (and rejections of Marxism) that were occurring in a variety of disciplines. Human geography has remained diverse in its approaches, in part because most critical human geographers understand the need for geography to be an intentionally interdisciplinary discourse (Dear 2001, 13). Thus, the many disciplines with which critical human geography now dialogues lead to a great diversity within critical geographical scholarship. No Grand Theory has recolonized the field.

At the same time, geography has maintained its role as a form of social theory. Human geography seeks to explain how different elements of social existence interact in order to constitute specific societies that function or fail to function in specific ways, with sensitivity to variation over space (Gregory, Martin, and

Smith 1994b, 10). Thus, geography is inexorably economic, political, and social (Gregory, Martin, and Smith 1994a). All current geographies must be fully conversant with social theory's triad of race, class, and gender (increasingly augmented by the category of age). Cultural geography examines rituals, behaviors, symbols, and practices, with a focus on how these combine into sets of shared meanings that are, to some extent, location-specific. Thus, the study of cultural geography requires attention to power relations (McDowell 1994, 147–48).

According to Derek Gregory and others, four themes run throughout this present enterprise of human geography (Gregory, Martin, and Smith 1994b). The first theme is contextualization. Not only is there no regnant Grand Theory, but attempts to construct grand theory have been overshadowed by the attention to smaller scales of geographic production. Second, geography attends to a consistent blurring of boundaries between humanities and social sciences. Thus, geography has increasingly allied itself with the growth of cultural studies, especially dealing with the problem of the strategies of representation. Third, geography has embraced concepts of spatialization, such as Lefebvre's insistence on materiality. Fourth, human geography has employed a rhetoric of difference and of othering. This is related to the emphasis on contextualization, with its concerns for situatedness and competing subject-positions, but it also involves postcolonialism's productions and representations of alternative geographies, and it empowers the notion of plural geographies. Michael Dear would emphasize the themes of spatiality and diversity, and add a focus on the relationship of geographic thought to social action (Dear 2001, 24).

Some critical geographers have asserted that these trends in geography indicate a postmodern phase of critical human geography, beginning perhaps at some point in the mid-1980s. Certainly, the interaction of geography and postmodern theory came to the fore with two massive works of 1989, Edward Soja's *Postmodern Geographies* and David Harvey's *The Condition of Postmodernity*. These two books cannot be said to have establish a new school within critical geography, but they certainly opened the dialogue between geographic theory and the wider movements of postmodernism.

Much postmodern geography was oriented to describing postmodern (mostly American) cities. At first glance, this appears to be less than helpful for researchers of ancient space. But in the postmodern move within geography, two important things occurred that make the new theoretical developments useful for biblical scholars. First, there was a shift from the assumption of industrial methods of production to the study of other economic systems, such as the postindustrial and postfordist. This is helpful to us because it opens up the questions of economics in interesting ways. For instance, the preindustrial may have more connections to the postfordist than to the industrial schemes. The relations of production and reproduction are brought once more into question, and issues of consumption also come to the fore. Additionally, the role of communication was also problematized once it was removed from the modernist industrial context.

By reintroducing such matters as variables in geographic theory, postmodern geography assists the study of ancient cultures as well as current postmodern and/or hypermodern ones. Second, postmodern geography has explored new relations of the global and the local, and within these new explorations may well be theories more relevant to the study of ancient cultures.

Such a postmodern geography attends much more closely to certain factors of epistemology that are frequent tropes of postmodernism, such as the slippery differences between materiality and representation (especially given the roles of narrativity in the construction of meaning); the undecidability of scale (in Soja 2001b, 285, this is explicitly a strategy to resist binarism); the vital role of conflict, diversity, and multivocality in all human engagements; and the functions of power and privilege in any cultural constructions. (See Dear 2001, 16–17 for a more developed list of postmodern concerns in geography.)

Postmodern geography maps the partialities, the fragments, and the differences. It examines micro and macro levels, as well as the marginal and the plural. Postmodern geography deconstructs the modernist logic of space in which reality leads to ideology. This can lead to the consideration of imagined spaces, such as the utopia, in which imagination leads to reality. But note that postmodern geography never allows the discourse to remain on the imagination, but instead returns always to the material and the spatial. Space consists of "socially constructed worlds that are simultaneously material and representational" (Jones 2001, 122; cf. Gregory 1984). This simultaneity separates critical spatiality from studies of (pure) ideology. We will return to these issues of imagined worlds.

The Tradition of Lefebvre and Soja

Lefebvre and Soja agree in their insistence on the materiality of space. Space is not just a metaphor, nor a lack or emptiness. Metaphorization of space leads to abstraction; Lefebvre prefers a materialization even of socially defined space. Lefebvre rejected the positivist notion of space and substituted a critical spatiality by problematizing the fixed notion of space. He developed a tripartite understanding of space, distinguishing between the physical, the mental, and the social (Lefebvre 1991a, 11). None of these is more "real" than another; a critical perspective on space requires analyzing space from all three understandings and integrating the results. Thus, Lefebvre maintained the physical space that the positivists had wished to study quantitatively, while setting two new concepts alongside of it. Mental space (or *l'espace conçu*) involved the perceptions of space and the ideas about space, whereas social space (or *l'espace vécu*) referred to practices of living in space in relationship to other people. Soja followed Lefebvre's tripartite conceptualization of space, but used a different terminology: Firstspace (the physical, positivist space), Secondspace ("imagined" space, or the space perceived, understood, and intended by people), and Thirdspace ("experienced" space, or the ways that people actually live in and use space). For Soja, imagined space and experienced space are not subject to scientific measurement or mathematical objectivity; they cannot be reduced to numerical analysis or statistical tables (McDowell 1994, 153). Thus, Lefebvre parallels de Certeau's split between the concept of the city (the orderly, rational image of the city that is the subject of mathematical modeling, cartographical mapping, etc.) and the fact of the city (the city as lived and experienced, thus as always diverse, fragmented, contradictory, and partially known) (de Certeau 1984, 95).

At the same time, Lefebvre writes against the illusion that separates pure form (i.e. empty space, or imagined space) from the impure content (i.e. lived time, everyday practices, etc.) (Lefebvre 1991a, 97; cf. Gregory 1997, 222). Lefebvre's Marxist-inspired scholarly program (as expressed through more than seventy published books, few of which have been translated into English) was in large part an effort to erase this binary split between pure and impure, imagined and real, or theoretical and empirical (Lefebvre 1992, 1995). While Lefebvre was writing his crucial work on postmodern spatiality, he was simultaneously writing his history of the body, which appeared as *Critique of Everyday Practices* (Lefebvre 1991a; cf. Gregory 1997, 205).

Edward Soja, whose work appeared in English before Lefebvre's, operates in a different context and in a changed technological setting. For Soja in particular, postmodern geography is necessitated by the crisis of modern geography, in which GIS (geographic information systems) becomes everything and geography falls under the tyranny of the binary. Postmodern geography resists this tyranny. Other postmodern geographers have followed in their recognition that humans do not live in the midst of geometrics, but in the midst of meanings (Adams, Hoelscher, and Till 2001b, xx–xxi).

Although Soja is best known for his work as a theoretician of city planning, he argues that there is no such thing as a purely postmodern city (Soja 2001a, 38). He writes more easily of a postmodern "transition" that may lead into something like a postmodern city or a postmetropolis. All cities, Soja argues, are hybrid forms with changing realities. This provides a good clue for our own work on ancient space, and Soja provides practical help in interpreting such hybridities. He suggests six outlines to this postmetropolitan transition: (1) globalization of capital, labor, culture, and information flows; (2) postfordist economic restructuring (such as high-technology manufacturing, craft-based/ design-intensive industries, and financial/business services, all of which participate in very complex patterns of concentration and dispersal); (3) restructuring of urban form (no centrality, with a methodological focus on multiple localities instead of the city as a whole); (4) restructuring the social order (older polarities are replaced with fragmentations and intense rise of inequalities); (5) "carceral cities" (that is, sites of incarceration, imprisonment, or similar controls as in resettlement camps) in which regulation is panoptical and pervasive; and (6) simcities (simulations or simulacra, including virtual realities and cyber-communities) (Soja 2001a, 40–45).

In all of these matters, Soja's work is an explicit challenge to and often a reversal of earlier assertions about space, reaching back to Marx's declaration of time's annihilation of space. Soja's emphasis on Thirdspace is a way to break beyond the binaries of GIS and of the material/ideological split, as well as the objectivities of modernism. Thus, Soja allows the introduction of otherness through Thirdspace, and in this way allies himself with postcolonial thinkers (Soja 1997, 246–47). Thirdspace is an act of resistance, a way of using space that points out its constructed nature. As a Los Angeles city planner, Soja would describe the spatiality of the city's extensive highway system in terms of all three spaces. Firstspace would indicate the physical objects of roads, onramps, offramps, bridges, and so forth, each with their own GPS positions and physical measurements. Secondspace would refer to the map of such highways, but also to the intentions for design (such as projected traffic flow) and to the meanings of the highways (whether seen as "connections" or as "isolating"). Thirdspace would point first to the uses of the highways (as intended for transportation, but also as a place of violence, an opportunity for road rage, a set for status symbols, and even as a place for homeless persons to gain shelter under the overpasses), but more importantly to the range of possible uses, even those that had not yet been thought or practiced. Over against the "tyranny of space" as a physical constraint and also over against the prescriptions of the powerful about how the elites intended for space to be used, Thirdspace always presents possibilities for resistance, for popular activity that redefines the realities of space.

Other Critical Spatialities

Lefebvre and Soja represent a major line of development within postmodern geography and critical spatiality. However, they do not represent the only formulations of such theory. Human geography has long studied the processes by which people interact with space, such as through the use of mental maps, symbols and icons of landscape, perceptions of the environment, and the every-day use of geography. One of the emphases within human geography has always been to examine the politics of place and place-making (Adams, Hoelscher, and Till 2001b, xv–xvi). Experience and identity are part of this, but these exist as corollaries of the imagination that allows the social construction of places.

Place and Spatialities of Meaning

Many spatialities draw a distinction between material spaces and mental or imagined spaces. Often, human geographers refer to this as space (the material) and place (the human-constructed meanings attached to specific spaces). (Cf. Jones 2001, 121, who refers to this notion of place as "lifeworld.") This is very similar to Soja's distinction between Firstspace and Secondspace.

This notion of "place" is an idea, a mental construct, or a meaning (Cresswell 2004). Thus, it can be imagined and narrated. Place as a social construct is inti-mately connected to the social construct of identity; geographers with concern for identity often argue that place and identity are simultaneously constructed (Richardson 2001, 267; Strohmayer 1997). Thus, critical geographies of place allow for integration of critical spatiality with imagination, narrative, and iden-tity. Edward S. Casey, for example, defines space as "the most encompassing reality that allows for things to be located within it," whereas place is "the immediate ambiance of my lived body and its history, including the whole sedimented history of cultural and social influences and personal interests" (Casey 2001, 404). Robert David Sack uses "place" to discuss "the countless areas of space that have bounded and controlled," that is, those "humanly constructed and maintained places" (Sack 2001, 232). "Arguments about spatiality and the social construction of space are really about the effects that places have on creating and sustaining projects" (2001, 233). From this, Sack wishes to construct a moral geographical theory, in which "good" places help us "see through to the real" and have a high level of variety and complexity (2001, 238). To take a final example, Steven Hoelscher discusses popular geographies—"an image of place created outside academic and scientific discourse that is available for mass public consumption" (Hoelscher 2001, 378).

Thus, the theories of "place" offer important opportunities for further critical spatial exploration. Since scholars working in critical spatiality have specific interests in spatialities of identity, narrative, and imagination, the work of Casey, Sack, Hoelscher, and others may well be of interest, as well as the extensive human geographic work of Yi-Fu Tuan (for an evaluation, see Entrikin 2001, as well as Olwig 2001, 93).

Non-Western Spatialities
Tuan represents an interesting case as a geographer. He clearly has developed as one of the key thinkers of place and its meaning(s). In this way, he falls directly within one of the mainstreams of critical geography. But is Tuan also an example of a non-Western spatiality? Although all of his academic career has been performed in the United States, his biography begins in China, and many of his spatial perceptions reflect his early Asian experiences. Perhaps in this way, Tuan forms a border figure for critical spatialities.

Other than Tuan, non-Western contributions to critical spatiality derive not from geography per se, but from areas such as postcolonial theory. This is not surprising, because of the particular history of geography within the West as a science of colonization. In this sense, the work of Edward Said has performed the key linkage between the fields. By considering orientalism (and its foundation in mappings and in imperializing geographies), Said deconstructed the imperial geographic project and substituted postcolonial theory. Does this mean that critical spatiality is only possible in the West (i.e. in the empire)? Or are there possibilities for critical spatialities that are fully non-Western and deimperializing? I believe the latter, but at present one must look not among the geographers but among postcolonialists.

As an example of a Third World postcolonial spatiality, consider Arjun Appadurai, who suggests five "scapes": ethnoscape, technoscape, finanscape, mediascape, and ideoscape. Each describes movements or flows through global culture, on the basis of power. Each scape can function as the building block of imaginary worlds, which may be able to be used in constructing real worlds. The attentive scholar notes the disjunctures between these scapes as their rate of flow shifts (Appadurai 1990; Grossberg 1996, 174–76). Such spatialities are fully conversant with the critical spatialities of Soja, Lefebvre, and others, but are not reducible to these European and American theorists, nor do they derive from them.

Feminist Spatialities

Critical spatiality, unfortunately, has remained a male-dominated discourse, as has much of geography. However, the last two decades have seen a plethora of new works in feminist geography (Spain 1992; Blunt and Rose 1994; Massey 1994; McDowell 1999; Domosh and Seager 2001; Moss 2002; Staeheli, Kofman, and Peake 2004). These writings cover a wide range of issues in human geography.

Daphne Spain's *Gendered Spaces* (1992) provides excellent overviews on basic issues of critical spatiality with special attention to gender segregation in cross-cultural settings. Her approach to space involves many of the classical issues of social anthropology, such as the division of labor and constructions of status in varying cultures. *Space, Place, and Gender* (Massey 1994) also focuses on many of the same issues, although within a more urban and industrial context. Feminist spatialities such as these suggest concrete ways that critical spatiality can interface with other sociologically oriented trends within biblical studies to understand better the practices of woman's lives in ancient societies.

Mapping Women, Making Politics (Staeheli, Kofman, and Peake 2004) concentrates on political geography and especially the issues of contemporary geopolitics. Likewise, *Feminist Geography in Practice* (Moss 2002) offers more insight into contemporary discourse of geographers. Although the implications for biblical studies are more difficult to see, the theoretical sophistication of these approaches provide opportunities for rethinking what biblical studies could accomplish.

The essays collected by Alison Blunt and Gillian Rose in *Writing Women and Space: Colonial and Postcolonial Geographies* (1994) reflect a set of issues that more fully engage postmodern and postcolonial interests. Thus, they problematize mapping to a higher degree and consider such topics as empire, race, and the body. Domosh and Seager (2001) explore many of the same topics, as well as the city and the environment. The connections between feminist spatialities and postcolonial geographies are manifold and quite suggestive of further research in the spatiality of religion.

Most feminist geographers share many of the interests in place and meaning, while also integrating the classic questions of social theory: gender, race, and class. Identity is often foregrounded (see Veness 2001 for one example). Questions of performativity of space, as well as the potentials for space (and the space of potential) are also vital (Gibson-Graham 1997). Together, these feminist trends within the field of postmodern human geography will push biblical studies and critical spatiality to consider deeper ways of integrating all people's lives into the development of theory and perspectives on biblical texts and the ancient world.

The Uses of Theory

Thus, the possibilities within critical spatialities are varied and extensive. As scholars of biblical studies and religious studies opening ourselves up to this range of critical spatialities, we confront both the vastness of the theoretical possibilities and the risks of eclecticism. In this situation, I would argue that Soja's work provides an important basis for moving forward in expanding critical spatialities (cf. Berquist 2002).

Although some have interpreted Soja's theoretical contributions as providing a new and tripartite ontology of space, Soja's work argues against any such ontology. The three spaces of Firstspace, Secondspace, and Thirdspace are not different realities of space or even different modes of spatiality. Rather, they represent what the interpreter sees when examining space in different ways. In this, Soja's work is very close to Foucault's notion of heterotopia (Foucault 1986; Soja 2001b, 285). Past representations of space are constructs and thus are products of power relationships. To interrogate those representations is to investigate the power relations that produced the constructs. In other words, the three spaces are new ways of seeing space, just as a heterotopia is a new way of seeing (as well as what one finds when one sees differently). These new visions of space (critical spatialities) are themselves products of power relations, of course, but they strive toward a self-awareness (and thus self-critique) and toward a diversity of voices (and thus a plurality of spatialities).

One could speak, therefore, of Soja's work not as an ontology of space but as a deconstructive method for spatial discourse. One uses Soja's theory not by parsing space into its constituent parts but by altering the power relations involved in seeing space, in variations that are not random but are certainly kaleidoscopic.

Within Soja's ways of seeing, there is room to study the meaning(s) of space, what Soja terms Secondspace and what others have preferred to call place. I do not find one terminology more compelling than another; I would suggest that Soja's theoretical framework allows an appropriate integration of meaning-space while continuing critical human geography's clarion call toward materiality. Critical spatiality examines theories and ideologies about space, but it is much more than that, because such ideologies are always brought into connection with the materiality of space. Space is more than ideology or metaphor for Soja, even though it is (as Secondspace) both ideology and metaphor. Whereas others can define space as a lack (Natter and Jones 1997, 149, state that space is "a *lack* to be filled, contested, and reconfigured through contingent and partially determined social relations, practices, and meanings"), Soja insists that space is not infinitely plastic nor empty (following Lefebvre's refusal to separate pure, empty, imagined space from the lived times, everyday practices, and so forth that are meaningful).

Soja also makes way for a connection between Western theoretical constructions of space and non-Western spatialities of postcolonialism. He does this precisely through the assertion of Thirdspace, which allows for the imagination *and enactment* of lived alternatives to dominant spaces. Despite the monolithic nature of a Secondspace such as imperialism, it remains possible to form and live Thirdspaces that resist, challenge, and subvert the Secondspace. This is not to say that Thirdspace and Secondspace are ontologically different, but instead engaging in the imaginative and active work of seeing and living differently, involved in alternative power relations (Buttimer 2001). Such Thirdspace is not a different ontology but rather a strategy for constructing alternates that have impact on imagination, perception, meaning, and materiality. In this sense, Soja also connects the feminist spatialities' concern with identity as well as with performance and potentiality.

Of course, Soja's own writing does not deal with the full range of possibilities that erupt from his theories. His work has remained focused on the issues of planning, especially around postmodernizing cities. The other theoretical contributions are vital for performing the alternative seeings and spatialities for which Soja argues. But Soja's three-space model remains helpful for calling us ever back to materiality and pushing us ever forward into actions of creating new spaces.

The Present Volume

This critical spatiality is strongly influenced by groundbreaking works such as those by David Harvey (1989) and Stephen Toulmin (1990). Several of the chapters in the present volume witness a great indebtedness to the theories of Henri Lefebvre (1991b) and Edward Soja (1989, 1996), as well as Yi-Fu Tuan (1977). But these essays also display the variety of methods, theories, assumptions, and interests that are becoming part of religious studies' discourse on critical spatiality (Knott 2005; Økland 2004; Skinner 2003).

This first part of this book deals with theoretical perspectives on spatiality. Mark K. George's chapter, "Historically Siting Critical Space: Conceptualizing Space in the Western World," reviews some of the history of spatial theories, beginning in the ancient Greek world with Plato and Aristotle, and continuing through Descartes, Kant, and others. Thus, George provides an appropriate context for understanding the present-day theories of Lefebvre and others, exploring the philosophical roots and connections of spatial theory.

"Toward a Narrative-Based Theory of Place-relations," by Wesley A. Kort, charts a new direction. Kort examines six novelists of the last two centuries, which he uses to suggest a more nuanced theory of how people can and should relate to places. He moves beyond simplistic dichotomies of sacred and profane spaces, and thus provides a literary and ethical treatment of spatial theory.

Mary R. Huie-Jolly links Lefebvre's spatial theories with psychological theory in her chapter "Formation of the Self in Construction of Space: Lefebvre in Winnicott's Embrace." She focuses on Winnicott's three developmental stages or spaces in object-relations theory, and relates them to Lefebvre's three spaces. Thus, spatial theory connects to psychology, the life of the mind, and human life-cycle. Huie-Jolly also writes the next chapter, "Language as an

Extension of Desire: The Oedipus Complex and Spatial Hermeneutics." This broadens her discussion of psychoanalytic theory to Freud, thinking more widely about spatial consciousness and the limit experiences of religion.

The book's second part is "Mapping the Bible." Mapping and cartography represent one of the most concrete expressions of spatiality within biblical studies, and Thomas B. Dozeman introduces these practices in his chapter "Biblical Geography and Critical Spatial Studies." His work provides insight into the connections between literature (describing space) and perception (imagining the space about which one reads), as well as the scholarship about both of them. He sets biblical geography in the larger context of the development of mapping—from the theologically based Religious Geography to the modern, critical field of Geography of Religion—proposing a dialectic rather than opposition of the two perspectives.

Burke O. Long's "Bible Maps and America's Nationalist Narratives" analyzes a cultural phenomenon of the twentieth century—map-making that constructs a concept of Bible lands. Long sees connections between these maps and the narratives of American nationalism, showing how modern map-making reads the present into the past.

The final part of the book studies two examples of "Space in Biblical Narrative." William Millar offers "A Bakhtinian Reading of Narrative Space and Its Connection to Social Space: The Case of the Levites." In this chapter, Millar investigates the usefulness of critical spatial theories for understanding the varied assessments of Levi and the Levites in Gen 49:5–7 and Deut 33:8–11.

Steven James Schweitzer authors this book's concluding chapter, "Exploring the Utopian Space of Chronicles: Some Spatial Anomalies." Schweitzer brings together critical spatiality and utopian theory in both literature and society. This theoretical combination undergirds his investigation of Chronicles as a text about utopia rather than about real spaces.

Works Cited

Adams, Paul C., Steven Hoelscher, and Karen E. Till, eds. 2001a. *Textures of Place: Exploring Humanist Geographies*. Minneapolis: University of Minnesota Press.
_____. 2001b. Place in Context. In Adams, Hoelscher, and Till 2001a, xiii–xxxiii.
Appadurai, Arjun. 1990. Disjuncture and Difference in the Global Cultural Economy. *Public Culture* 2, no. 2:1–32.
Benko, Georges, and Ulf Strohmayer, eds. 1997. *Space and Social Theory: Interpreting Modernity and Postmodernity*. The Royal Geographical Society with the Institute of British Geographers Special Publications 33. Oxford: Blackwell.
Berquist, Jon L. 2002. Critical Spatiality and the Construction of the Ancient World. Pages 14–29 in *"Imagining" Biblical Worlds: Studies in Spatial, Social and Historical Constructs in Honor of James W. Flanagan*. Edited by David M. Gunn and Paula M. McNutt. JSOTSup 359. London: Sheffield Academic Press.
Blunt, Alison, and Gillian Rose, eds. 1994. *Writing Women and Space: Colonial and Postcolonial Geographies*. Mappings: Society/Theory/Space. New York: Guilford.
Buttimer, Anne. 2001. Introduction: Moralities and Imagination. In Adams, Hoelscher, and Till 2001a, 223–31.

Casey, Edward S. 2001. Body, Self, and Landscape: A Geophilosophical Inquiry into the Place-World. In Adams, Hoelscher, and Till 2001a, 403–25.

Crang, Mike. 2001. Rhythms of the City: Temporalised Space and Motion. Pages 187–207 in *Timespace: Geographies of Temporality*. Edited by Jon May and Nigel Thrift. London: Routledge.

Cresswell, Tim. 2004. *Place: A Short Introduction*. Short Introductions to Geography. Oxford: Blackwell.

de Certeau, Michel. 1984. *The Practice of Everyday Life*. Berkeley: University of California Press.

Dear, Michael. 2001. The Postmodern Turn. In Minca 2001, 1–34.

Domosh, Marna, and Joni Seager. 2001. *Putting Women in Place: Feminist Geographers Make Sense of the World*. New York: Guilford.

Entrikin, J. Nicholas. 2001. Geographer as Humanist. In Adams, Hoelscher, and Till 2001a, 426–40.

Foucault, Michel. 1986. Of Other Spaces. *Diacritics* 16:22–27.

Gibson-Graham, Julie Kathy. 1997. Postmodern Becomings: From the Space of Form to the Space of Potentiality. In Benko and Strohmayer 1997, 306–23.

Gregory, Derek. 1984. *Geographical Imaginations*. Oxford: Blackwell.

_____. 1997. Lacan and Geography: The Production of Space Revisited. In Benko and Strohmayer 1997, 203–31.

Gregory, Derek, Ron Martin, and Graham Smith, eds. 1994a. *Human Geography: Society, Space, and Social Science*. Minneapolis: University of Minnesota Press.

_____. 1994b. Introduction: Human Geography, Social Change and Social Science. In Gregory, Martin, and Smith 1994a, 1–18.

Grossberg, Lawrence. 1996. The Space of Culture, the Power of Space. Pages 169–86 in *The Post-Colonial Question: Common Skies, Divided Horizons*. Edited by Iain Chambers and Lidia Curti. London: Routledge.

Harvey, David. 1989. *The Condition of Postmodernity: An Enquiry into the Origins of Cultural Change*. Oxford: Blackwell.

_____. 2001. *Spaces of Capital: Towards a Critical Geography*. New York: Routledge.

Hoelscher, Steven. 2001. Conversing Diversity: Provincial Cosmopolitanism and America's Multicultural Heritage. In Adams, Hoelscher, and Till 2001a, 375–402.

Jones, John Paul, III. 2001. Introduction: Segmented Worlds and Selves. In Adams, Hoelscher, and Till 2001a, 121–28.

Knott, Kim. 2005. *The Location of Religion: A Spatial Analysis*. London: Equinox.

Lefebvre, Henri. 1991a. *Critique of Everyday Life*. Vol. 1, *Introduction*. London: Verso.

_____. 1991b. *The Production of Space*. Oxford: Blackwell.

_____. 1992. *Elements de Rhythmanalyse: Introduction à la Connaissance des Rhythmes*. Paris: Editions Syllepie.

_____. 1995. *Henri Lefebvre: Writings on Cities*. Edited by E. Kofman and E. Lebas. Oxford: Blackwell.

Massey, Doreen. 1994. *Space, Place, and Gender*. Minneapolis: University of Minnesota Press.

May, Jon, and Nigel Thrift, eds. 2001a. *Timespace: Geographies of Temporality*. London: Routledge.

_____. 2001b. Introduction. May and Thrift 2001a, 1–46.

McDowell, Linda. 1994. The Transformation of Cultural Geography. In Gregory, Martin, and Smith 1994a, 146–73.

_____. 1999. *Gender, Identity, and Place: Understanding Feminist Geographies*. Minneapolis: University of Minnesota Press.

Minca, Claudio, ed. 2001. *Postmodern Geography: Theory and Praxis*. Oxford: Blackwell.

Moss, Pamela, ed. 2002. *Feminist Geography in Practice: Research and Methods*. Oxford: Blackwell.

Natter, Wolfgang, and John Paul Jones III. 1997. Identity, Space, and Other Uncertainties. In Benko and Strohmayer 1997, 141–61.

Økland, Jorunn. 2004. *Women in Their Place: Paul and the Corinthian Discourse of Gender and Sanctuary Space*. JSNTSup 269. London: T&T Clark International.

Olwig, Kenneth R. 2001. Landscape as a Contested Topos of Place, Community, and Self. In Adams, Hoelscher, and Till 2001a, 93–117.

Relph, Edward. 2001. The Critical Description of Confused Geographies. In Adams, Hoelscher, and Till 2001a, 150–66.

Richardson, Miles. 2001. The Gift of Presence: The Act of Leaving Artifacts at Shrines, Memorials, and Other Tragedies. In Adams, Hoelscher, and Till 2001a, 257–72.

Sack, Robert D. 2001. Place, Power, and the Good. In Adams, Hoelscher, and Till 2001a, 232–45.

Shields, Rob. 1997. Spatial Stress and Resistance: Social Meanings of Spatialization. In Benko and Strohmayer 1997, 186–202.

Skinner, Matthew. 2003. *Locating Paul: Places of Custody as Narrative Settings in Acts 21–28*. Academia Biblica. Atlanta: Society of Biblical Literature.

Soja, Edward W. 1989. *Postmodern Geographies: The Reassertion of Space in Critical Social Theory*. London: Verso.

_____. 1996. *Thirdspace: Journeys to Los Angeles and Other Real-and-Imagined Places*. Cambridge, Mass.: Blackwell.

_____. 1997. Planning in/for Postmodernity. In Benko and Strohmayer 1997, 236–49.

_____. 2001a. Exploring the Postmetropolis. In Minca 2001, 37–56.

_____. 2001b. Afterword. In Minca 2001, 282–94.

Spain, Daphne. 1992. *Gendered Spaces*. Chapel Hill, N.C.: University of North Carolina Press.

Staeheli, Lynn A, Eleonore Kofman, and Linda J. Peake, eds. 2004. *Mapping Women, Making Politics: Feminist Perspectives on Political Geography*. New York: Routledge.

Strohmayer, Ulf. 1997. Be*longing*: Spaces of Meandering Desire. In Benko and Strohmayer 1997, 162–85.

Toulmin, Stephen. 1990. *Cosmopolis: The Hidden Agenda of Modernity*. New York: Free Press.

Tuan, Yi-Fu. 1977. *Space and Place: The Perspective of Experience*. Minneapolis: University of Minnesota Press.

Veness, April R. 2001. But It's (Not) Supposed to Feel Like Home. In Adams, Hoelscher, and Till 2001a, 355–74.

Part I

THEORETICAL PERSPECTIVES

SPACE AND HISTORY:
SITING CRITICAL SPACE FOR BIBLICAL STUDIES

Mark K. George

Scholars in biblical studies increasingly are turning their attention to the critical analysis and study of space. To be sure, scholars have been interested in space, such as sacred space, for some time. A variety of questions have been asked about space in antiquity, including what objects are in space, what objects identify a space as that of one social group over another, how spaces of different sorts—temples, homes, churches, cities, gates, public buildings, and the like— were used, by whom, where they were located, and how they changed over time. Where the recent critical study of space, sometimes called critical spatiality, differs from that prior work is that the question of space itself has become of interest. In light of theoretical work on space, including that of Michel de Certeau (1984), Yi-Fu Tuan (1977), Gaston Bachelard (1994), Michel Foucault (1986), and particularly Henri Lefebvre (1991, 2000) and Edward Soja (1989, 1996), this critical approach understands space as a thoroughly social project and product. Central to the critical work biblical scholars are undertaking on space, then, is the understanding of space as a social, cultural creation and prod-uct. Analysis of the space or spaces produced by a society thus offers another means of studying and understanding the society and culture that produced it.

To understand space as a social product, the result of social ideas and prac-tices, is not to make a claim about matter, motion, or other physical properties of the universe. Rather, it is an understanding and recognition of the role human beings, individually and collectively, play in creating the spaces they occupy and inhabit. Space is more than matter, motion, or physical properties, just as it is more than the symbolic, mythological, or religious meanings spaces come to have for people and societies. As Lefebvre has helpfully argued, space is all these things at once (Lefebvre 1991, 2000). Social practices are required to transform matter and physical reality into socially meaningful and recognizable spaces and places. The social practices utilized in this process differ from society to society. As a result, each society produces its own social spaces. These become the spaces and places within which that society lives and exists. They have socially significant meaning, be that meaning symbolic, religious, metaphorical, or mythical. They also embody the mental ideas of space of that society, that is, those conceptual or cognitive ways of identifying, organizing, and arranging space that are particular to that society. To speak of a society's or culture's space thus is to speak of three inter-related aspects: physical space and how physical reality is arranged and practiced, the mental organizational and conceptual systems that map space and make it possible to "think" space, and the socially significant meanings that are ascribed to such spaces (Lefebvre 1991, 33; cf. also Flanagan 1999; Zevit 2002).

The understanding and approach to space taken by biblical scholars in critical spatiality is part of a much larger and longer discussion in the Western world about space. For millennia, scholars and thinkers have debated, among other things, whether space is something that is absolute or relative, something known by abstraction or on the basis of human experience, how space works, and the relationship between space and the absolute (often assuming the divine to be part of the absolute). Understanding space as a social product is another aspect of this larger debate and has its antecedents within it. This essay will survey the history of this debate and highlight some of the ways in which critical spatiality reflects and responds to it. In this way, I hope to set or "site" the work biblical scholars are doing on space within that discussion. Following this survey, I will discuss Lefebvre's theories of space and how his work seeks to hold together what are typically divergent understandings and approaches to the question of space. Lefebvre's understanding of social space as a social product pushes that discussion in new directions, but it is his focus on how spaces are produced as the result of social processes specific to a time and place that I think makes his spatial theory quite useful for the analysis of ancient spaces and societies.[1]

Space and Place in Western Thought[2]

Plato and Aristotle
In ancient Greece, a number of persons wrote about space and place (cf. Jammer 1993, 7–26), but it is the work of Plato with which I want to begin. As part of his discussion of the universe in *Timaeus*, Plato argued that space, at least empty space, was identical with matter, and thus was a receptacle that receives all matter and gives that matter form, without having form itself.

> In the same way that which is to receive perpetually and through its whole extent the resemblances of all eternal beings ought to be devoid of any particular form. Wherefore the mother and receptacle of all created and visible and in any way sensible things is not to be termed earth or air or fire or water, or any of their compounds, or any of the elements from which these are derived, but is an invisible and formless being which

1.   For a helpful discussion of critical spatiality in the twentieth century, see Berquist 2002.

2.   My discussion of the history of space is guided by two excellent books. The first, Jammer (1993), is a history of theories of space. The second, Huggett (1999), provides excerpts from the primary texts, along with commentary. I refer to the primary texts whenever possible in what follows.

receives all things and in some mysterious way partakes of the intelligible, and is most incomprehensible. (Plato *Timaeus*, 51a–b)

For Plato, space is that which contains all physical things. Space is a container, something that is one and the same with matter, and that container is given its shape by means of geometry and geometric forms. In this way, Plato argues that the physical world and empty space are equated with geometry and geometrical surfaces, which are the organizing principles of reality.[3]

For Plato, there are two possible ways of considering or understanding space. One way is through the body and personal experience. The other way is through what Plato called "pure reason." A person's body, and the experience of the world one has through one's body, give a person legitimate knowledge of the physical world and space (Plato, *Timaeus*, 51d–e). Experience, however, cannot provide a person with knowledge of the ideal world of forms. Such knowledge is possible only by means of pure reason. What brings together these two ways of knowing space is geometry. The physical world is organized by the principles of geometry (as copies of ideal forms), and thus geometry allows a person to obtain knowledge about the world's ideal forms.

Plato's search for a means of knowing space introduced themes that have characterized the discussion about space ever since. Of particular note here are the themes of the role of experience in understanding space, and the role of reason and abstract reasoning in explaining and defining it. Some, such as Descartes and Kant, argue that space is something known through reason, not experience, while others, including Aristotle and Leibniz, argue knowledge of space is derived from the experience of space. Plato himself, ironically, falls somewhere between these two claims, since he claims both reason and experience provide one with knowledge about space and place.

Aristotle, Plato's student, developed his own views about space by focusing on the question of place. Indeed, in his *Physics*, Aristotle does not take up space, but rather discusses place as a theory of positions within space.

In Book IV of his *Physics*, Aristotle makes four assumptions about place, which form the basis for his subsequent conclusions:

> (1) That the place of a thing is no part or factor of the thing itself, but is that which embraces it; (2) that the immediate or "proper" place of a thing is neither smaller nor greater than the thing itself; (3) that the place where the thing is can be quitted by it, and is therefore separable from it; and lastly, (4): that any and every place implies and involves the correlatives of "above" and "below," and that all the elemental substances have a natural tendency to move towards their own special places, or to rest in them when there—such movement being "upward" or "downward," and such rest "above" or "below." (Aristotle, *Physics* 4.4.211a1–5)

In his first assumption, Aristotle states that a place is separate from that which contains it. In the second assumption, the place of an object corresponds exactly to the size and shape of that object. Third, he rejects the claim of Plato that space

---

3. On the philosophical problems faced by Plato by this conception of space and matter, see Huggett 1999, 4–7.

and matter are the same thing. Rather, Aristotle argues that place (and thus space) cannot be matter, since it can contain matter. Place cannot simultaneously contain an object and be an object, since that would imply two objects occupying the same place at the same time, an implication that defies common sense. A vessel can contain water, then air (when the water is poured out), then another substance, so Aristotle concludes, "the place or space into which or out of which they passed was something different from both" (Aristotle, *Physics* 4.1.208b5–7). In his fourth assumption, Aristotle claims that the difference between up and down, left and right, is not simply relative to the body, but is absolute.

These assumptions about place are the basis upon which Aristotle posits four theories about place. Place is either "[a] the shape, or [b] the matter, or [c] some sort of extension between the extremities, or [d] the extremities" (Aristotle, *Physics* 4.4.211b7). Aristotle eliminates [a]–[c] as impossible. "Shape" is the outer surface of an object, and therefore cannot be place, because the outer surface cannot be separated from that object. Because it cannot be separated in this way, it violates Aristotle's third assumption about place. Similarly, place cannot be matter (thereby refuting Plato's claims), because it cannot be separated from the body itself. Once again, such a situation violates the third assumption. Finally, place cannot be some sort of extension between the extremities. The extremity Aristotle has in mind here is the inner surface of whatever contains the body (for example, the inner surface of the vessel containing water). As Huggett explains, "The 'extension between' this surface is the volume enclosed; however, this 'volume enclosed' is not the matter enclosed, but something independent of the object" (Huggett 1999, 76). Because space cannot be matter, this theory does not hold. Thus, by a logical process of elimination (theories [a]–[c]), Aristotle concludes that place must be defined as his fourth theory, [d], namely, as the extremities. To put this another way, place is the boundary between a containing body and the thing contained (Aristotle, *Physics* 4.5.212b6). According to Aristotle, this is a theory compatible with experience and common sense.

On the basis of these theories about place, Aristotle derives his views on space. As discussed above, place has extension in three dimensions, but place is not matter. Because place is not the same as matter (that is, it is separable from what can fill a place), space exists, for space is the sum total of all places.

The arguments of Plato and Aristotle on space (especially those of the latter), particularly their concern with the physical and material aspects of space, were a significant influence on the discussion about space and place for the next two thousand years in the Western world. A number of important arguments about space and place were made in the period from Aristotle to Descartes, including arguments by Muslim thinkers and scholars, which laid the groundwork for the modern mathematical and scientific discussion of space (such as the work of Copernicus and Galileo). Theological ideas also shaped the discussion and focused it on the physical and material aspects of space (Jammer 1993, 27–52; Huggett 1999, 85–90). Whereas Greek thought tended not to associate the divine with space, other religious and theological traditions (such as in Jewish thought) viewed space as an attribute of the divine. Indeed, theologically influenced understandings of space would continue well beyond this period, as the work of Newton and Locke demonstrates; non-theological explanations of space are a relatively recent development. Nevertheless, even these theological arguments about space largely were extensions of the concerns of Plato and Aristotle about the physical and material aspects of space, demonstrating the lasting influence of these two Greek philosophers. It was not until the work of Descartes that the real break from the ideas of Plato and Aristotle was made, marking the transition into the modern discussion.

The Modern Period: Space from Descartes to Kant
In *The Principles of Philosophy*, René Descartes (1596–1650 C.E.) sought to articulate a secure position from which he could understand and explain the world (Descartes 1955). As his famous dictum, "*cogito, ergo sum*," suggests, Descartes found that position in reason, rejecting experience as fallible (and, in the process, rejecting the empiricism of Plato and Aristotle). In Descartes' worldview, there was mind and matter, and he utilized his reason to examine and define matter as something characterized by extension: length, width, and height (Descartes 1955, 2.4). Matter and space were the same thing in Descartes' view, and thus, because matter was extension, so, too, space was pure extension, a volume with no properties (Descartes 1955, 2.11–13, 15). Space was, therefore, a substance (because measurable through extension).

Descartes' material understanding of space aligned his work on space with that of Plato. At the same time, it placed Descartes in opposition to Aristotle and his assumption that matter and place are not the same thing. Descartes addressed Aristotle's assumption by distinguishing between two related aspects of space, the particular and the general. A stone has a particular extension (or dimension) in space, one that moves with the stone whenever it is moved from one place to another. The particular extension of the rock, however, is only one aspect of space and matter. The other is general extension. The stone has a general extension in space, that of its volume. The volume of the rock is specific to the place occupied by it before it is moved, and it remains in that place after the rock moves, because that volume is determined relative to other objects. In the particular case of the rock, extension is inseparable from the rock, whereas in the general case, extension *is* separable from it. Place thus is determined relative to other objects in space that humans consider to be fixed (cf. Descartes 1955, 2.13).

Descartes' claim that space and place "merely" indicate position relative to other bodies signals the transformation of the discussion about space into the modern period. Descartes' views pick up ideas from Plato (about that which contains space and that which fills space), yet moves them in new directions. Space is relative, a theory acknowledging that space, even the "same" space, will vary in position and motion, depending on the reference point used to determine the position of that space or place (a theory known as relationism).

Descartes' views on space were challenged almost immediately. One of the first and most important challenges came from Sir Isaac Newton (1643–1727 C.E.). Newton's work on mechanics, the theory of motion in space, led him to argue space is absolute, a claim he attempted to prove by means of mechanics. Newton's larger arguments and proofs for absolute space are beyond the scope of this study (for details, see Huggett 1999, 116–41; Jammer 1993, 95–116), but the essential points of his argument are important for the debate and discussion about space in the Western world.

Newton held a Euclidean notion of space. Thus, space has a three-dimensional structure, and space should be understood to be a container for material objects. On the basis of this understanding of space, Newton rejected Descartes' equation of space with matter, and thus that space is a substance. Relational space and the equation of matter with space cannot explain certain motions in space, including inertia and the question of the position of objects in space (as Descartes argued; 1955, 2.13, 2.25). The only way to explain these motions is if space is absolute.

Newton did not deny that relative space—space that is evident to common sense—exists. On the contrary, he readily acknowledged that it does (Newton 1999, 409). When the position or motion of something is being considered, the location of that object is determined relative to some other object or objects. Such reference frames constituted relative space for Newton (for more details on Newtonian relative spaces, see Huggett 1999, 131–33). But Newton denied that there is only relative space. Abstracting from the senses, Newton explained absolute space as space that is immutable, infinite, and three-dimensional, the precondition for matter and existence (even the existence of God, whom Newton believed to be everywhere), a rigid, unchanging container that exists through time (Newton 1962). This explanation ascribed to absolute space an independent, ontological status (Jammer 1993, 102). An absolute reference point, and thus absolute space with absolute positions within it, was required to explain the motion of a body moving in a straight line and validate the first law of motion, "Every body perseveres in its state of being at rest or of moving uniformly straight forward, except insofar as it is compelled to change its state by forces impressed" (Newton 1999, 416). From this initial claim, Newton was able to make arguments about other aspects of motion to support his claims about absolute space.

Newton's views were quickly challenged by Gottfried Wilhelm Leibniz (1646–1716 C.E.). Through a series of letters with Samuel Clarke, Newton's spokesperson, Leibniz argued for a relative understanding of space.[4] In his third letter to Clarke, Leibniz refuted Newton's claim that space was absolute and thus had an ontological status, arguing that space is nothing but a system of relations, "an order of coexistences" or a "situation of bodies among themselves"

---

4.   Clarke is widely considered to have conferred with Newton in drafting responses to Leibniz's objections to Newton's theories of space. The Leibniz–Clarke correspondence, between 1715–1716, therefore is widely considered to be essential in gaining a better understanding of the differences between the competing views of absolute and relative space.

(Alexander 1956, 25, 26; Leibniz 3.4, 5).[5] In a relative system, the locations of various objects or bodies are determined in terms of some reference point. Virtually anything can serve as that reference point, with the result being that, on the basis of multiple reference points and reference systems, people come to have an awareness of space. In other words, space is that which comprehends every place, both the situations or distances between materials, and the system of relations between these materials (Alexander 1956, 69; Leibniz 5.47).

Leibniz illustrated the relative nature of space by using genealogical trees. Within a genealogical tree, the position of any person within a particular genealogy appears absolute. If, however, one posits the fiction of a metempsychosis (the migration of a soul) from one person to another, then the persons in that genealogy might change places. "And yet those genealogical places, lines, and spaces, though they should express real truth, would only be ideal things" (Alexander 1956, 71; Leibniz 5.47). Space, Leibniz argued, is no different from this genealogy: genealogical positions appear to be absolute, but in reality they are relative to one another, and thus there is no such thing as absolute space.[6]

Despite the skill and persuasiveness with which Leibniz argued against Newton's ideas, it was Newton's views of space, as something absolute, that gained general acceptance, and his views have had long-lasting effects on the discussion about space. In large measure, the acceptance of Newton's views were a result of the corresponding arguments he made about absolute motion; with the advent of modern science and its concern with the physical properties of the universe, the relationalism of Leibniz, along with Cartesian theories about space, fell out of favor (Jammer 1993, 127). The fact that Newton identified absolute space in relation with the divine also helped his ideas achieve prominence in the seventeenth and eighteenth centuries.

It was in this historical and intellectual context that Immanuel Kant (1724–1804 C.E.) began his work, and it is with Kant's work that scholarship on space in religious and biblical studies most often begins. Kant is important in the historical discussion in part because his ideas about space changed during his career. In his early work, Kant sought to reconcile the views of Leibniz and Newton. Kant argued that the relationship between places in space reflects causal interaction between them, and such interaction can only be a result of divine interaction. This led Kant to argue that space is an "independent existent" of absolute reality and, as such, is absolute (Kant 1929b; Jammer 1993, 131). In short order, however, Kant abandoned his attempts to reconcile Leibniz and Newton in favor of understanding and explaining space in terms of geometry.

Kant's 1768 work, "On the First Ground of the Distinction of Regions in Space," signals the change in his thinking and his adherence to Newton's understanding of space. Kant's aim in this essay was "to investigate whether

5.   The Leibniz–Clarke correspondence is numbered by letter and paragraph within the Alexander 1956 volume; therefore, citations will include references to each author, letter, and paragraph.

6.   I have simplified Leibniz's arguments with Newton here. Leibniz employs so-called "shift arguments" to refute Newton's claims of absolute space, but detailing his arguments is not important for this essay. For more information, see Huggett 1999, 159–68.

there is not to be found in the intuitive judgments of extension, such as are contained in geometry, an evident proof *that absolute space has a reality of its own, independent of the existence of all matter, and indeed as the first ground of the possibility of the compositeness of matter*" (Kant 1929a, 20; italics original). Kant thus approached the question of absolute space not through mechanics, as had Newton, Leibniz, and others before him, but through geometry, as had Plato. Kant argued that "the parts of space in relation to one another" (Kant 1929a, 20) presuppose something toward which they are oriented, and that something was, in Kant's view, absolute space.

Kant made several preparatory observations to begin this essay, including one that is particularly significant for later scholars of space: that the initial reference point for experiencing space is the human body. The six directions—up–down, right–left, and before–behind—are determined in relation to the human body, and thus it is the body that allows a person to derive a concept of space and its regions (Kant 1929a, 21–23). The experience of space relative to the body, however, does not result in relative space. On the contrary, the body itself provides evidence of the necessity of absolute space, through the distinctions between right and left. Kant argued that a person's right and left hands are exactly identical (ignoring various imperfections on either hand). Relative distances on either hand—for example, the distance between the thumb and index finger of the right and left hands—therefore are the same. Because of this, there is no way to distinguish between right and left hands or the relative distances between points on each hand. Nevertheless, the two hands are incompatible, since neither can be substituted for the other or fitted into the exact same space, such as a right glove. This incompatibility Kant called the "incongruent counterpart" (Kant 1929a, 26). The differences between each hand cannot be explained apart from absolute space. No change in the relative distances between the parts of each hand can be introduced to explain the differences, whereas absolute space does provide an explanation. The differences are due to each hand occupying a unique position in absolute space (Kant 1929a, 28).[7]

Kant backed away from asserting the existence of absolute space in his later works, particularly in his *Critique of Pure Reason* (Kant 1996).[8] In this work, Kant attempted to explain that space must exist, even though he then distinguished between the existence of space and how human beings perceive and understand that space. To accomplish this goal, Kant made two important

7. Kant's attempt to use handedness (the distinction between right and left) to prove the existence of absolute space has been refuted by a number of scholars. Cf. Huggett's discussion of this essay and its flaws (e.g. that various spatial manipulations, such as employing a Möbius loop or three-dimensional space, quickly overcome the question of handedness; Huggett 1999, 203–12). See also Jonathan Z. Smith's additional information on critiques of Kant's proof (Smith 1987, 135–36 n. 17).

8. I rely on Huggett's explanation of Kant in this section, and refer readers to that source for a more detailed explanation, including how assuming non-Euclidean space challenges Kant's claims (Huggett 1999, 221–34).

distinctions, one between different types of knowledge, and the other between different types of judgments (or statements).

Kant argued that there are two distinct types of knowledge: *a posteriori* and *a priori*. The former type of knowledge, *a posteriori*, is knowledge gained from experience and empirical data. This type of knowledge includes such things as what types of flies to use when fly-fishing in a particular mountain stream. Both general knowledge (such as biological information about trout) and specific knowledge (such as the type of insects that hatch along a certain section of a river) can be gained through experience. Hence, it is experience that provides the justification for all *a posteriori* knowledge (Kant 1996, 43–44).

Since *a posteriori* knowledge is based on experience, all other knowledge must be *a priori* knowledge, the justification of which must not derive from experience (Kant 1996, 45). Kant therefore understood *a priori* knowledge to be universal and true, and he cited as examples mathematical propositions. Likewise, Kant argued that knowledge of space is *a priori* knowledge.

The second distinction Kant made in *Critique* was between analytic and synthetic judgments (or statements). Analytic statements are true by virtue of definitions alone. The classic example of an analytic statement is that a bachelor is an unmarried man. Because analytic statements are definitional, they are also *a priori* statements. Analytic statements are structured in subject-predicate form: the predicate tells one something about the subject. Analytic statements, therefore, don't provide additional information about their subjects, since they simply make explicit part of the definition (Kant 1996, 51). By contrast, any statement that does not meet these requirements, because it provides new information about the subject, is a synthetic statement, and hence is an *a posteriori* statement.

On the basis of these two distinctions, Kant took up the concept of space, beginning with geometric theorems. Axioms of geometry are, according to Kant, *a priori* synthetic statements, because they are necessarily and universally true, and because they are genuinely new. "Geometry is a science that determines the properties of space synthetically and yet *a priori*" (Kant 1996, 80; italics original).[9] Euclidean, geometric space, according to Kant, thus exists and is real, prior to human experience or perception of such space.

When human beings have an experience of geometric space, that experience, according to Kant, occurs in two parts. First, there are the sensations caused by the objects in that space. Second, these sensations are organized into a single, coherent visual field. Kant called the organization of these sensations, "the *form* of appearance" (Kant 1996, 73; italics original), and argued that this form cannot be something learned from experience (i.e. it is not *a posteriori* knowledge), but must be something *a priori* in the mind. When the form of appearance organizes the sensations caused by objects in experience, a sense of space is created. "Thus the general spatial properties of experience are not themselves learned from experience, but rather both precede all experiences and are necessarily

---

9. Kant termed such statements "elucidatory," because they make the definition clear.

present in all experiences. They are, in other words, known *a priori*: they are 'pure intuition'" (Huggett 1999, 225).

Kant's views on space mark a significant development in the history of the discussion. By arguing that the concept of space involves a subjective component, that is, the work the mind does arranging and organizing sensations produced by objects, Kant acknowledged that space is not something that can be experienced either directly or objectively. There is an experience of external things (that is, external to the viewer, and hence not simply constructed by the viewer), but the way in which those experiences are arranged and conceived occurs in the mind. One might think of space, for instance, as sacred space and hence absolute space, but, following Kant's logic, such space is neither sacred nor absolute at all. It is, rather, thought to be absolute because of the form of experience, which organizes one's experiences of such space according to the *a priori* category of absolute space, arranges those experiences into that category, and thereby allows one to think of space as absolute. Kant's notion of a transcendental ideality of space (a "pure intuition" of space) is something that later philosophers (not all of them concerned with space) would challenge.

Critical Spatiality: Henri Lefebvre and Social Space

Work on space after Kant followed two general directions. One direction focused on the physical aspects of space. This line of approach was undertaken primarily by mathematicians, physicists, and other scientists, including Ernst Mach, Henri Poincaré, and Albert Einstein. The other direction focused on cognitive and philosophical aspects of space, leaving the physical properties and aspects of space to science. Other aspects of space, such as how communities and individuals experience and shape space, have been the concern of this approach to space. This largely is the work of philosophers, social scientists, anthropologists, and geographers, especially human geographers.

In the study of religion, it is the latter approach to space that has been taken up, as the work of Émile Durkheim demonstrates. Durkheim was strongly influenced by Kant and the neo-Kantians, especially Charles Renouvier, Octave Hamelin, and Émile Boutroux, because his sociological epistemology was a development of Kant's arguments about intuition and *a priori* knowledge (Lukes 1972, 54–58). The way in which Kant described the experience of space, as dependent on the form of experience in one's mind, set the stage for the socialization of space by Durkheim.

In *The Elementary Forms of the Religious Life*, Durkheim provided his well-known definition of religion as the distinction between the sacred and the profane (Durkheim 1915, 37).[10] Durkheim employs the sacred and profane as a means to bring together both empiricist and cognitive (*a priori*) theories of knowledge. The sacred (and sacred space) is one universal pole of knowledge,

---

10.   As Smith notes, this classification presupposes a spatial division (Smith 1987, 39). Colpe's examination of each term's etymology confirms Smith's reading of Durkheim (Colpe 1987).

that of ultimate authority and external reality, while the profane, the other universal pole of knowledge, is common space experienced by individuals. Durkheim argues, however, that because society constructs and shapes the framework of knowledge in the human mind, the sacred and profane are social constructs. Furthermore, because space is a result of thought, which in turn is a result of society and social forces, space reflects social understandings and society. Space is the external expression of human consciousness, with the symbolisms, organizations, arrangements, and other aspects derived from social structures and meanings. In short, space is an abstraction of the concept of society (Durkheim 1915, 442). Thus, the Kantian notion of the form of experience in a person's mind, which exists *a priori*, is, in Durkheim's theory, not "pure intuition," but a product of society, which creates and shapes a person's mind and the ways in which that person thinks. Durkheim thus shifted the understanding of space from a natural one to a cultural one, from the individual to society.[11]

The work in critical spatiality pursued by biblical scholars is, in large part, an exploration of this idea that space is a social construct, although less because of Durkheim's work than because of the work of the French philosopher Henri Lefebvre, among others. Like Durkheim before him, Lefebvre drew upon Kant's work in order to make an argument about space being a social construct. Lefebvre went beyond Durkheim, however, in various ways, including a desire to bring together the two directions taken after Kant in the study of space. This desire was not an attempt to form a unified theory of space. Rather, Lefebvre recognized that space is not simply a mental construct shaped by societies. Social space (understandings of space shaped by social ideas) produces real, tangible effects in (and on) the material, physical world. Thus, for Lefebvre, to study one type of space, be that physical space or mental space, without the other is to ignore something central about the nature of social space.

Lefebvre drew on the work of both Kant and Hegel. From Hegel, Lefebvre made use of the idea of the concrete universal. The concrete universal is not something formed abstractly or ideally (that is, it is not an absolute), but through social interactions between people, and the consciousness that one's actions effect a communal end (Lefebvre 1991, 15; cf. also Williams 1997, 71–73, 201–5). Lefebvre linked this Hegelian idea with the Marxian concepts of production and the act of producing, a linkage that allowed him to speak of the production of (real) space. While he admitted that the idea of producing space might be somewhat unusual or strange, Lefebvre argued that it was an appropriate concept for examining space because it allowed him to bring "the various

---

11.   Scholars have demonstrated that Durkheim's sociological epistemology is problematic (cf. Schwartz 1981, 10–33). Smith, however, argues that, while the genetic relationship Durkheim posited between classificatory systems and social organizations is flawed, the relationship he and Mauss (Durkheim and Mauss 1963) saw between social arrangements and a classificatory system is correct. Smith argues that an isomorphic relationship exists between social arrangements and classificatory systems; the same mode of relation exists between these two, if not a causal one (Smith 1987, 38).

kinds of space and the modalities of their genesis together within a single theory" (Lefebvre 1991, 16). Furthermore, this concept enabled Lefebvre to bring Hegel's work into conversation with Kant, specifically Kant's ideas that space is something of which individuals (and, by extension, societies) become aware because of the ways in which they arrange their experiences of space in their minds.

In Lefebvre's view, space is produced in a dialogical fashion between people and their experiences of real, physical space (their surroundings). Similarly, spatial codes—the mental systems that organize and classify space—are produced through the interaction of people's experiences of space and their mental arrangement of those experiences, since people produce language to describe and speak about space (Lefebvre 1991, 16). Lefebvre was not arguing for the existence of a general or universal spatial code (as did Kant), but of specific codes, unique to individual cultures and societies, in particular places and times, with varying social and spatial effects (Lefebvre 1991, 17). In effect, Lefebvre was arguing for a historicist critical spatiality, that is, an understanding of space that is historically and culturally specific (cf. Elden 2004, 169–210). As the product of historically specific cultures and times, both space and the spatial codes that make such space possible could be read, whether they be ancient or modern.

The combination of ideas from Hegel and Kant (along with the work of Marx) provided Lefebvre with a theoretical starting point for his examination of space. A study of space must examine the particular spatial codes of an existing space in order "to elucidate their rise, their role, and their demise" (Lefebvre 1991, 17–18). In order to accomplish such an examination, Lefebvre argued, one must place critical emphasis on the dialectical character of these codes and material reality. The practical focus of such an emphasis was to highlight the social practices inherent in the forms of space being considered, because these spatial codes are a social product (Lefebvre 1991, 18).

Lefebvre encapsulated his understanding of space in the proposition that "*(Social) space is a (social) product*" (Lefebvre 1991, 26; italics original). In his view, every society, whether modern or ancient, produces a space that is uniquely its own, and thus every space can be analyzed and explained in social terms, as can its relations of production (Lefebvre 1991, 31).[12] Following Marx, Lefebvre assumed every society assigns places to social relations of reproduction and to social relations of production. In light of capitalism and neocapitalism, Lefebvre modified this Marxist assumption, arguing that each society assigns space for (1) social relations of reproduction, that is, relations between the sexes, age groups, and social groups; (2) social relations of production—those social arrangements whereby labor is organized, divided, and arranged; and (3) symbolic representations that serve to maintain social relations in a state

---

12.   Lefebvre acknowledges that any such analysis will be incomplete, given the complicated nature of spatial production, and the limitations of Western epistemology and analysis in attempts to study non-Western spaces and cities. This acknowledgment similarly applies to the analysis of spaces in the biblical text and the ancient Near East.

of coexistence and cohesion (Lefebvre 1991, 32). The content of these spaces is specific to each society and to particular times within that society's history.

On the basis of these three assumptions about production and their being located in space, Lefebvre developed a conceptual triad to examine social space. This triad distinguishes between spatial practice (*la pratique spatiale*), representations of space (*les représentations de l'espace*), and spaces of representation (*les espaces de représentation*; Lefebvre 1991, 33; 2000, 43).[13] Spatial practice is Lefebvre's analytical term not only for physical space, but also for the social practices employed to transform real, physical space into the uses a society has for that space. Thus, spatial practice examines the ways in which humans modify space in predictable ways, including the routines, uses of space, and physical changes they make to space. For example, modern-day cemeteries in the United States typically are located on the outskirts of towns and cities (unless the town or city has expanded and surrounded the cemetery), are enclosed by a fence or wall, and have a park-like appearance (due to the lawns, trees, flowers, and other plants contained in them). They generally have neat rows of grave markers or (stone) headstones, which are inscribed with such information as the name and dates of the deceased, and which are spaced at predictable intervals (irregular spacing often is a sign of the age of a cemetery). If there are buildings on the grounds (other than mausoleums), they are few in number and they tend to be situated inside the grounds, rather than on the borders. Any roads in the cemetery, if it is large, may appear to wander through the various sections of the cemetery, rather than to be laid out on a systematic grid. But such is only an appearance, since the road is designed to reach all areas of the cemetery. All of these elements—the park-like setting, the regular intervals between graves and markers, the road—are part of the cemetery's spatial practices. It is these practices that produce (and reproduce, since they can be applied in other places) the particular social space of cemeteries.

Representations of space are the conceptual systems societies develop and employ to arrange, organize, systematize, divide, and thus "know" physical space. Lefebvre argued this is the space of urban planners, social engineers, and others who produce cognitive arrangements of space. Primarily mental space, representations of space usually employ verbal signs and intellectual concepts (Lefebvre 1991, 39). The representations of space in a modern U.S. cemetery include the organizational concepts and maps that divide the cemetery into sections and determine such things as the order in which each section is used,

13.   Nicholson-Smith translates *les espaces de représentation* as "representational spaces," a translation I find more confusing than "spaces of representation" (cf. Soja 1996, 10). Lefebvre also employs another set of terms for the examination of space: perceived space (*l'espace perçu*), conceived space (*l'espace conçu*), and lived space (*l'espace vécu*; Lefebvre 1991, 38–39; 2000, 48–49). The first triad, spatial practices, representations of space, and spaces of representation, are Lefebvre's analytical terms for social space, that is, the conceptual study of social space. Perceived, conceived, and lived space are Lefebvre's terms for the human, embodied experience of social space. Lefebvre uses them when he analyses or discusses space from the perspective of an individual (Lefebvre 1991, 40).

how many grave sites can be included in a particular section, and the orientation of those grave sites. It determines how the roadways and paths will be placed in it. It undertakes various economic considerations, such as how to price grave sites and services, and how to manage the cemetery. The scheduling of the space, from how many burials can occur in a day to who may perform the interment services, also is part of the cemetery's representation of space, the mental system that organizes and structures this space. Cemeteries are businesses, and capitalist concerns affect how cemetery space is conceived.

Spaces of representation are the symbols, myths, and metaphors that give space significance for people. Spaces of representation attempt to synthesize both spatial practice and representations of space into a larger symbolic framework. As such, spaces of representation are the lived spaces of a society, because they give meanings to a society's spaces.[14] They also are contested spaces, because symbolic meanings, which may only be partially understood in the first place, overlap and conflict with one another. The spaces of representation in a modern U.S. cemetery are numerous. Religious meanings, from various religious traditions (especially Christianity), are part of this space. One aspect of the Christian symbolism in cemetery symbolic space is that only the physical, mortal bodies of the dead lie in this space, because the souls of the dead have departed to go to heaven or paradise (typically, few are said to go to hell!). Thus the cemetery is the "final resting place" of the deceased. It is the place where people may go to "visit" the dead (even if, at some level, these people believe the deceased have gone to heaven and thus cannot be "found" at the cemetery). Certain emotions and behaviors, such as weeping by men, are permitted in this space, while being prohibited or discouraged elsewhere. Religious symbols are inscribed on grave markers, and flowers, stones, and other tokens adorn grave sites. Less comforting symbolisms also are part of cemeteries' spaces of representation. Cemeteries are for the dead, and death generally is not a popular social topic in the United States. Cemeteries are considered to be more ominous in the dark. Ghosts, the spirits of the dead, haunt them at night (regardless of claim that the spirits of the dead go to heaven). One must respect to the dead, lest they be offended. These symbolic meanings shape how society lives in cemetery space.

Critical Spatiality and Biblical Studies

The way in which Lefebvre goes about studying space is significantly different from that of Plato, Aristotle, and others who preceded him. And yet similarities remain. Experience (or common sense) plays a role for them all, even if the ways in which that experience functions in space and the understanding of space is different. They all assume space is something to be explained, although what needs to be explained, and how, differs. Plato sought to explain the ideal world of forms. Newton sought to explain certain motions in space. Kant sought to

---

14. Lefebvre views spaces of representation as dominated spaces, because the symbols produced in symbolic space are experienced passively by the majority of society.

explain how the idea of space comes to be thought by individuals. Lefebvre sought to explain how space is a social product, one that reflects the society and social system that produced it. Reason and abstraction play a role in their different explanations of space, whether as the means whereby the "true" meaning of space is to be discerned, or as part of the social production of space. Lefebvre's theories about space take the discussion in a particular direction, yet they remain very much a part of the larger discussion and debate about space in the Western world.

It is the particularity of Lefebvre's understanding of space, as something specific to a time, place, and society, that appears to have made his work, or at least a critical spatiality derived from his work, appealing to biblical scholars.[15] Each society practices space, thinks about space, and ascribes social meanings to space in different ways, and these change over time. Space, as a reflection and product of particular societies, has a story and a history to tell. The task of spatial analysis, in Lefebvre's view, is to read that story and history in order to understand the society that produced that space and how it did so. As a Marxist, Lefebvre expected these spatial stories to reflect the views of those with the most power within the society that produced the space (cf. Boer 2003). At the same time, he expected to find instances and signs of resistance to those with power, ways of living in and representing the meaning of such space that enabled those without power (or oppressed by power) to resist the "authorized" meanings of social space.

There are many spaces biblical scholars encounter in their work, including the land of Israel, Persian Yehud, Roman Palestine, Jerusalem, Babylon, Rome, Alexandria, the Temple, the tabernacle, house churches, and the "house of the father." Critical spatiality provides scholars with a means of examining and analyzing such spaces in terms of the social practices and forces that created them. Space is not simply the neutral medium in which biblical and related narratives and events took place. It is not an absolute, ontologically independent container within which the events of history occurs as some in history have thought. Rather, space is a product of a particular time and place in the ancient world. Space is a complex social phenomenon, one that involves not only physical space, but also the conceptual systems created and employed to organize it, and the symbolic and mythological meanings societies develop in order to live in space. In this way, the concerns of Plato with the experience of space and how one interprets those experiences continue to be argued and addressed.

Works Cited

Alexander, H. G., ed. 1956. *The Leibniz–Clarke Correspondence, Together with Extracts from Newton's* Principia *and* Optiks. New York: Philosophical Library.
Aristotle. 1995. *Physics*. Edited by Jonathan Barnes. Princeton: Princeton University Press.
Bachelard, Gaston. 1994. *The Poetics of Space*. Boston: Beacon.

15.   The work of Edward Soja (1996) is used more commonly than that of Lefebvre or others, although Soja himself is indebted to Lefebvre (Soja 1989; 1996, 26–82).

Berquist, Jon L. 2002. Critical Spatiality and the Construction of the Ancient World. Pages 14–29 in *"Imagining" Biblical Worlds: Studies in Spatial, Social and Historical Constructs in Honor of James W. Flanagan*. Edited by David M. Gunn and Paula M. McNutt. JSOTSup, 359. London: Sheffield Academic Press.

Boer, Roland. 2003. *Marxist Criticism of the Bible*. London: T&T Clark International.

Certeau, Michel de. 1984. *The Practice of Everyday Life*. Berkeley: University of California Press.

Colpe, Carsten. 1987. The Sacred and the Profane. Pages 511–26 in vol. 12 of *The Encyclopedia of Religion*. Edited by Mircea Eliade. 16 vols. New York: Macmillan.

Descartes, Rene. 1955. The Principles of Philosophy. Pages 201–302 in vol. 1 of *The Philosophical Works of Descartes*. Translated by Elizabeth S. Haldane and G. R. T. Ross. New York: Dover.

Durkheim, Émile. 1915. *The Elementary Forms of the Religious Life*. Translated by Joseph Ward Swain. New York: Macmillan.

Durkheim, Émile, and Marcel Mauss. 1963. *Primitive Classification*. Translated by Rodney Needham. Chicago: University of Chicago Press.

Elden, Stuart. 2004. *Understanding Henri Lefebvre: Theory and the Possible*. London: Continuum.

Flanagan, James W. 1999. Ancient Perceptions of Space/Perceptions of Ancient Space. *Semeia* 87:15–43.

Foucault, Michel. 1986. Of Other Spaces. *Diacritics* 16:22–27.

Huggett, Nick, ed. 1999. *Space from Zeno to Einstein: Classic Readings With a Contemporary Commentary*. Cambridge, Mass.: MIT Press.

Jammer, Max. 1993. *Concepts of Space: The History of Theories of Space*. New York: Dover.

Kant, Immanuel. 1929a. On the First Ground of the Distinction of Regions in Space. Pages 19–29 in *Kant's Inaugural Dissertation and Early Writings on Space*. Translated by John Handyside. Chicago: Open Court.

Kant, Immanuel. 1929b. Thoughts on the True Estimation of Living Forces. Pages 3–15 in *Kant's Inaugural Dissertation and Early Writings on Space*. Translated by John Handyside. Chicago: Open Court.

_____. 1996. *Critique of Pure Reason*. Translated by Werner S. Pluhar. Indianapolis: Hackett.

Lefebvre, Henri. 1991. *The Production of Space*. Oxford: Blackwell.

_____. 2000. *La production de l'espace*. 4th ed. Paris: Anthropos.

Lukes, Steven. 1972. *Émile Durkheim: His Life and Work; A Historical and Critical Study*. New York: Harper & Row.

Newton, Isaac. 1962. De Gravitatione. Pages 123–46 in *Unpublished Papers of Isaac Newton: A Selection from the Portsmouth Collection in the University Library, Cambridge*. Edited by A. R. Hall and M. B. Hall. Cambridge: Cambridge University Press.

_____. 1999. *The* Principia*: Mathematical Principles of Natural Philosophy*. Translated by I. Bernard Cohen and Anne Whitman. Berkeley: University of California Press.

Plato. 1961. *Timaeus*. Pages 1151–1211 in *The Collected Dialogues of Plato Including the Letters*. Edited by Edith Hamilton and Huntington Cairns. Bollingen Series 71. Princeton: Princeton University Press.

Schwartz, Barry. 1981. *Vertical Classification: A Study in Structuralism and the Sociology of Knowledge*. Chicago: University of Chicago Press.

Smith, Jonathan Z. 1987. *To Take Place: Toward Theory in Ritual*. Chicago: University of Chicago Press.

Soja, Edward W. 1989. *Postmodern Geographies: The Reassertion of Space in Critical Social Theory*. London: Verso.

_____. 1996. *Thirdspace: Journeys to Los Angeles and Other Real–and–Imagined Places.* Malden, Mass: Blackwell.

Tuan, Yi-Fu. 1977. *Space and Place: The Perspective of Experience.* Minneapolis: University of Minnesota Press.

Williams, Robert W. 1997. *Hegel's Ethics of Recognition.* Berkeley: University of California Press.

Zevit, Ziony. 2002. Preamble to a Temple Tour. Pages 73–81 in *Sacred Time, Sacred Place: Archaeology and the Religion of Israel.* Edited by Barry M. Gittlen. Winona Lake: Eisenbrauns.

SACRED/PROFANE AND AN ADEQUATE THEORY
OF HUMAN PLACE-RELATIONS

Wesley A. Kort

Introduction

Theories of time are stabilized by conventional categories and problems, while theories of place and space are far more shaped by the interests of those who sponsor them—philosophical, architectural, geographical, social scientific, cultural critical, and so on.[1] One consequence of the fact that theories about place and space come from diverse sponsors and are not controlled by conventional terms is that questions of space and place and of our relations to them appear more elusive and complex than, perhaps, they need to. Another consequence is, as Michel de Certeau points out about dealing with the everyday, that in this area there are many competent and interesting contributors but no dominant or authoritative voice, school, or method.

Why have spatial theories taken second place to theories of time? One answer is that time, due to its vulnerability to abstraction and measurement, is more philosophically engaging. Kant (1929, 19–29), in his early discussions of space, subordinates spatiality to temporality precisely because spatial relations are more physical. Time, thereby, is judged more universal, and time, he contends, includes, with everything else, space. Michel Foucault (1980), viewing the situation from another angle, gives a second answer. Questions of place and space have been the province primarily of military and political interests, and such interests are too impure for philosophers. A third answer lies in an argument I recently made that a major shift in modern culture occurred when Vico applied to reading the histories of non-biblical peoples Bacon's practice of reading nature as a second scripture that was not optional but necessary if one is to know God (Kort 1996, 51–58). Hegel added a crucial ingredient to Vico's shift when he dissolved the distinction between the histories of biblical and non-biblical peoples and posited reading history as the way by which the effects of Providence are actualized. As reading nature as scripture first complemented and then displaced reading the Bible as scripture in the eighteenth century, so in the eighteenth and nineteenth centuries reading history as scripture, while at first it complemented reading the Bible, eventually displaced the Bible as scripture.

---

1. For a discussion of theories of human time in relation to works of modern fiction, see Kort 1986.

Without attempting to be exhaustive, I want to add a fourth answer to the question of why, in modern culture, theories of time and history upstaged theories of place and space. Modern culture was able to adjust to the loss of shared religious beliefs as they apply to temporality as it was not able to adjust to that loss in regard to spatiality. The loss of an ultimate beginning and ending, of Creation and Apocalypse, was redressed by the elevation of moments within history as decisive. Christianity already had done this by affirming the birth of Jesus as a beginning point that rivaled, if it did not overshadow, the beginning marked by Creation. Marking historical watersheds and distinguishing periods in history from one another is part of the tradition and becomes an obsession in the modern period. Monarchies, revolutions, radical cultural shifts: these all serve to mark decisive beginnings and endings, and modern culture can, per-haps, be no more accurately characterized than by the assumption it carries about itself as a period sharply distinguished in nature and value from what preceded it. But the erosion of a dominant religious view regarding ultimate places and their stabilizing and normative status, that is, heaven and hell, could not so readily be redressed.

The emergence of interest in theories of place and space within the last few decades is largely due to the questionable standing of modern culture's temporal self-description. Disillusionment with the culture's history—due to increasing alienation from and within rapidly emerging urban areas, increasing ambiva-lence about relations to non-Western peoples, and the First World War—turned into a sense of betrayal, of being part of modern history as though one has been, in the words of William Golding (1966, 100), conned into a great "mincing machine." Western history became not the emergence of Providence or even human potential but a record of violence, oppression, and terror. Consequently, cultural self-definition shifted from historical to spatial terms, and by the close of the twentieth century place and space emerge as primary matters of attention. That shift is basic to what is often referred to as the rise of a post- or anti-modern culture. As Fredric Jameson remarks (1984, 64), "I think it is at least empirically arguable that our daily life, our psychic experience, our cultural languages, are today dominated by categories of space rather than by categories of time, as in the preceding period of high modernism proper." We find our-selves in a difficult and complex situation, therefore: the culture's self-definition has shifted from temporal to spatial terms, but there is little in and across discourses regarding spatiality that stabilizes them, gives them continuity with one another, and provides norms.

One effect of this situation is that place-relations are often valued at the expense of mobility and the temporal associations carried by mobility. Indeed, this evaluation of place-relations over mobility often implies a contrast between attitudes that are in some way or to some degree judged as traditional and "sacred" in contrast to mobility and temporality, which are judged as modern and "profane." For example, Akhil Gupta and James Ferguson, in their own essays and in others collected in their *Culture/Power/Place: Explorations in Critical Anthropology* (1999), point out a pervasive assumption in recent ethno-graphic studies that the close relations of indigenous peoples with their locations carries a moral and spiritual value that the modern ethnographer, by being mobile and unattached, lacks. Ignoring the obvious advantages of mobility that ethnographers enjoy as participants in modern culture, they overvalue the less mobile by assuming that rootedness is morally and spiritually superior. Another example is a noticeable shift among Americanists in locating the moral and spiritual values of American culture not so much in its history and destiny as in its "sacred" sites. Such books as John Sears' *Sacred Places: American Tourist Attractions in the Nineteenth Century* (1989) and David Chidester's and Edward T. Linenthal's edited volume *American Sacred Space* (1995) reveal a growing validation of sites as securing the moral and spiritual aspects of American identity. From another quarter, cultural geographers like Yi-Fu Tuan (1996, 6) theorize human place-relations with an eye toward restoring "place as the locus of human fulfillment." As well, the interest in myth and ritual, ranging from popular to sophisticated, can also be seen as a fascination with what transcends, stabilizes, or defies history. And the value imputed to Native American cultures and the spiritual authority of their place-orientations has mass-media standing.

The high value currently placed on rootedness affects the status of the category of "sacred space." It becomes easy to pit "sacred space" against the "profane," identified as modern history. The effect is to deploy the category of sacred space as though such space were simple rather than complex, abstracted from rather than related to power, and universal rather than diverse. In a recent collection of essays to which the editors, John Eade and Michael Sallnow, add their own contributions, anthropological studies reveal that "sacred" places, such as goals of pilgrimage, are so highly valued and effective not because they are simple, politically pure, and universal but because they are complex, controlled, and particular.

When posited as a contrary to profane history, sacred space becomes not only abstract but also dependent on the profane. The general, negative judgment of modern history as evil or profane serves as a warrant for various constructions of space as good or even sacred. During the twentieth century, particularly due to the two World Wars, a cultural confluence emerged from contrary sources, religious and secular, political and aesthetic, that posited modern history as evil. Current attention to spatial at the expense of temporal orientations is supported by a shared certainty regarding history.

Let us take Mircea Eliade as an example. His influence continues not because of the Idealism of his phenomenology of sacred space but, I should think, because he posits sacred space as a contrary to modern history, which is profane. As he says at the beginning of *The Sacred and the Profane*, "The first possible definition of the *sacred* is that it is *the opposite of the profane*" (1959, 10 [his emphasis]). There is no uncertainty for Eliade about what is profane; it is Western history and Western understandings of history. A displaced Romanian, he militated against Hegelian and other progressive theories of history and historicism. Contrary to what he termed the "terror of history" he advocated a reinstatement of place and placement. Spatial orientation serves as an antidote to the dislocation, alienation, and trauma caused by modern history in general and the history of war and Western European domination in particular. Homo religiosis, as central, original, and normative "man," subordinates time to place and understands time as cyclical and subsumed under natural processes. While he also imputes an ontological standing to sacred space, the clarity and stability of his theory is derived from the position of certainty that he gives to the profane, which, for him, is primarily modern history and assumptions that history produces novelty, is irreversible, lacks inherent significance, and is constituted by discrete events.

In other words, Eliade's theory of sacred space retains currency in present cultural and religious discourses, because it shares with so many other theories the assumption that the "profane" is known and its negative evaluation culturally shared. The profane, namely, modern history, provides the secure, common base upon which various "sacred" spatial alternatives are erected. Whether the sacred is a political or social utopia, the collective unconscious (Jung), internal freedom (Bultmann), the Church (Barth) or whatever, it draws its viability from its contrary relation to what is taken as certain, namely, the profane. Theorists who otherwise share little assume in common that modern Western culture, especially as defined by its history and understanding of history, is deeply deficient, even evil. This standard assumption is problematic because it conceals the fact that the negative is stabilizing, affecting, and even controlling the positive, even while the negative is denounced. In addition, the assumption depends on what Julia Kristeva (1987) identifies as symptomatic of narcissistic tendencies in the culture, namely, forming relationships negatively by constructing a common enemy, an action she diagnoses under the heading of "Romeo and Juliet." One does not need the kind of psychological insights of Kristeva to recognize that in a society as diverse and mobile as ours there is a need to create some sense of cultural commonality, and this commonality can most easily be secured by creating a common problem or evil, namely the profane as modern history.

In my opinion, theories of sacred space, if they are to regain substance, should be based on a more adequate theory of positive place-relations rather than on history constructed as sacred space's negative contrary. However, in my view, it is not convincing to posit sacred space as a free-standing or ideal category from which a theory of positive place-relations can be derived. Rather, the procedure should be one that first develops a more adequate theory of positive place-relations that then formulates what accounts for their positive qualities, and that finally develops a norm that allows sacred and profane spaces to be distinguished from one another.

In service to the task of forming a more adequate and stable theory of positive place-relations, I have examined works of English fiction written between the closing decades of the nineteenth century and the closing decades of the twentieth, texts that, in my opinion, advocate positive place-relations, to determine what kind of implicit theory of positive place-relations can be extrapolated from this fiction and placed in conversation with other spatial theories. I would argue that narrative discourse, although discounted by much postmodernist theory, gives place to spatial language, that the language of place and space is always a part of narrative discourse, and that the language of place and space shares with

the other languages of narrative the potential for prominence and even dominance. I have chosen to work with three early and three later modernists whose
work reveals both awareness of the problem of spatial orientation in a time of
rapid and radical dislocations and whose work gives prominence, if not dominance, to the language of space, place, and place-relations. I have extrapolated
from their narratives the implicit or incipient theory of positive human place-
relations by which present spatial orientations in the culture are questioned and
alternatives to them proposed.[2] I then place this theory in conversation with
other, recent theories of human spatiality. Finally, I take up the question of
norms for evaluating places and place-relations, turning, only then, to a discussion of sacred place.

I

The first component of the theory of human place-relations drawn from these
narrative discourses is the proposition that place-relations are of three kinds:
cosmic or comprehensive, social or political, and personal or intimate. The three
kinds are distinct but also clarify one another by reason of their differences.
However, while kinds of place-relations are discernible because they differ from
one another, positive place-relations of one kind tend to occlude those of another
kind.

The narratives of the six writers, while all shaped by a language of place and
space that is prominent if not dominant, differ from one another as to which of
the three kinds of place or space is of chief significance. They do this while also
attending to the other two kinds of places. This allows a number of hypotheses
to be drawn: (1) an adequate theory of place-relations will include awareness of
the complex, three-part repertoire of human spatiality, and a theory of human
place-relations that neglects one or more of the three kinds or transfers qualities
of one kind of place-relation to one of the other kinds damages our understanding of human spatiality; (2) a positive place-relation will be of one kind
and will occur at the expense of the other two kinds; and (3) the differential
character of human place-relations forms a valuable source of critical awareness
of actual or potential negative factors in relation to places, since it allows
comparison of a place not only with places of the same kind but also with places
of the other kinds. Curtailing the complex or three-fold nature of human
spatiality serves to produce or exacerbate negative place-relations.

In my opinion the narratives of Thomas Hardy and Graham Greene, however
different they are in other respects from one another, can be yoked together as

---

2.   For the narrative theory that underpins my work, a theory that defines narrative discourses in
terms of four languages, any one of which can be dominant, that relates the languages of narrative to
sets of beliefs, and that relates those beliefs to the necessary components of a workable world, see,
especially, the introductory section of my *Story, Text and Scripture: Literary Interests in Biblical
Narrative* (Kort 1989, 6–23). This theory warrants my interest in the narrative language of place and
space and my contention that it can play a prominent, if not dominant role in a narrative and does so
in the fiction of these writers.

directing attention to the primacy of cosmic or comprehensive space. That is, their narrators and characters attempt to retrieve or to search for place-relations that can be accessed outside of, prior to, between, or beyond places that are humanly constructed and controlled. Their narratives imply that the problems of human place-relations can be addressed only if attention is first of all given to comprehensive space.

Since for both writers cosmic or comprehensive space is sharply contrasted to places constructed and controlled by humans, it is a space encountered as unpredictable and even threatening, and this characteristic makes it both discomforting and beneficial. What makes comprehensive space salutary in narratives by both writers is that spaces of the other two kinds, especially social space, have become too confining, despite the magnitude of social space. The contrast created between comprehensive space and social spaces is sharply dawn, then, and a critique of the propensity in social space to presume the status of comprehensive space is implied.

In addition to countering the excesses of social space, cosmic or comprehensive space in these texts reveals other benefits. It has a limiting and sobering effect on human pride. It also allows human beings, despite the many ways in which they differ from one another, to feel a degree of kinship because comprehensive space, unlike social space, is inclusive of people and not structured by lines that primarily separate and even exclude people. Finally, cosmic or comprehensive space allows for some sense of commonality with other creatures, since it is a space that humans share with them.

A major difficulty concerning cosmic or comprehensive space is its dependence on beliefs about "Nature."[3] This question is part of the narratives of both authors. While in Hardy's *The Return of the Native* and Greene's *A Burnt-Out Case* we find characters in significant relations to natural places, nature is not simply there. The heath and the forest, while distinguishable from social, economic, and political space, are affected by it. Natural places, while central to the narratives, are also recognized as marginal in relation to dominant social spaces. In addition, heath and forest, rather than themselves constituting cosmic or comprehensive space, grant access to it. A significant move in the fiction of these two writers is that the power and significance of comprehensive space are related to but not identical with the "natural." Narratives by both writers depict nature as in retreat. For Hardy, the heath is becoming more a memory to be retrieved than a reality to be encountered. His material is from an earlier generation, and his narratives do not advocate the emptying of urban populations onto the heaths and moors of England. But attention to the heath as it once was provides a discipline of bracketing constructs, and this bracketing allows one to see the limits of those constructions and possible accesses to comprehensive space provided at their edges, in gaps, and by transitions. Greene also does not expect the denizens of modern Western culture to leave it all behind for ventures

---

3. For an informative and comprehensive study of the various roles played by "nature" in Western cultural history, see Coates 1998.

into central Africa. But distant places reveal, if not the limits of Western culture, at least its odd and frazzled edges. There, too, the peculiarly destructive effects of modern culture's constructions can be seen. Such exposures, even when achieved indirectly, can help to bracket social space.

In support of Hardy's and Greene's use of the heath and the forest as sites to access comprehensive space, we can say the "natural" still operates in our culture as contrary not to "supernatural" but to "artificial." It directs attention to what precedes, comprehends, and evades humanly constructed and controlled places. As D. W. Meinig says (1979, 37), "Nature is fundamental only in a simple literal sense: nature provides a stage." Indeed, despite its retreat and suppression, the "natural" continues to carry moral force and meaning as that which precedes human constructions and that upon which such human constructions depend. The fact that the word "natural" helps to sell products reveals both how thoroughly the category has been included in the market and how tenacious the qualities of goodness and reliability in "natural" as opposed to "artificial" are. Because of the importance of "nature" as a cultural site of access to comprehensive space, it should, as long as possible, be retained.

When we turn to social space, we face the problem not of reference or accessibility but of size. Social space tends to displace comprehensive space and to swamp personal space. There is, in the work of all six writers, agreement that social space in modern culture threatens or has already taken over the role of comprehensive space and dictated the conditions of intimate space. Joseph Conrad and William Golding, for whom social space is most important, are critical of social spaces constructed in modern, especially urban, settings and attempt to substitute differing kinds of social spaces for those characteristic of the culture. Conrad does this primarily by exposing not only the size and power of modern urban spaces but also their dependence on and determination by abstract, formal relations. The tendency toward abstraction makes social spaces not only increasingly self-enclosed and divorced from their contexts but also impersonal and lifeless. The implied correctives are to relate social space more fully to specific conditions, to consider Western social spaces as specific to their culture rather than as universally transportable, and to allow social spaces to be marked by uncertainty and self-criticism. Golding's critique of modern social space emphasizes the importance of change and movement in social space and the role of visionaries, principally artists, in providing the direction for such change. In addition, the kind of social space that appears to be advocated in his fiction is one in which differences are not absorbed by some abstract whole but, rather, one in which differences are unified by and toward a social goal. Vision and goal in his work hold social contraries and tensions in productive relations to one another.

One characteristic of modern social space that Conrad and Golding put clearly before us and subject to critique is its domination by rationality. The consequence of that domination is to make the placements of people, the distinctions between them, and the relations between their positions not only formal and impersonal but fixed and ends in themselves. The binding of social space to rational categories secures what Lefebvre calls "mental space" (1991, passim, especially 3–5, 94–95, 103–4, 295–300). Modern social spaces, especially because of the importance for them of bureaucracy (Weber 1968, 3:950–1136), are easily imagined, Lefebvre points out, as neutral, universal, and homogeneous. Society becomes an abstract container, a mental frame that contains diverse spaces and subjects them to an overall rational structure. This understanding of social space as a unified and controlling container is extended by the increasing power of communication, transportation, and commercial relations that modern social spaces require and foster.

Social spaces, it should be remembered, are always particular human constructs, and they ought neither to be identified with rationality nor thought of as universally extendable. Lefebvre's emphasis on social spaces as products counters these errors by stressing both the particularity of social spaces and their limits. The problem is that social space is largely constructed by invisible lines that designate particular places for various kinds of activities, objects, and, even, people. These lines are necessary if social space is to protect people and human interests from, while also relating them to, one another. However, these lines should operate to enhance more than to restrict human life. In addition, they overlap and penetrate one another so that social spaces should not be read as single texts but as inter-textual. The positive potential of social place-relations is to elicit from persons their contributions to a life that is larger and richer than could be provided by and for particular persons or small groups. Crucial to the construction of positive social spaces is the belief that human activities and interactions are basic to social structures and not only or primarily determined by them.

The narratives of E. M. Forster and Muriel Spark emphasize place-relations that occasion and support personal identity and intimate relations. The principal difficulty for securing personal or intimate space is to distinguish it from the cultural authority of ownership and individuality. Personal space does not depend on ownership, and it is relational. In *Howards End* (1911), the houses that are owned by the Wilcox family reveal how fully places have been absorbed by social and economic power and interests. And, in Spark's *The Only Problem* (1984), Harvey's ownership of a house in the northeast of France is only a first step toward the work he undertakes to secure some sense of his own particularity and integrity in response to a society intent on dissolving his particularity into social categories.

In addition, personal space, if it is to secure a role in a theory of human place-relations, cannot be defined only negatively. The force and significance of personal or intimate places arises from their enhancement of potentials within persons and their relations, potentials that have content, so to speak, of their own. However, it is difficult to designate this content, since the personal and intimate largely elude categorization. The qualities of actual, positive place-relations under the heading of personal or intimate space are variable and elusive.

The need for and the benefits of personal attachments to particular places may be more necessary and complex than we realize. For example, Gaston Bachelard, in his *The Poetics of Space* (1964), argues that our earliest and most formative memories are ordered not temporally but spatially, and this ordering is determined largely by the house or houses of our youth. He deals extensively, for example, with the verticality of the house and the different qualities of the attic and cellar. While he privileges the past in his discussion of personal space, he also includes the future, since he contends that people imagine an alternative life for themselves often in terms of an abode. In addition, he discusses hiding-places within the house of one's youth that secure, he argues, the sense of worth the child needs to develop. He deploys his theory of personal space against the early Heidegger, who assumes that we are cast into the world and not placed in it, and Bergson, for whom personal experience is temporally defined and for whom spatialization has a depersonalizing consequence (Bachelard 1964, 7).

Virginia Woolf, in *A Room of One's Own* (1929), in ways similar to Forster and Spark, ties personal place-relations to self worth, human relationships, and creativity. She marvels that, given the lack that women have suffered in personal place-relations, there have been any women writers at all. This fact is even more surprising when one considers that people of genius, rather than less sensitive to negative criticism and acts of personal devaluation, are more sensitive than others to them.

Personal space is the site, finally, from which moral critiques of society can take shape and where personal potentials can be actualized, new forms of personal identity secured, and new kinds of human relations created. Forster makes clear that personal place-relations potentially counter social space because they can support moral and spiritual awareness and social critique. For Muriel Spark, the spiritual qualities of personal identity and relationships require intimate space to counter the forces and designs of modern social space. People who engage in disciplines that cultivate a relation to personal space are perceived by society as odd or dangerous. Exiting society and culture in order to enter a personal or intimate space is a radical, threatening act.

II

Now that we have clarified the first component of an adequate theory of human place-relations, namely, that there are three kinds, we can turn to the second required component. Place-relations have two aspects, physical and spiritual.

This two sidedness of place-relations comes into view when the earlier modernists—Hardy, Conrad, and Forster—are compared to the later—Greene, Golding, and Spark. The earlier modernists try to redress the problems of spatial orientation by retrieving from their earlier years or the previous generation primarily the physical qualities of places and relations to and within them. In contrast, the later modernists, due to the disillusionment with the culture received from the past, a disillusionment caused primarily by warfare, turn not to the past but to the future and not so much to the physical as to the spiritual aspect of place-relations. While the earlier modernists are not indifferent to the spiritual and the later modernists are not indifferent to the physical, the stress of the earlier is on the physical and of the later on the spiritual side of place-relations.

All three kinds of human place-relations are two-sided; both sides need always to be present, although one side will likely dominate the other. As these writers seem drawn to stress one *kind* of place-relation at the expense of the other two kinds, so they seem to stress one of the two *sides* of place-relations rather than hold them in balance.

Physicality grants space value because physicality grounds and steadies human life and forms modes of relationship not only between people but also between their bodily identities and physical contexts. For Hardy, the physical aspects of space are associated with the cosmic context of human life shorn of cultural attempts to conceal, tame, or ignore its force. Human beings, rather than being related primarily to the partial and fragile world of human constructions, ought primarily to be related to a world comprehended by a physical space that has force and that grants human life an integrity that only relation with the "real" can provide. For Conrad, the physical aspect of social place-relations is provided by human labor. Human labor, in Conrad, while it carries unavoidable ties to economic and political factors, is directed basically toward the threats and potentials of the physical world. Labor becomes distorted when it is defined primarily by the economic and political ties it carries. Behind Conrad's many depictions of distorted social space stands the model of social place-relations formed primarily by the crews of sailing ships at sea, social place-relations established more or less directly by physical labor. Finally, the physicality of space for E. M. Forster is provided by the human body's accustomed residence in a place and its relations there with other bodies. Intimacy, which is defined primarily but not exclusively in terms of sexual relations, needs and establishes its own places. The validity and integrity of personal identity and relations give them a primacy that has potential consequences for society that are morally beneficial.

Kant, in his early writings on space, makes clear that human place-relations and spatial orientation are grounded in physicality (1929, 19–29). While he privileges absolute space, imputing to it a reality independent of the existence of all matter and as a ground for the existence of anything material, he recognizes that human judgments about space are radically affected by physicality. Entities have relations to one another determined by the body, distinctions between left and right, front and rear, above and below, for example. This gives rise to the understanding that things are distinguishable from one another because they occupy differing places. Perception, then, presupposes and does not construct spatiality, and that presupposition is grounded in the body.

It is not surprising that a theorist like Lefebvre, working out of a generally Marxist framework, would emphasize the physicality of human place-relations. He develops his theory on the conviction that "the material conditions of individual and collective activity" antedate the ways by which people are related to locations, that the language of space derives from and is secondary to labor, and that the body and forms of physical activity are basic to the construction of space (Lefebvre 1991, 71). This is what lies behind his relentless exposure and vigorous attack on what he calls "mental space." The effects of mental space in its repression of the body and physical labor are, for him, devastating. That evil is vastly compounded by the conflation of mental with social space. He counters that evil by decrying the absorption of labor and its constructions by an all-inclusive social, political, and economic space. He sees the subjugation of particular spaces to a general, uniform space as a means of control, and he opposes the inevitable denigration of what he considers to be human reality, particularly the labor of human bodies. He posits the laboring body as "base and foundation, beyond philosophy, beyond discourse, and beyond the theory of discourse" (Lefebvre 1991, 407).

As I stated earlier, the fictions of Greene, Golding, and Spark extend the language of space not in a backward and downward direction toward the past and the physical but in a forward and upward direction, toward the future and the spiritual. While positive human place-relations for the earlier modernists have to be largely *re*covered, for the later modernists they need primarily to be *dis*covered. So, in Greene's work, the place for which his characters look is located at the edges of materially constructed space and in the interstices between competing human institutions. For Golding's fiction, the visionary is identified as crucial to the possibilities for human creativity in social space. Without such visions, social space hardens and fragments, and people perish. Social space must be oriented upwardly and towards the future by goals and aspirations. Finally, Muriel Spark's fiction discovers that personal place-relations are not only distinguishable from materially constructed space but also opposed to the virtual non-material space constructed by the media and reproduction. In a culture of image, almost nothing personal can be articulated, and the culture so mimics the aura of spirituality that it is difficult to define personal space in an upward and forward direction without being usurped by the social. Taking exception to social space and categories demands intense personal attention and discipline.

Joseph Frank (1963) provides a theory of space derived from and directed toward what he refers to as "the spiritual attitudes that have led to a predomi-nance [in modern literature] of spatial [rather than temporal] form." What he means by "spatial form" is a coincidence between the "art medium" and "human perception," a theory that he derives from Lessing. By being an instance of inter-relationship, "form" is abstracted from time and made spatial. Using this category, he reads modernist work as designed to produce such moments. Modern narratives and poems tend to suspend sequence and reference and to defer recognition until the whole is read, its sundry parts then combining to occasion a spontaneous, self-referential, and momentary unity with the reader. We reach the clearest declaration of Frank's aim when he discusses Wilhelm Worringer's *Abstraction and Empathy* (1908) and its theory of the relation of art to history. Following Worringer, Frank argues that sequential and referential styles are typical of cultures in which people have a positive relation to their historical conditions while non-naturalistic styles, which for him define literary modernism, arise when such rapport is lacking. Spatial form in modern literature provides readers with moments of wholeness that stand in contrast to historical circumstances. Frank then goes beyond Worringer to endorse the philosophical conclusions to which his argument leads. He affirms the implicit idealism of several of the writers he considers and turns, in his last paragraph, to the religious idealism of Mircea Eliade. Modern literature, he concludes, transmutes time into timelessness, transcends history, and is revelatory of what art is and should be, namely primarily spatial rather than temporal, and, in some sense, sacred—or at least myth-like.

Raymond Williams offers an alternative to Lefebvre's materialism and Frank's idealism. His inclusive cultural theory sponsors an understanding of human spatiality that affirms both its physical and spiritual sides. He puts the options nicely when he says,

> Either the arts are passively dependent on social reality, a proposition which I take to be that of mechanical materialism or a vulgar misinterpretation of Marx. Or the arts, as the creation of consciousness, determine social reality, the proposition which the Romantic poets sometimes advanced. Or finally, the arts, while ultimately dependent, with everything else, on the real economic structure, operate in part to reflect this structure and its consequent reality, and in part, by affecting attitudes toward reality, to help or hinder the constant business of changing it. (1983, 274)

Williams stands behind the third option. If one pushes his theory a bit, there seems to be within it a primary emphasis on social space created by the "common loyalty" of workers (1983, 326).

What I find particularly intriguing about Williams' theory is its emphasis on a "whole way of life" and, even more, its dependence on a theory of internal relations. The relations he poses between aspects of human culture, such as physical and spiritual, are grounded in a sense of human life itself as basically relational. As he says, "Politics and art, together with science, religion, family life and the other categories we speak of as absolutes, belong in a whole world of active and interacting relationships, which is our common associative life" (Williams 1961, 39). These relationships include not only the relations of people to one another but also the relations of "man's ideal development" to "his 'animal nature' or the satisfaction of material needs" (1961, 43). Elsewhere, he puts it this way in another place:

> Yet I am saying that cultural theory is at its most significant when it is concerned precisely with the relations between the many and diverse human activities which have been historically and theoretically grouped in these ways [i.e. literary and social] and especially when it explores these relations as at once dynamic and specific within describably whole historical situations which are also, as practice, changing and, in the present, changeable. (1989, 164)

Finally, Williams, rather than posit realities that either archeologically (Lefebvre) or teleologically (Frank) antedate language, views language as constitutive, integrative, and inclusive. "Language, then," he says, "is not a medium; it is a constitutive element of material social practice" (1977, 165). While I think that Williams tends to favor the material over the spiritual and while he is attentive exclusively to social space, I agree with his position in many other respects.

III

The third component of an adequate theory is the norm for evaluating the qualities of place-relations. I believe that the fictional narratives I have already have mentioned provide a single norm that runs across kinds of place-relations and includes, in varying degrees, their two sides.

Perhaps it would be best to approach the matter of norm by way of the lack of relation to place, that is, placelessness. Placelessness can be both imposed and chosen. It is imposed by exclusion and confinement. Imposed placelessness is to some degree unavoidable; we are understandably excluded from some places, and we are required to be in places where we would prefer not to be. However, imposed placelessness can be a major aspect of some parts of our lives or of the lives of some people, and that is when its negative character becomes recognizable. However, placelessness is also chosen. We maintain stances of detachment from places because we frequently do not want the responsibilities and limitations associated with relations to places.

Placelessness, detachment, or unrootedness need not be taken, then, as wholly questionable or negative when compared to place-attachment. In his *Out of Place: Englishness, Empire, and the Locations of Identity* (1999) Ian Baucom detects this negative appraisal of mobility in nineteenth-century English cultural theory by pointing out how Carlyle and, especially, Ruskin, evaluated the mobility of industrial workers as making such people less English and more like Arabs and Gypsies (Baucom 1999, 20). Mobility, it should be seen instead, is crucial to human place-relations because, for one thing, it allows movement between the three kinds and the two sides of place-relations that constitute the full spatial repertoire. However, mobility as constant in a person's or people's lives appears also to suggest deficiency, and detachment from place altogether suggests some kind of self-abstraction. I agree with J. E. Malpus who says that subjectivity is likely to be deformed when wholly detached from place because "place is not founded on subjectivity, but is rather that on which subjectivity is founded" (1999, 35). Exile or alienation is no less a potentially negative condition when self-imposed than it is when imposed by others.

Let us move from placelessness to its opposite, ownership and the questions that it raises. Ownership counters placelessness not only by the inclusion it grants the owner but also by the power it grants to exclude others. Ownership also provides an alternative to elected placelessness. Ownership allows a person to have things the way he or she wants them, and it counters the fact that people have very little to say regarding the many places in which they commonly find themselves. Ownership and imposed and chosen placelessness are mutually clarifying. And since not all placelessness is evil, ownership is not wholly negative. The latent negative effects of ownership for place-relations arise first of all from the control that ownership provides. Ownership is inclined to eliminate reciprocity between person and place, to eliminate relationship. The negative effects of ownership arise, secondly, from the fact that ownership along with its contrary, placelessness, have become primary in our culture, perhaps even exhaustive. They should, it seems to me, have a more limited status. What is missing between them is a whole center-range of human spatiality that can be described neither as placelessness nor as ownership.

An important aspect of current spatial theory is the attention being given to the need for and experience of relations to places that include feelings, memories, and beliefs. It becomes clear that such attachment can mark all three kinds of place-relations. Sociologists emphasize social spaces as sites attached to and enhancing social relationships.[4] Leroy Rouner's edited volume, *The Longing for Home* (1996), turns attention to intimate spaces, to their enhancement of personal tastes and interests. And Yi-Fu Tuan (1996) stresses the counter-positioning of hearth and cosmos as kinds of spaces with which people have meaningful relations. This interest in "place attachment," especially by social theorists, attempts to do justice to the physical specificity of human place-relations and the meanings that accumulate in sites by virtue of what people have done and can do to and in them. My misgiving with this line of theory is that "place attachment" stresses projection or deposit almost exclusively, making the site passive. I think this weakness becomes clearer when people, taking this approach, analyze "sacred" places entirely in terms of their significance as an accumulation due to what people have done to, in, and on them.[5]

A contrary to such an emphasis is spatial theory oriented to place-relations described under the figure of "home." This need not be a house. William James speaks of feeling "at home" in the universe. I am uneasy with this designation as a norm for positive place-relations because it stresses too heavily arrival and completion, finality. The term neglects the positive potential of mobility and the way by which home, especially as house, can also become a prison. Nonetheless, there is a steady stream of studies of human spatiality that counter modern mobility with an emphasis on the significance of being placed, rooted, or at home.[6] While "place-attachment" over-emphasizes construction and projection, making the location passive, "home" over-emphasizes the inherent qualities of the location, making the person or people passive.

The designation I have come to use, rather than "attachment" or "home," is "accommodation." I mean several things by it. First, it suggests a mutual adaptability in positive place-relations, an adjustment, an achieved reciprocity between persons and places. Places draw something from and add something to persons, and persons draw something from and add something to places. Second, accommodation suggests capaciousness. Positive place relations are commodious. They unify physical and spiritual, past and future, restfulness and stimulation.

---

4.   See, for example, the edited volume of Altman and Low (1992), which is a collection of sociological studies of place relations.
5.   See, for example, Smith 1987.
6.   See, for example, Hogan 1995; Hamma 1999; Lane 1988.

Third, accommodation suggests that place-relations are not final. They are enabling, even liberating, and the positive qualities of a place-relation are closely
associated with non-finality. Finally, accommodation suggests the ingredient of
place as gift. There is something unplanned and surprising about a positive
place-relation, something new. One is unexpectedly incorporated, confirmed,
exhilarated, and enriched by a place, whether comprehensive, social, or intimate.
"Accommodation," then, suggests these qualities as basic to positive place-
relations: reciprocal, capacious, liberating, and gift-like.

In narratives by the six writers already mentioned, these positive place-
relations are narrated or implied, especially in their narratives' endings. These
moments can be accurately described by the term "accommodation," as I have
defined it. I shall venture a few comments about a text by each of them.

Clym Yeobright, in Hardy's *The Return of the Native*, returns to the heath
with expectations and plans that are unrealistic. His exposure to it requires
accommodation to its harshness. That adjustment explicitly yields wisdom. The
heath, in turn, becomes a fitting arena in which Clym can carry on his pedagogi-
cal program, since it also is a teacher of wisdom. In addition, the heath is commodious enough to grant a sense of continuity with the past, expressed primarily
in rituals still extant there, and with the future, adumbrated in Clym's teaching
ministry. And the relation of physical and spiritual to one another in the place is
secured not only in and by the rituals but also in and by the moral integrity and
charitable qualities that are recognizable in people, who, like Venn, live close to
the heath. However, the heath is too difficult and unpredictable a place to allow
Clym's return to carry a sense of finality or completion. Finally, the gift-like
quality of relation to the heath is that the heath not only is anything but humanly
constructed but also that by so being it is a welcome relief to the sense of
superficiality and self-deception that Clym judges to be characteristic of Parisian
life. The gifts bestowed by relation to the heath, especially because of its
magnitude and vicissitudes, are truthfulness, integrity, and an identity relatively
free from illusion.

In Conrad's *The Secret Agent* (1907) we encounter a wholly negative image
of social space and social place-relations. We have to infer from these negative
characteristics what a positive social space and relation to it would be like. So,
for example, it is mutual adjustment that is exactly what is missing in the
relation of Verloc to his social environment. He and the political bureaucracy
stand in no mutuality at all. The social space is also negative because it does not
allow Verloc to experience past and future as related to one another. Nor is there
any relation between the physical and the spiritual in the lives of the Verloc
family. Rather than capacious, the social space is confining and reductive.
Indeed, it is imprisoning; there are no alternatives available. Efforts toward
greater freedom only create more confinement. Finally, there is nothing gift-like
about this social space. All the surprises are bad ones.

Mutual adjustment between persons and place is very much a part of the
situation of Ruth and Helen at the close of Forster's *Howards End*. The house
can accommodate change, suggested by Helen's pregnancy and her interest in
the larger world, as it can also accommodate the Schlegel furniture. The ability

of the women, especially Ruth, to adjust to the house and its legacy is also clear. The close of the narrative also makes clear the commodious character of personal space, its ability to hold past and future, as well as physical and spiritual, together. Ruth continues the spiritual presence of Mrs. Wilcox, and, by taking in Helen and her child, Ruth adumbrates a future that will differ from the past. And the spiritual legacy of Mrs. Wilcox is related by Ruth's presence in the house to the material assets of the Wilcox males. However, the house, while stabilizing relations, also provides no permanent location. Helen especially will not allow herself to be confined by the kind of space it represents. Finally, the house is very much a gift, a bequest to Ruth by Mrs. Wilcox. The gift quality of the place is extended by Ruth's hospitality to Helen.

Querry and the heart of Africa evoke something from one another by the end of Greene's *A Burnt-Out Case*. The location has a positive, quickening effect on Querry, however complicated the place is due to the effects of European imperialism. And by allowing him to take up his work again, Querry is able to have an effect on the place. The attention the place draws to physical realities, especially to the forest and to the bodies of the ill, are tied very closely for Querry to questions of moral integrity, charity, and a lack of anxiety concerning his own dying. However, there are enough ambiguities in Querry's relation to the heart of Africa to keep it from becoming final. Indeed, he always recognizes that he must move on to something further. Finally, the heart of Africa and the comprehensive space to which it grants Querry access are gifts. He did not go to Africa as part of a plan or with expectations. The asylum it grants from constructions imposed on him by the culture he left behind and the sense of mystery it provides make the place gift-like.

The mutual adjustments between Jocelyn and the cathedral in Golding's *The Spire*, while not by any means without their painful and injurious sides, are evident in the fact that the cathedral evokes in him the aspiration to build the spire, and the spire is completed largely because it draws so much from him. The social space is changed by the contributions of persons to it, and the location elicits those contributions from the people. The capaciousness of the social space is also clear. The cathedral joins past and future and physical and spiritual together. The question of foundations, for example, is crucial to the construction of the tower and spire, and the completion of the spire has a reorienting effect on the social context. Finally, the spire is a gift, a surprise. Despite the storm, it stands. While planning and skill go into its construction, it is also improvised, and the result, to some degree, is unexpected. Golding weaves a language of grace and a language of judgment together in the narrative to convey the very ambiguous nature of human social constructions, their costly and edifying sides.

In Spark's *The Only Problem*, Harvey, at the end, seems to have discovered a personal place that is at least partially outside of and free from the determinations of social categories and identity constructions. The effects on him of this place are registered by the caring roles he assumes at the end. The past that he takes to his discovery of personal space is his long-standing interest in the exiled position of Job, and the future opens to his caring for others, particularly the young. The physical and spiritual are interrelated in that the location and

Harvey's sense of personal integrity are inseparable. His newly achieved relation to personal space is temporary, however, if for no other reason than that he is preoccupied with the nurturing of children. Finally, securing personal space is a matter not only of concentration and determination, but also of gift. The painting by Georges de La Tour of Job and his wife, which supports Harvey's quest for personal space, and the discovery of what constitutes exit from the determinations of the social space come as gifts, as unexpected.

The four connotations of "accommodation"—namely, mutually adjusting, comprehensive of past and future and of physical and spiritual factors, accepting and releasing, and gift-like—serve to give content to the norm for positive place-relations that runs through these narratives. What is advocated by the fictions as a response to the negative spaces that result from the dominant culture is a spatiality constituted by place-relations of three kinds, by place-relations with two sides or aspects, and by place-relations evaluated by a single norm, which I call "accommodation."

Conclusion

Returning to the question raised in the introductory section of this paper, I repeat that a theory of sacred space and its alternative, profane space, should be based on an adequate theory of human place-relations rather than either on abstraction or on the putative certainty and cultural agreement regarding the profane, in particular the profane as modern history. Sacred places, then, become sacred not (or not only) because they are so different from other places but because they are so much related to and like places and relations to them that are positive. The ingredients that go into constituting the sense of placement a person or people may have in what could be called "sacred space" are the ingredients characteristic of positive place-relations more generally.

One could say, then, that in "sacred" place-relations the four aspects of accommodation come into focus: place as mutual adjustment, as inclusive of contraries, as freeing, and as gift-like. In addition, the two sides of place-relations are also affirmed; the relation between physical and spiritual is confirmed. Finally, the three kinds of place-relations flow together—a sense is granted of what comprehends human constructions, of inclusion within a humanly consti-tuted fullness, and of having one's value as a particular and relational person verified.

Works Cited

Altman, Irwin, and Setha M. Low, eds. 1992. *Place Attachment*. New York: Plenum.
Bachelard, Gaston. 1964. *The Poetics of Space*. Translated by Maria Jolas. New York: Orion.
Baucom, Ian. 1999. *Out of Place: Englishness, Empire, and the Locations of Identity*. Princeton: Princeton University Press.
Coates, Peter. 1998. *Nature: Western Attitudes Since Ancient Times*. Berkeley: University of California Press.
Conrad, Joseph. 1907. *The Secret Agent: A Simple Tale*. London: Methuen & Co.

Eliade, Mircea. 1959. *The Sacred and the Profane: The Nature of Religion*. Translated by Willard R. Trask. San Francisco: Harcourt, Brace, Jovanovich.

Forster, E. M. 1911. *Howards End*. New York and London: G. P. Putnam's Sons.

Foucault, Michel. 1980. Questions on Geography, and The Eye of Power. Pages 63–77 and 146–65 in *Power/Knowledge: Selected Interviews and Other Writings, 1972–1977*. Translated by Colin Gordon et al. New York: Pantheon.

Frank, Joseph. 1963. Spatial Form in Modern Literature. Pages 3–62 in *The Widening Gyre: Crisis and Mastery in Modern Literature*. New Brunswick, N.J.: Rutgers University Press.

Golding, William. 1964. *The Spire*. New York: Harcourt, Brace, & World.

_____. 1966. *The Hot Gates*. New York: Harcourt, Brace & World.

Greene, Graham. 1961. *A Burnt-Out Case*. London: Heinemann.

Hamma, Robert M. 1999. *Landscapes of the Soul: The Spirituality of Place*. Notre Dame, Ind.: Ave Maria.

Hardy, Thomas. 1878. *The Return of the Native*. London: Smith, Elder & Co.

Hogan, Linda. 1995. *Dwellings: A Spiritual History of the Living World*. New York: W. W. Norton.

Jameson, Fredric. 1984. Postmodernism and the Cultural Logic of Late Capitalism. *New Left Review* 146:53–92.

Kant, Immanuel. 1929. On the First Ground of the Distinction of Regions in Space, and Dissertation on the Form and Principles of the Sensible and Intelligible World. Pages 19–29 and 35–85 in *Inaugural Dissertation and Early Writings on Space*. Edited and translated by John Handyside. Chicago: Open Court.

Kort, Wesley A. 1986. *Modern Fiction and Human Time*. Tampa: University of Florida Press.

_____. 1989. *Story, Text and Scripture: Literary Interests in Biblical Narrative*. University Park, Pa.: University of Pennsylvania Press.

_____. 1996. *Take, Read: Scripture, Textuality and Cultural Practice*. University Park, Pa.: Pennsylvania State University Press.

Kristeva, Julia. 1987. Romeo and Juliet: Love–Hatred in the Couple. Pages 209–33 in *Tales of Love*. Translated by Leon S. Roudiez. New York: Columbia University Press.

Lane, Belden C. 1988. *Landscapes of the Sacred: Geography and Narrative in American Spirituality*. Mahwah, N.J.: Paulist.

Lefebvre, Henri. 1991. *The Production of Space*. Translated by Donald Nicholson-Smith. Oxford: Blackwell.

Malpus, J. E. 1999. *Place and Experience: A Philosophical Topography*. Cambridge: Cambridge University Press.

Meinig, D. W. 1979. The Beholding Eye. Pages 32–48 in *The Interpretation of Ordinary Landscapes*. Edited by D. W. Meinig. New York: Oxford University Press.

Rouner, Leroy S., ed. 1996. *The Longing for Home*. Notre Dame, Ind.: University of Notre Dame Press.

Smith, Jonathan Z. 1987. *To Take Place: Toward Theory in Ritual*. Chicago: University of Chicago Press.

Spark, Muriel. 1984. *The Only Problem*. New York: G. P. Putnam's Sons.

Tuan, Yi-Fu. 1996. *Cosmos and Hearth: A Cosmopolite's Viewpoint*. Minneapolis: University of Minnesota Press.

Weber, Max. 1968. *Economy and Society: An Outline of Interpretive Sociology*. Vol. 3. Translated by Ephraim Fischoff et al. Edited by Guenther Roth and Claus Wittich. New York: Bedminster.

Williams, Raymond. 1961. *The Long Revolution*. London: Chatto & Windus.

_____. 1977. *Marxism and Literature*. Oxford: Oxford University Press.

_____. 1983. *Culture and Society: 1780–1950*. New York: Columbia University Press.
_____. 1989. *The Politics of Modernism: Against the New Conformists*. Edited by Tony
    Pinkey. London: Verso.
Woolf, Virginia. 1929. *A Room of One's Own*. London: Hogarth Press.

FORMATION OF SELF IN CONSTRUCTION OF SPACE: LEFEBVRE IN WINNICOTT'S EMBRACE

Mary R. Huie-Jolly

Can You Nail Down Dimensionality?

The Constructions of Ancient Space Seminar of the AAR/SBL explored the spatial dimension of biblical texts, ancient worlds, and their contemporary impact on social construction. Henri Lefebvre's *The Production of Space* and his post-modern interpreter, Edward Soja (*Thirdspace* [1996]), informed much of this group's thinking. Lefebvre, a post-World War II French social activist and critical theorist, situated his thinking about spatiality within a dynamic "trialectic." According to Lefebvre, "space may be said to embrace a multitude of intersections" that can be described in terms of the physical spatiality of things in everyday life, which presupposes the use of the body and is "the practical basis of the perception of the outside world"; "lived space," which "overlays physical space, making symbolic use of its objects"; and conceptions of space that impose structure on ordinary life (Lefebvre 1991, 33, 39 40). The trialectic, however, represents movement more than an attempt to define three dimensions of spatiality as categories. Lefebvre regularly contradicts his own explanations of distinctions between them. Their boundaries are blurred. They morph from one to another and shift in the lenses of various users. And they gain new resonance when placed in conversation with other theorists, as we shall see below.

This lack of clarity, to which the Spatiality seminar grew accustomed, is not simply a failure to be precise. Rather, the puzzle of finding language adequate to spatiality has to do with contradictions inherent in the attempt to nail down a dimensionality, to hold gravity alongside transformation within the duration of one's life experience. A bit like Heraclites' asking "How can you step in the same river twice?," the paradox eludes us. To call it "temporal" is to abstract the change over time from its grounding in physical substance and in memory, smell, touch, sound, sense, velocity, temperature, and the inexorable wet pull of the current.

In this contribution to the theoretical conversation, I will use "home" as a metaphor to frame critical spatiality within a theory of the self. I do this by interpreting Lefebvre's spatial critique of alienation through Donald W. Winnicott's developmental view of the self. Winnicott was a British pediatrician and psychoanalyst during the middle of the twentieth century. His work continues be influential in the revision of Freudian psychoanalysis known as Object Relations.

Home is an apt metaphor for Winnicott's theory of the formation of the self in relationship to the maternal environment. Though Winnicott did not intentionally focus on spatiality, his theories were grounded in observation and interpretation of his pediatric and psychoanalytic encounters with clients, many of whom were children accompanied by their parents. He quite spontaneously described these encounters spatially, sometimes including maps of the consulting rooms in his publications (e.g. *The Piggle*—Winnicott 1978) and describing movement between the parts of the rooms, and body language, in as much detail as the conversation. Also, he saw in the emerging self three developmental "spaces." Though apparently his use of spatial language was quite unintentional, Winnicott's developmental "spaces" bear comparison with Lefebvre's more self-consciously spatial trialectic.

Lefebvre's first space of physical things in the space of everyday life is similar to Winnicott's first developmental space in the formation of the self. Winnicott's first space is the holding environment of the infant in a relationship of total dependence, both within the womb and securely held in early infancy.

Winnicott's second developmental space is similar to lived space in Lefebvre. For Winnicott, the second developmental space concerns the ability to distinguish self from other through mirroring and recognition. It is the safe and free space of play within parental boundaries; within the room where the mother is busy, the child can play "alone" but in the presence of the mother. The mother's recognition of the child's accomplishment ("Mommy look what I made!") and games like peek-a-boo mirror back the child's growing perception of herself as an identity distinct from the mother. Consciousness of space is formed in the play of presence and absence that characterizes the relationship between the mother and the infant.

Winnicott's third developmental space—transitional space—has some resonance with the space constructed by architects and planners that is imposed on society, which Lefebvre calls conceived space. Transitional space concerns the child's ability to project and use illusion in order to try out new configurations and identities that help to connect the inner symbolic world of relationship with the demands and realities of the external world. Winnicott's transitional space is sometimes marked by the child's taking a teddy bear or blanket as an object of make-believe and fantasy. The child uses that space to pretend and act out various roles, creating an imaginative buffer that enables movement from dependence upon parents to participation in the larger social world.

In this essay I will invite Lefebvre's trialectic into Winnicott's home, allowing Winnicott's understanding of the spatiality of the self to act as a metaphor for Lefebvre. Winnicott understands the human self to be based in the relationship of the child with the mother (or the maternal environment). I am arguing that spatial sense emerges from this relationship.

The Self is Lodged in a Habitat

Winnicott reckoned there is no such thing as a baby; instead he spoke of the mother and child dyad as a nursing couple (Winnicott 1975, 97). He understood this primary relationship as a symbiotic, homeostatic union from which the self and consciousness of the individual as distinct from the mother, other persons, and the external world are formed (Winnicott 1975, 300). He coined the term "facilitating environment" to refer to a situation in which (during the first crucial months of life) the mother is given over to preoccupation with the infant and facilitates a total adaptation of the environment to the infant. The mother's adaption of herself to the needs of her child nurtures the infant's emerging self as an entity who is born from the center (of the environment/individual set up). The healthy self becomes localized in the baby's body. The self becomes a kind of internal house. It creates an external world, while acquiring a limiting membrane and an inside (Winnicott 1975, 98). The mother's preoccupation with the infant provides a sense of identity between the two; this spatial feeling of connection becomes the basis for the infant's ability to rest and find an integrating center within the infant's own body that, at the earliest stage of infancy, is inseparable from the maternal environment.

Gaston Bachelard, in the *Poetics of Space*, describes the house in the same way one could describe the human self, as a community of affection, concentrated courage, and resistance: "[it] seems as if it could greet us every day of our lives in order to give us confidence in life" (1964, 54). The body is at home within a facilitating maternal environment that allows the child to grow to meet the challenges of the outside world. It acquires the physical and moral energy of the human body as an intimate space supposed to defend intimacy.

> A house that stands in my heart...
> Open to the winds of my youth.

Bachelard (1964, 54) describes this "house" as "a sort of airy structure" open to another time. His language recalls the self that is formed, centered, and lodged within the body of the infant through her relationship with a facilitating maternal environment. An infant develops a sense of gravity, centered in himself through maternal care, that allows the infant's needs for love and food and secure holding to be met. When this happens, Winnicott says, the maternal environment has centered upon adaptation to the needs of the infant. It allows the center of gravity, the self-awareness of the child that is being formed through the environment/individual set up, "to lodge in the center, in the kernel rather than the shell" (Winnicott 1975, 98).

Winnicott's location of the center of the self in the infant's body resonates with Lefebvre's reflection on the body as the "point of return." He says, "We grasp and perceive only what corresponds to our own rhythms, the rhythms of our organs" and we extend their capacities to a micro and macro level (Lefebvre 2003, 170). He alludes to an "immense spectral presence" to which the rhythms of each body move. Similarly, Winnicott saw the house of the self grounded in an inner connection with the "ongoing continuity of being."

A House of Presence in Absentia

Winnicott describes transitional space, the use of illusion for constructing transitions to the outer world, developmentally. People are not just an inner and outer world. There is an intermediate area of experiencing to which inner reality and the external life both contribute. Though the mother does not know what is to be created at first, the mother presents her breast and the urge to feed. "The mother's adaptation [to the need of the infant]...gives the infant the illusion that there is an external reality that corresponds to the infant's own capacity to create"; that is, between what the mother supplies and what the child demands (Winnicott 1975, 238–39). Winnicott bases the idea of interchange between the mother and the baby on an illusion of the baby's ability to create or summon the breast as his object designed to meet his need, when in reality it is part of the mother. This illusory transitional space of interchange between infant and mother forms the basis for the establishment of the ego, which manages connections between the inner feelings and drives of the child and the external realities of the child's wider social world.

This illusory transition space is an unchallenged area mother and baby agree never to ask the question, "Did you conceive of this or was it presented to you from without?" The important point is that no decision on this point is expected (Winnicott 1975, 239–40). No claim is made for the transitional space of illusion except "that it shall exist as a resting place for the individual engaged in the perpetual human task of keeping inner and outer reality separate yet interrelated" (Winnicott 1975, 230).

The growing child begins to develop a separate identity by appropriating the security that she associated with the presence of her mother to an object, for example her thumb, or sometimes a blanket or teddy bear. This is the child's first possession or object. It relates to "the intermediate area between subjective experience and that which is objectively perceived," between primary creativity and object perception based on reality testing (Winnicott 1975, 230, 238). The infant uses her object to play with a sense of her own power and to reconfigure and try out roles and identities. By constructing an illusory imaginative space, the child begins to gain a sense of her autonomy; she creates and manages her own space.

The spaces that Winnicott links to the formation of the self are all grounded in the child's relationship to the maternal facilitating environment, either as
- dependence (the holding space),
- perception (the me and not-me space), or
- appropriation (the transitional space of creative reconfiguration between fusion with the mother and differentiation from her).

Lefebvre criticizes the inhospitable economic and social patterns of urban neocapitalist life that alienate people from awareness of themselves in connection with a facilitating environment. He calls for a recentering of the self by attending to the spatial dimension that restores awareness of this primary sense of relatedness or presence. "One loves a presence... Thus speaks the thought which wishes to determine the object of love...it operates through the encounter," says Lefebvre (quoted in Shields 1999, 62). Spatial awareness facilitates a feeling of belonging to a presence within a facilitating maternal environment. It is transformed by returning this feeling to the heart of everyday life.

Alienation Disconnects

Lefebvre's *Production of Space* addresses the alienation resulting from capitalist economics imposed on ordinary life patterns. Lefebvre regarded alienation as the central problem for progressive thought (Shields 1999, 17). He sought the origins of alienation within "a junction between the space of physical nature... and social space, an imagined synthesis between real and supra-real which had rendered the entirety of space—mental, physical, and social—tragic" (Shields 1999, 25). Lefebvre understood alienation as a spatial concept referring to the displacement or distance

- of the worker who is treated as an object,
- of creative self-fulfilling aspects of labor which become alienated by the assembly line,
- of the alienation of people from their needs for self-actualization, and from their bodies and actual needs (Shields 1999, 40).

Lefebvre finds no room for give and take in malls and expressways. Their physical structures of ubiquitous conformity embody their systemic corporate dominance. The airport, the nauseating predictability of fast food chains, the unresponsive space of neocapitalistic society makes no space, no possibility for adaptation from lived experience to spatial concept.

Unlike Winnicott's facilitating environment in which the mother provides for the healthy formation of the child by adapting to his needs, neocapitalist social structures were designed for profit alone and imposed from above, not in response to the needs of the people. Their social structures embody such concepts as profit and commodification. These ideologies become metanarratives that structure people's everyday lives. In Lefebvre's terminology, these concepts that control society from above are "conceptual space." They dominate by imposing themselves upon the patterning of people's lives without consultation or adaptation to their needs. Conceptual space alienates because it is not concerned with or adaptive to the ongoing well-being of their lives (Lefebvre 1991, 43–44).

Lefebvre used the Freudian idea of regression, rather like a modern day shaman, as an antidote to the de-personalization of space, to facilitate a more primitive and dynamic self-awareness among moderns. Lefebvre linked spatial awareness to a three-stage approach of returning back to the past before moving to the present in order to progress forward to the future; he saw regression as a spatial challenge to the neo-capitalist commodification of the patterns of everyday life. Regression in the service of progression is noted as a theme common to Lefebvre and Freud (Lefebvre 2003, 109).

Lefebvre regarded psychoanalysis as a herald of a new era: the reconfiguration (or "appropriation") of primal connection with one's faciliating environment, psychoanalysis allowed for cathartic regression to an earlier age, in order
to gain the inner courage to progress beyond the dominating structure of industrial society (Lefebvre 2003, 28). Lefebvre saw completely unalienated persons
as "true to themselves" by being at one with their desires: in all his books and
articles, he said, his concern in the first instance was "only love" (Shields 1999,
137). Freudian psychoanalysis, he said, is "a clumsy effort, but evidence of a
change of direction…the appropriation of desire, the appropriation of the body,
of time and space, and of new possibilities" (Lefebvre 2003, 182).

Lefebvre understood the problem of alienation and its spatial impact on social
life poetically and symbolically. Gallic crosses dotted the hilltops of his childhood in Landes, in southern France. They featured a circle centered on the cross,
an icon of the puritanical Catholicism that was a dominant religio-cultural force
in his home region. He inverted the usual theological designation for the glory
surrounding the cross to make it a designation for his own sense of himself as a
"crucified sun," whose creativity and power was put to the rack, crucified by the
imposed constructs of his social context: "Like my ancestors I continued to
crucify the sun in me and to carry in me the sun spiked to a cross" (Lefebvre,
quoted by Shields 1999, 8).

As a university student Lefebvre had been influenced by a medieval Catholic
mystical view of festivals as the collective appropriation of seasons, of life
transitions, of time-embodied formative social and geographical space (Shields
1999, 31–32). The festival modeled a way of holding daily life within a form
emerging from the season; its collective observance corresponded to an inner
desire to connect with the rhythm of nature. The festival does not abstract time
from ideas, or ideas from embodiment in communal practice.

Lefebvre attempted to live out communal actions that served as signs of his
own time as a 1960s philosopher, activist, revolutionary who never held a university post but supported himself as a taxi-driver. A poster constructed by
Lefebvre in 1972 called for a critique, not just of economics, but of all fields of
life, including "the experience and creation of human nature, the realization of
the self, including the creation of the city, the idea of "absolute love," psychoanalysis, the decision to change one's life—in short, the creation of new situations' (Lefebvre, cited in Shields 1999, 136). Instead of using abstract and linear
notions of time, Lefebvre holds time in space, and uses the language of
"moments" to describe events with transformational potential. He helped inspire
the revolutionary student occupation of the Sorbonne as a festive moment, a
"happening."

Lefebvre's language of first, second, and third space aims simply to envision
a dynamic synthesis of transformation that places value on movement between
three foci, as an alternative to the dualism of binary opposition. His irritat-
ing contradictions are indicative of his distaste for a taxonomy that separates
and defines. He is more interested in movement between differentiation. He
sees revelatory Moments as awareness of Presence within ordinary life. For

Lefebvre, everyday life is the site of multiple confrontations between private and public, between what comes from nature and the artificial, what through culture has become detached and opposed to nature (Lefebvre 2003, 100–101). The Moment is a mode of spatial awareness that discloses Presence within everyday life, unasked. It recognizes the form that experience takes in connection with dependence upon its origins. Moments have the power to reattach a person, to effect a primal sense of connectedness with nature and one's environment.

Just as the festival in its era was medicine against communal alienation, Lefebvre regarded psychoanalysis similarly, as a remedy for individuals on "autopilot, in a daze, having alienated mind from body" (2003, 100–101). Like the individual's post-industrial version of the festival, psychoanalysis also facilitates return to original sources of vitality and appropriates them. However, the fact that the focus was on the individual in psychoanalysis was symptomatic for Lefebvre of the destruction of communal life. The industrial capitalist milieu from whence it emerged commodified and depersonalized social patterns. Neocapitalism divided everyday life into discrete compartments, cutting off connection with a sense of ongoing presence within the whole.

Though they were contemporaries in England and France respectively, Winnicott probably did not know Lefebvre. Yet in many ways Winnicott's vocational clarity complements Lefebvre's desire for critical spatiality to bring transformation. Like Lefebvre, Winnicott also sought to facilitate reconnection; he thought that his role as a psychoanalyst required him to simulate an adaptive maternal environment. He maintained that it is the role of the analyst to facilitate a relationship of security and unconditional love. Within this environment a patient who had suffered from inadequate care could regress to the place of neglect and be healed by the sufficiency of the analyst's unconditional love for the patient.

Lefebvre understood critical spatiality similarly, as a process of regression in order to progress. Awareness of a moment of presence was a disclosure, hidden within everyday life. Presence in the moment reconnects, like the psychoanalytic process of regression back to earlier developmental states. Lefebvre saw psychoanalysis as a therapeutic parallel to his desire for symbolic appropriation of archaic forms of nature within spatial awareness. In a similar vein, Lefebvre develops the notion of "appropriation" (Lefebvre 2003, 130–32, 181–82) as the human task of reaching back (regression in psychoanalytic terms) to the physical or bodily source of an affective experience and appropriating it, bringing it to bear upon the present, by consciously acknowledging or interpretively representing it in one's constructive expressions in ordinary life.

Following Lefebvre and Winnicott, I will argue that appropriation occurs when space is created for ongoing continuity of being in the present; it allows the facilitating maternal environment to be reconfigured in constructive efforts to transform one's everyday life in the world. Connection with the primary sense of gravity, and helplessness, and the need for recognition and love is appropriated when it is acknowledged, it is held in the present, it not hidden. Psalm 131 is an example:

Ground of my being, my heart is not hardened,
And my eyes are not high;
I do not concern myself with greatness
and in expanding beyond myself.
Surely I have calmed, I have quieted my inner being,
like a weaned child rests upon her mother,
like a weaned child within me is my inner being.
Wait, Israel, upon the Ground of being,
from now on and for a long time. (my translation)

Regression back to the body, to infantile desires and satisfactions in continuity with being heals alienation. The development of the self is nascent in poetic expression. It reconfigures the primary relationship of dependence; it is appropriated in a new form that is "weaned" in relationship but differentiated from its source. Appropriation allows for the expression of gratitude, for satisfaction of the feelings of dependence within a new adult relationship of interdependence.

When the weaned child trusts the friendliness of the maternal environment he is able to switch back and forth, from assertion of a new identity, to infantile feelings of absolute dependence, and back again in response to the challenges in the adult world. The emerging self moves back and forth. The external structures, roles, and expectations of the larger world are on one side; the inner world of dependence upon the maternal environment is the resting place that allows for reappropriation of primary feelings through the medium of external space on the other. Illusory transitional space acts as a buffer. It quiets the soul. It creates a bridge.

This back and forth process weaves feelings of the past into new configurations, adapted to respond to the needs of the present. Trust in a relationship of ongoing being appropriates earlier feelings of absolute dependence (such as, gravity, hunger for food and love, and the frustrated lust for attention and power).

Can a Person Be Born Again When They Are Old?
Can They Enter Into Their Mother's Womb a Second Time and Be Born?

The narrative of spatiality emerging from primal relationship is not unique to Winnicott's psychoanalytic observations. The story of Maori creation evokes a spatial reconfiguration of primal relationships. (I am conscious that my interpretation of Maori spatial perception is simply that. It does not attempt to express a Maori point of view.)

The Maori creation story begins in the embrace of the primal parents. As the children become conscious of themselves, they feel crowded between them, suffocated in their embrace. To make room to breathe the children conspire to push apart their parents. They push their mother Papatuatuku down below; she becomes the earth. They throw their father Ranginui up; he becomes the sky. The space pushed apart from within the parents allows fresh air and light. Within the space they have pushed open for themselves between their parents, the children find their own places. One becomes the seas, another all the trees of the forests, another the root crops, another the wind. Only one of them, named Tu, which means standing upright, stays with Papatuanuku the earth, their mother. Human beings descend from Tu.

Spatially, the story is appropriated in the social practices of Maori. When they gather formally in the *wharenui*, or meetinghouse, it is acknowledged as the center of communal life by reciting the genealogy of ancestors, as well as of the land and the meetinghouse, all of whom are seen as ancestors of the tribe gathered in the midst of these. The meetinghouse represents the collective body of the ancestors. They sleep side by side on the floor, which represents their primal mother Papatuanuku who was pushed down to become the earth so they could have room to live. The descendants, with the new additions to their families, sit and discuss in the same place. The floor, representing their mother, holds the rest and the deliberations of her transformed and growing children. The roof signifies Ranginui, the sky father. The space between floor and roof beams is held up by the internal pillars that represent the children holding their parents apart by propping up the sky, who make it possible to move in the light by holding up the space between earth and sky. Between the floor and roof there is light and air, space for living. The meetinghouse gives space. In the Maori *hui* (or gathering together to plan and discuss) present-day Maori understand themselves as descendants of the mythic children. By gathering together in the meetinghouse they make space to reunite in the body of their ancestors before returning to their urban homes. Gathering within a space that embodies their ancestors allows them to rise to their full stature in their communities, to see and breathe freely, to deliberate on present actions. The *whakapapa* (genealogy) is ritually recited by an orator each time the people are gathered at the *wharenui*. The genealogy is taken all the way back to Papatuanuku and Ranginui, earth mother and sky father, the primal parents of the tribe, showing the people to be descended from the very land that they inhabit. The meetinghouse embodies living in the space between earth and sky, a space infused with the tension of the parents' desire to be joined once again. They are separated by the space created by their modern-day descendants whose task is to prop up the sky, to allow space to continue living by holding apart the earth and the sky.

"The most 'profound' philosophers have tried to reach a definition of 'habitation,'" says Lefebvre (2003, 122). The growth of the human person as a self in relationship to others is a spatial process. It involves movement from absolute dependence to a bounded safe and free space in which the identity is mirrored, to an illusory creative space of potentiality in relation to the outside world, and back again. The children held within parental embrace differentiate themselves though their need to push mother and father, earth and sky, apart in order to have light and air. Separation is held in tension with the longing to be fused again. I place this myth alongside Lefebvre's spatial dynamic, for it helps to explain the passion of dependency struggling for power of its own. People struggle to make space for themselves. To re-appropriate and to reconfigure a debt of love in a space that one has made for oneself is to hold differentiation and change in tension within a sense of belonging and relatedness.

Winnicott identifies a facilitating maternal environment as the core whence spatial differentiation and awareness develops, and as the home-like environment of regression to which people return in order to find lost or missing parts of themselves. Winnicott commented, regarding his therapeutic role in his psychoanalytic practice, that he constantly needed to remind himself that he was not, in fact, the patient's natural mother, though he understood himself to be offering unconditional maternal love to his patients. By unconditional acceptance, he says, the analyst effectively communicates to the client,

> I have love for you, that is my capacity to be identified with you—love with no ifs, buts, or sanctions; the only way to start is by the analyst coming to you with love—you had no idea of it, I came and fetched you; to make adaptation to your need I must come to you with love before you know about the need. (Winnicott 1989, 149)

The analyst facilitates healing regression by acting as a second mother for the client. Regression to a facilitating environment of loving acceptance allows the client to revisit earlier developmental phases to understand the deprivation and heal what was broken. Winnicott valued regression, the patient's willingness to return to a painful situation in the past and experience its emotions. Like a shaman on a journey seeking missing bodily parts, regression allows the patient to revert to an earlier stage of emotional development, to revisit and sit with the feeling of the original deprivation of one's basic needs. In the therapeutic situation, the psychoanalyst comes from the opposite of deprivation, says Winnicott, by creating an environment of loving acceptance that is willing to hold and to allow patients to appropriate for themselves the painful emotion.

Winnicott's "regression in the service of healing" is reminiscent of the redemptive mythic journey of recapitulation that Ireneaus attributed to Jesus. In a redemptive return to all the sites of brokenness, his descent into Hell released the captives of death, his return to the Garden as the Second Adam healed the alienation of the first. The journey regresses back to formative sources to allow one to remake the present by appropriating or reconfiguring earlier forms.

Appropriation is basic to Lefebvre's sense of the transforming potential of spatial awareness. His trialectic does not intend to define three distinct categories or modes of space. Instead, it is an attempt to give expression to a continuous dynamism within spatial awareness—a constantly changing and reconfiguring movement back to primal source, forward to emergent expression and back again. This restorative movement of recapitulation is appropriation.

Lefebvre sees the psychoanalytic process of regression as necessary for progression. It allows people to return to the place of trauma or alienation. It enables the developing self to establish continuity with the healing presence of ongoing being. It reconstructs the self by returning to primal sources of sustenance and desire.

Love is Self Forming, Self is Space Forming,
Space Derives from Love

Winnicott maintains that the self grows developmentally through the back and forth movement of distance and nearness to the mother who preoccupies herself with responding to the demands, cries, and instinctual needs of the infant. On the basis of her responsiveness, the infant establishes basic trust.

In the beginning the environment is a physical holding environment. The completely dependent child is held in the womb and in the arms of the mother after birth. After the self begins to develop outside of the holding environment, the mind—which is rooted in the body's need for a perfect adaptive environment—is able to use mental activity to idealize even the relative failures of the good enough mother and turn them into perfect adaptive success (Winnicott 1975, 244–46). Trust in the sufficiency of maternal care is able to cope with disappointment and rage. Trust sustains the relationship when the child's demands are momentarily not met.

A mother who is reliable in providing a safe space for the infant to rest and grow is, in fact, not constantly physically present; she goes out, she leaves the room. Trust enables the infant to compensate for her absence by hypothesizing her return. The ability to imagine her presence provides comfort, through the illusion of presence even in the event of absence. The ability to use illusion in order to endure the necessity of waiting to meet one's need is the basis for emerging consciousness of the difference between the child and the mother.

The infant pushes apart from the mother, as if by an elastic cord. Fusion between the infant and the mother is strained, stretched, creating spatial awareness of the boundary between what is me and what is not me, between what is part of me and what is part of the environment that holds and feeds me. Spatial consciousness of one's own body emerges in relation to movement between the mother and the external environment; it is given within the back and forth play, from presence to absence, when the mother is momentarily lost from view.

In Winnicott's terminology, the "good enough" mother is adequate for the infant to establish basic trust. That trust is elaborated by the mind; the infant, who has idealized the goodness of the mother, rationalizes her temporary absences and lapses in consistent care by using the mind to idealize and justify and compensate for what is lacking in her care. The healthy self develops when the infant can continue to express her instincts freely and increasingly test them against responses from the external world. The mind imagines and tests the relation with the external world in a play of spatial presence and absence. Her ability to keep alive what she loves and to retain a belief in her own love for the mother, even in her absence, forms the self. "One loves a presence... Thus speaks the thought which wishes to determine the object of love...it operates through the encounter," says Lefebvre (quoted in Shields 1999, 62). "Presence can be a person, thing, tree, flower, event or landscape, there is infinite variety, but the important thing is the intensification of experience; persuasive space thus conceptualized is a play of presences and absences" (Lefebvre 2003, 55).

The self grows through the spatial interplay of presence with absence in the relationship, in constant tension and testing between inner (idealized) and outer (imperfect) reality (Winnicott 1975, 61). Love, according to Lefebvre, is a model of Presence, originally and most intensively associated with the mother; it is appropriated through new relationships.

Shall I Forget My Nursing Child?

The problem posed by Lefebvre in the *Production of Space* concerns the persistent absence of presence, the retreat of nature, the alienation of daily life practices from desire for and recognition of primal connection with archaic sources of sustenance. I will try to minister to Lefebvre by bringing him into Winnicott's home.

Alienation is a state of being disconnected from ongoing belonging; it results in a loss of trust. The child loses trust in the goodness of her environment when she must constantly react to impingements that interrupt and interfere with the ongoing relationship of being in rhythm with the environment.

A comparable process of alienation occurs socially. On a macro level, structures that are themselves alienated from their source in the facilitating environment impinge on the practice of daily life. For example, for several generations, Maori, the indigenous people of New Zealand, were "strapped" (i.e. flogged with a leather belt) or expelled if they spoke their own language in the public schools, because the colonial government had decided that English was the official language of New Zealand. "Like all social practice, spatial practice is lived directly before it is conceptualized; but the speculative primacy of the conceived over the lived causes practice to disappear along with life, and so does very little justice to the 'unconscious' level of lived experience per se" (Lefebvre 1991, 34).

Spatial experience of one's habitat gives rise to language in a way that is grounded in its connection with the rhythm of ongoing being; in contrast, interference interrupts the interplay between the social practice and the facilitating environment. In neocapitalist society, the adaptive connection with the facilitating environment has become dysfunctional; nature is rendered passive and is receding, dying. Lefebvre's *Production of Space* depicts this domination of ordinary life. It is alienated from a reciprocal and nurturing connection with its substance in nature.

Nature as Human Property?

Lefebvre regards the human impact on the natural environment as having two modes: domination or appropriation. Domination of the physical environment is the result of technology. It ravages nature while allowing societies to substitute its technological products for nature itself. In contrast appropriation does not ravage nature but transforms it "into human property" (Lefebvre 2003, 130).

Lefebvre's notion of transforming nature into human property appears to rely upon Karl Marx's early thought. Marx saw production as a process of alienation or separation that emerged from an originally unalienated connection between humans and nature. The process of production, according to Marx, presupposes an original absolute dependence on nature. Production requires a separation from and control over one's physical, spatial context, exemplified in the master–slave relationship. It alienates people from nature and from mutuality with their fellow humans.

Lefebvre stands within the Marxist materialist tradition that regards humans and nature as part of the same interdependent ontological reality. He regards the earth as a relatively stable and self-regulating homeostatic system (Lefebvre 2003, 23–27). The human body is the organ of accumulation, experience, and memory; it appropriates "nature" around and within the human being by its own nature, sense and desires (Lefebvre 2003, 27). Lefebvre's concept of the human appropriation of nature as "human property," is, I suggest, a revision of Marxist materialism. Marx saw humans living on nature as if human and nature were one body:

> Inasmuch as nature is 1) [the human's] direct means of life, and 2) the material, the object and the instrument of his life-activity... Man lives on nature—means that nature is his body, with which he must remain in continuous intercourse if he is not to die. That man's physical and spiritual life is linked to nature means simply that nature is linked to itself, for man is part of nature. (Marx 1978, 75)

Humans are totally dependent on air and food, water and fire for their very being. Marx spoke of nature as the body of humans. This is what I think Lefebvre means by appropriation: an attempt to reconfigure in the present to a relationship of ongoing being with the environment through one's body. To turn nature into "human property" is Lefebvre's way of saying that it is a property of being human to live as if one belongs to nature, to acknowledge "an attachment to being [as a relationship to a] Presence which precedes surprise, the flower of life (the Rose without why)" (Lefebvre 2003, 52).

This awareness is spatial awareness (as it were, before the Fall) of moments of unalienated, uninterrupted, primordial relationship with the continuity of ongoing being of nature in daily life.

Lefebvre describes a house constructed so that its inhabitants could signify their environment, so that it becomes meaningful and appropriates conditions of their existence symbolically. This is an example of turning nature into human property. In his work on urban planning and geography, *The Urban Revolution*, Lefebvre asks how relationships between human being and habitation might facilitate rich possibilities of childhood and adolescence, "how to create a 'habitation' that will give form without impoverishing, a shell that will allow the young to grow without becoming prematurely closed up" (Lefebvre 2003, 138–39). Lefebvre's question invites comparison with Winnicott's developmental spaces of the self.

Winnicott's True and False Self

The true self emerges when the maternal environment adapts to the infant, facilitating a growing confidence in her ability fruitfully to give expression to her needs. This healthy self is porous. It allows for give and take between the inner feelings and impulses of the child and ongoing reality-testing in the external environment. However, when maternal care is consistently inadequate, the habitual need to react for self-protection causes the ego to form a protective shell whose function is not to connect inner feelings and outer realities, but instead to react to protect and hide inner feelings from the disappointment of an unresponsive or harsh maternal environment (Winnicott 1975, 296).

In the New Zealand of the 1970s, the government routinely supplied weekly visits by infant health nurses from the Plunkett Society to every mother of a newborn. The nurses advised on best practice. Feeding at four hourly intervals, not on demand when the baby was hungry, was widely encouraged. One nurse advised putting a fretful newborn in a closed room at the end of the house all night, as this would "train" the baby to sleep through the night. It is easy to grasp that the spatial is social; it is harder to grasp that the social is spatial, Soja observes (2000, 8).

When the mother does not adapt herself to the infant, the infant must emotionally, physically, and mentally adapt himself to the maternal regime in order to survive. The construction of a false self occurs when the infant's instinctual cries for nourishment and care are ignored repeatedly until the child gives up expecting that the mother will respond. The baby is not facilitated in trusting that his cries will be answered, but instead is dominated by the external imposition of a regime. "Impingement" is Winnicott's term for this kind of "[i]nterference with the personal 'going on' of the infant in a state of being in homeostatic union with the facilitating environment. Impingements create the need for the infant to react, and interrupt the infant's ability to maintain a sense of ongoing being or identity with the mother" (Winnicott 1975, 183). For Lefebvre, similarly, alienation is concerned with the impositions of structures upon ordinary life that interrupt the mutuality of human connection with nature. In contrast, the healthy self is formed with consciousness of one's basic dependence upon primal relationships for vitality, sustenance, and nurture.

Winnicott's transitional or potential space helps me to understand Lefebvre. It relates to the presence of a dependable, caring mother figure who evokes from the infant's earliest days a continuous sense of being (Fuller 1980, 203). The self is free and yet conscious of its dependence.

The Ivory Tower of Abstraction

Mental activity of the infant can convert the mistakes of the mother into good enough care, as the trusting infant rationalizes her occasional lapses. But when the mind is abstracted from the home of the self, centered in the body, mental activity can also act as the enemy of the psyche (Winnicott 1975, 225).

Elaboration of bodily functioning within the psyche, as an extension of the body, is distinct from intellectual work, which, Winnicott says, "so easily becomes artificially a thing in itself, and falsely a place where the psyche can lodge" (1975, 251).

When the maternal habitat is perceived as unresponsive, in order to survive in the external world, the mind constructs a self that maintains an illusion of autonomy over the environment. It does this by disconnecting from the unhappiness associated with the feeling of despair at the mother's unresponsiveness; the mind alienates itself from the feeling of bodily neediness that has been frustrated at its core. The mind provides a survival mechanism. Logic can operate distinct from feeling. The knowledge that it produces has a kind of magic, it can seem to create worlds unto itself.

The child who is abandoned by the mother meets the interruption of the presence of "on-going being" with the deepest dread. He adapts as best he can, and develops an identity of care for himself as an entity separate from the absent or unresponsive mother.

Lefebvre observes that social practice that has been dominated by neocapitalist systems is separated into discrete compartments of work, religion, leisure, and home. Winnicott's false self similarly defends itself by construction of barriers. It compartmentalizes to protect deeply hidden feelings from an unresponsive environment. Flat affect, a taboo on tenderness, these are responses of a self that has buried, or lost, the desire to see herself as reciprocally connected with the maternal environment.

The mind can be seduced away from connection with the needs of the body. Abstract thought betrays the original, intimate relationship between the mind and the body to which it belongs. The child can create transitional space defensively, protectively, or even aggressively. The mind compensates for the lack of motherly love by allowing the child to construct a sense of himself unto himself in order to mother himself. This compensation is necessarily abstract because it is disconnected from a feeling of connection with the maternal environment. In turn, the false self uses abstraction, the compensation for lack of connection with the environment, to neglect or dominate the maternal environment, as he was neglected or dominated. This unconscious revenge is the failure, in adult life, to recognize or appropriate the maternal environment as his source.

The self relies on the mind to construct an inner world to compensate for the absence of adequate maternal care. Like a castle, it is a world unto itself. It can create illusions of self-sufficiency. It can adapt one's ability to persist for oneself against all odds in reaction to an unresponsive or harsh external maternal environment. In the false self, the mental constructs of the self are imposed upon the external world as a defense against connection with one's bodily dependence upon the world outside oneself. When socially constructed space is imposed upon everyday life as a defense against nature, the structure it imposes does not facilitate the play of connection with tangible sources of sustenance.

The alienated self generates an alienated social practice. The social practices that construct dislocated space express a collective false self. They reinforce each other. The socially alienated self does not appropriate consciousness of feelings of the body in relation to the habitat. If the maternal habitat was unresponsive, the feelings are too painful; they have been buried under a protective internal shell. The metaphor for this condition is a life without love. People without love survive by going through the motions of existence without ever appropriating the source of their vital energy. The taboo on tenderness in public discourse respects the disconnection.

The Green, Green Grass of Home

Implicit within Lefebvre's commitment to the discourse of space is the assumption that the very consciousness of one's own spatiality is itself transformative Awareness of being at home within one's own body—of an inner sun, an outer cross, of tension between parents—spatial awareness connects with ongoing being, now resting, now pushing apart, to let in light and air. It builds a house. It appropriates a human positioning and owning of oneself as belonging to the physical habitat.

Earlier, in *Leaves of Grass*, Walt Whitman's poem "Kosmos" expressed a comparable awareness of spatiality that grounds social construction in earth, in one's own body:

> Who includes diversity and is Nature—
> Who is the amplitude of the earth, and the coarseness and sexuality of the earth,
> and the great charity of the earth and the equilibrium also...
> Who, out of the theory of the earth and of his or her body understands by subtle
> analogies all other theories,
> The theory of a city, a poem, and of the large politics of these States...
> Who, constructing the house of himself or herself...
> Sees races, era, dates, generations
> The past, the future, dwelling there, like space inseparable together. (Whitman 1891, 308)

Lefebvre's dynamic spatiality presupposes belonging, in a vast conflictual becoming, within the matrix of nature. The task of critical spatial awareness is to recognize the survival of this continuity within the limits, markers, and boundaries we impose by our perception, and to resist disconnection from it (Lefebvre 2003, 197).

Lefebvre invited a regression backwards in order to progress forwards. The progression of spatial awareness is a paradoxical movement toward experience of everyday life that is transparent to moments of connection with ongoing being. He regarded ordinary life as a work of art with the potential poetically and symbolically to appropriate a sense of presence; each activity is an opportunity either for alienation or connection. Lefebvre considered that to so live ordinary life, to make such choices, involved experiencing the body as the "point of return"; the self at home in the body is at the heart of space (Shields 1999, 70). Lefebvre sees the human body as an extension of nature and reasons that civilization is formed by the seed of nature. He understood poetry, its return to feelings and appropriation of forms from nature into ordinary life, to be consistent with spatial consciousness. Like psychoanalysis and the festival, poesis and appropriation are part of the cure. They bring memory and story into connection with place. They hold time and space together, allowing an acknowledgment of the parts within the whole, allowing what has become separate to return to its source of nourishment.

Our way of organizing ourselves spatially is in fact our way of relating to the world itself (Fuller 1980, 173). Habitual patterns of domination or appropriation of the environment are related to primary organization of the self. Lefebvre's cure for alienation is "to bring presence into the heart of the actual" (2003, 55). Winnicott, like Lefebvre, experiences love as the mode of presence. Like spatial awareness, it is a modality of presence that transforms everything.

Works Cited

Bachelard, Gaston. 1964. *The Poetics of Space*. Translated by Maria Jolas. Boston: Beacon.

Chodorow, Nancy J. 1994. *Femininities, Masculinities, Sexualities: Freud and Beyond*. Lexington: University of Kentucky Press.

Fuller, Peter. 1980. *Art and Psychoanalysis*. London: Writer's and Reader's Cooperative Ltd.

Lefebvre, Henri. 1991. *The Production of Space*. Translated by Donald Nicholson-Smith. Oxford: Blackwell.

_____. 2003. *Henri Lefebvre: Key Writings*. Edited by Stuart Elden, Elisabeth Lebas, and Eleanore Kofman. New York: Continuum.

Marx, Karl. 1978. Economic and Philosophic Manuscripts of 1844. Pages 66–125 in *The Marx–Engels Reader*. 2d ed. Edited by Robert C. Tucker. New York: W. W. Norton.

Meszaros, Istvan. 1970. *Marx's Theory of Alienation*. London: Merlin.

Shields, Rob. 1999. *Lefebvre, Love and Struggle: Spatial Dialectics*. New York: Routledge.

Soja, Edward W. 1996. *Thirdspace: Journeys to Los Angeles and Other Real and Imagined Places*. Cambridge, Mass.: Blackwell.

_____. 2000. *Postmetropolis: Critical Studies of Cities and Regions*. Oxford: Blackwell.

Whitman, Walt. n.d. *Leaves of Grass, comprising all the poems written by Walt Whitman, following the arrangement of the edition of 1891–92*. New York: Modern Library.

Winnicott, Donald W. 1975. *Through Paediatrics to Psychoanalysis: Collected Papers*. London: Karnac.

_____. 1978. *The Piggle: An Account of the Psychoanalytic Treatment of a Little Girl*. Edited by Ishak Ramzy. London: Hogarth.

_____. 1989. *Holding and Interpretation: Fragment of an Analysis*. London: Karnac.

LANGUAGE AS EXTENSION OF DESIRE: THE OEDIPUS COMPLEX AND SPATIAL HERMENEUTICS

Mary R. Huie-Jolly

Introduction

In this essay I use psychoanalytic theory to interpret spatial consciousness. I treat the relationship between a mother and infant as the matrix from which other kinds of relationships and perceptions and communications grow. I use the oedipus complex hermeneutically to explore the tension between spatiality and language.

The oedipus complex exemplifies the relationship between spatiality and the hermeneutical use of language to resolve inner tension. I chose the oedipus complex as a model for thinking about spatial awareness because it links pre-oedipal transferences of feeling, largely associated with the child's relationship with the mother, with the child's later struggles to find equilibrium in the symbolic order and within the larger adult world. In this process, it connects language with primary needs and emotions. This is essential in a spatial model if one is to avoid entering language as an abstract world of discourse, unconnected with the body and the living of everyday life.

The oedipal task is to resolve primary tensions, tracing back to childhood, in adult relationships with significant others. Appropriation of bits of stories or songs that seem to fit one's feelings transfers the structure of the storied language into the structure of one's inner life. It challenges the notion that texts can be transmitted and understood abstractly by acknowledging the emotional resonance that causes people to think they can understand the meaning of the text. The language becomes spatial when people connect it to the difficulties of life and when parts of everyday life are ordered by its sequence. The symbolic language that is chosen provides a socially understood plot. It plots the resolution of their particular struggle.

My particular interest is the relationship between spatial consciousness and religious feeling, when religion is understood as experienced at the limit, beyond the control or understanding of human experience.[1] The language that bridges between bodily feelings and the acting out of human purposes within society is spatial. It endeavours to reach out from bodily feelings to express itself in the

---

1. See David Tracy (1986) and Rudolf Bultmann (1958) regarding this interpretation of religion.

world outside the body. Jacques Lacan regarded language as a form of transcendence from the body. He saw free speech as the formative source of the self (Lacan 1988, 191). He described this kind of language as a cry, generated by absence from the body of the mother (Mitchell 1982, 4, 6, 25). His poignant image of speech as a sign of absence evokes a rethinking of spatiality in the tension between bodies and the abstraction of language. I will use his image of language as absence from the body metaphorically in order to explore the oedipus complex as a bridge between the body and the symbolic order. In the oedipus complex, language functions spatially to allow people to connect the feelings in their bodies with purposeful social actions designed to resolve the tensions of their inner feelings.

Recently, I saw the ancient Greek play "Alcestis" by Euripides.[2] The script was translated and adapted by the British poet Ted Hughes, the widower of poet Sylvia Plath. The program booklet commented that Hughes' translation is haunted by the ghost of his dead wife, Sylvia. The plot conflates a number of Greek myths. It opens with the god Apollo declaring the fate of the king, Admetos. He must die. Or else, someone in the royal family must die in his place. The king is in despair. He has begged his aged and mortally ill father to die as his substitute, but his geriatric father and all his other relatives refused. Only his wife Alcestis responds by offering her own life for his, on the condition that he must never take another wife. She dies. The king grieves her death and his own cowardice. The king's friend, Heracles, arrives unexpectedly. The king hides the fact of Alcestis' death rather than refuse hospitality to his friend. In gratitude, Heracles returns the hospitable love of the king by journeying to find another wife for the him. The king resists, mindful of his promise never to marry again, but when the woman is unveiled, he finds it is Alcestis. Heracles defeated Death to return her alive to the king.

While viewing the play, I imagined what it felt like for Ted Hughes to translate Alcestis after his own marriage to Sylvia had broken up and she had taken her own life. I also noticed a dramatic similarity between "Alcestis" and a popular Christian meta-narrative. Like Alcestis', Jesus' death was interpreted as a sacrificial gift of love, a death to save the life of others who are unable to save themselves. As in "Alcestis" the tragedy is overturned when Death is defeated. Both Alcestis and Christ surprise those who love them by reappearing alive from the dead. Stories like these are cathartic. Identifying with the characters can assist people in finding a way to move through their own personal passion narrative. When this happens, the language of the story becomes spatial; it becomes an extension of the desire of the person for resolution of their own inner conflict; it provides a bridge for the resolution of feelings; it becomes an extension of desire.

2. Performed by Theatre Emory and Out of Hand Theatre, directed by Ariel De Man at Emory University, Atlanta, Georgia, October 6–16, 2005.

Lefebvre's Challenge to the Idea of Space
as a Mental Construct

My understanding of spatiality is informed by Henri Lefebvre's pioneering work on critical spatial awareness. Lefebvre's thought is, in part, informed by psychoanalytic theory.[3] Lefebvre shares, with the psychoanalytic theorists Donald Winnicott and Jacques Lacan, the Freudian view that the human body is a physical nexus motivated by drives that, like a river or electric charge, excite currents of feeling or desire within the body. These drives link human beings with primal forces that are repressed by the imposition of conceived space, or "civilizing" impulses which alienate the body from desire. Lefebvre rejects a use of "space" to denote a mental construct of language that envelops social and physical notions of space (Lefebvre 1991, 5); this abstract semiotic, epistemological notion of space, closely resembling discourse, is supposedly given in language (1991, 136), not formed separately from language. Instead, for Lefebvre, "space—my space—[is not textuality] it is first of all my body, then the intersection between what touches, benefits, threatens it and all other bodies (1991, 184).

Lefebvre hypothesizes that if space is a product of the energies of "my body" interacting in society, the object of interest is to shift from "things in space" to actual production of space. His major work, *The Production of Space*, is a Marxist critique of the dominance of "conceived" space, the space imposed upon everyday life by architects and planners that causes any connection with nature to retreat. However, in spite of his critical emphasis on conceived space, Lefebvre understood spatial awareness as a potentially liberating dynamic process of interaction, a tensive movement within a threefold dialectical (trialectic) process, often encapsulated in the phrases perceived space (or spatial practice), conceived space, and lived space (see Lefebvre 1991, 33–46, and other essays in this volume). I am most interested here, however, in the holistic language of feeling and embodiment that Lefebvre uses to express his understanding of spatiality.

> The spatial practice of a society secretes that society's space. (Lefebvre 1991, 38)

> The past leaves its traces.... Yet this space is always...a present space, given as an immediate whole, complete with its associations, connections and their actuality. (Lefebvre 1991, 36–37)

> Signifying practices occur in a space that [is in the present moment] and therefore cannot be reduced to or confined within discourse or texts. (Lefebvre 1991, 136)

If feelings and tactile perceptions within our bodies are basic, and pertain to spatial awareness, then in what sense are words related to these bodily feelings? In what sense are words transcendent?

---

3.   See the discussion of Lacan in Lefebvre's major work, *The Production of Space*. See my other contribution to the present volume for a discussion of Lefebvre's debt to psychoanalytic theory in his theorizing of spatiality.

The Emotional Bridge Between the Body and Language

Psychoanalytic theory attends to the connection between the body and the symbolic order of language. It assumes that responses from infancy and early childhood are formative of adult patterns of emotional response. If feelings associated with early childhood are contained in the human body, then in what sense is language, as an expression of feeling, spatial, even though it is "abstract"? How is language connected to emotion? In what sense is language grounded within a body? Is it a compensation for physical presence, shaped out of absence in order to bridge distance between discrete bodies? Sigmund Freud's oedipus complex bridges between primal tensions in the body and the language of myth (1959, 164). I use it hermeneutically to explore these questions in relation to developmental plots that drive people to place themselves within stories.

The dynamics peculiar to one's experience in a primary family become imprinted within each child and continue to operate consciously or unconsciously in the outworking of choices one makes in adult life. The Greek myth of Oedipus is not a universal norm for the psychodynamic struggle toward maturity. There are as many myths as there are patterns of relationships in families. Dynamics associated with one's experiences of parents continue to effect the dynamics of relationships with significant others. Intense feelings of love and hate, dependency and neediness, fear and gratitude, are reappropriated when, in adult life, one transfers complex feelings from childhood onto new configurations of relationships.

Psychoanalysis is like archaeological investigation in the sense that it starts with what presents in the moment and works backwards from there. In *Civilization and Its Discontents*, Freud's analogy of the city of Rome is apt to this kind of exploration. In Rome, people live and work in quite functional modern structures which are built upon structures going back to the Renaissance, and under these are remains of more ancient roads, aqueducts, and sewers indicating the primary organization of the city originating from ancient times (Freud 1989, 725–26). In investigating the presentation of the "oceanic feeling," a primordial sense of being part of a larger whole, Freud reflected upon a comment of his friend, a clergyman, who attributed to this feeling the matrix of religious feeling.[4] His friend regarded this feeling of absolute dependence—a bodily, affective feeling—as more basic to religious consciousness than rules about living or concepts of God (Rizzuto 1979). Freud agreed that this "oceanic" feeling must be associated with regression to a pre-oedipal, even pre-natal feeling of fusion with the body of one's mother, but he appears to dismiss the comment of his friend, that this feeling of absolute dependence is the basis for religious sensibility. Freud typically gives little attention to the primacy of the relationship between the child and the mother (Chodorow 1994, 4). In his comments on religion, here as elsewhere, he focuses instead on the task of separation from the

---

4. Freud identifies his friend as Romain Rolland in a footnote added to the 1931 edition of *Civilization and its Discontents* (Freud 1989, 723 n. 2).

mother and on the idealizing and adversarial struggles of the male child to be identified with the father.[5] Accordingly, his view of religion focuses on its role as an internalized parent, or superego, that draws boundaries regarding socially acceptable behavior.

From a critical spatial perspective, I wish to take the part of Freud's friend. I also see the "oceanic feeling" of an intimate fusion of physicality and dependence in the first space that humans inhabit, as the maternal matrix of all subsequent spatial and religious consciousness.

Oedipus and Spatiality of the Self

Freud regarded the oedipus complex, the triangular love between the child, the mother and the father, or other significant parent substitutes, as the primal dynamic of love and hate, jealousy and indifference, idealization and desire. Conflicted feelings between child and parent(s) or significant caregivers form a pattern of relating that becomes primary in the preconscious and conscious experience of the child. As the child grows and meets significant others in adult life, earlier patterns of primary pleasures, tensions, and unresolved conflicts persist (consciously or unconsciously), informing feelings attached to relationships in later life. The particular dynamics of love and work in adult relationships are, according to Freud, an (often unconscious) replay of psychodynamic patterns in childhood. In the Greek myth, Oedipus' natural attachment for his mother was denied when he was abandoned at infancy; later, in adulthood, he acted out a pattern of rivalry against his (unrecognized) father and he desired his (unrecognized) mother. Unconscious of their identity as his father and mother he murdered his father to marry his mother. Freud uses Oedipus as an example of one possible configuration of the complex tensions, the ambiguity and shadow, that adults hold within themselves.

Children build defenses to protect against the terror of their own feelings toward people upon whom they are dependant. Oedipus' is but one story of how the paradox between desire and the repression of feeling in social behavior that defends society from desire.

Conflicted love between child and parents remains central in contemporary psychoanalytic thought.[6] Freud did not intend the Greek myth of Oedipus to be the only myth used to interpret life stories; but rather any narrative or image that fits the needs of an individual to work through conflicts from childhood in later adult life may function as an oedipus hermeneutic (Chodorow 1994, 26).[7] A range of myths express various configurations of "family romance." For

5. See the discussion of Freud's perspective on feelings of dependence in Chodorow 1994, 4, 26–32.
6. For example, Benjamin (1988), Mitchell (1982), and Chodorow (1994) all accept that early patterns of relationship are formative of and influential upon later development, while they challenge and reinterpret various aspects of Freud's analysis of the oedipus complex.
7. For this reason I do not capitalize "oedipus" when referring to the Freudian complex as it may be linked dynamically to any coming of age myth, not solely the Greek story of Oedipus the king.

example, in the myth of Persephone (Spring), the maiden is captured by Hades (the Underworld) and abducted from Demeter (Summer), her mother, to the cold subterranean world of winter. There she grieves until she is allowed periodic visits to return to her mother in the world above. Chodorow sees the Persephone myth as an expression of another version of the oedipus complex, one better suited than the Oedipus story to many women's experience of separation from their mothers (Chodorow 1994, 10). The Maori myth of Rangi and Papatuanuku, in which the children separate the embracing parents in order to make space for living is a primordial story of coming of age, as is another cultural text, the Genesis story of disobedience in paradise. Freud's fixation on mimetic dynamics between father and son to the near disregard of the mother now appears to be his particular take on the pluriform versions of family romance that he termed "the oedipus complex" (Chodorow 1994, 4–5).

Freud regarded the daydreams or fantasy life of adults to be expressions of their infantile desires for pleasure that have not yet been suppressed by the necessity of conforming to realities of civilized life in the real world.[8] For him, a mature acknowledgment of such wishes, willingness to embrace the ambiguity and tension between instinctual feelings and the norms of socially acceptable behavior, is healthy. For Freud, it is desirable to follow these feelings and to stay connected to them while living within the restraints of public and social life; though it is desirable to fulfil infantile wishes, living within the norms of society means that their gratification must be deferred. As in the fairytale, you may ask for your three wishes to be granted, but, in order to live well, movement toward their fulfilment in real life must be sublime or indirect, translated into a socially acceptable form of wish fulfilment—as in the expression of music, art, or religious feeling—in one's chosen work and relationships.

In my view, Freud's description of religion as a form of wish fulfilment for the masses is respectful of its function for psychological health. Religion, according to Freud, satisfies the psychic needs of those who have insufficient independence to work through the primal mythic structures that constitute their own unconscious interior lives. In spite of Freud's protest that he, as scientific thinker, was not religious, his view of religion presupposes its value for health within his own frame of reference. Wish fulfilment is, for Freud, a necessary process of projection of desire outwards by using fantasy or idealization of real persons or events, in order to reach toward a deeply felt need for pleasure and satisfaction. To see religion as a form of wish fulfilment, albeit collective wish fulfilment, implies that it provides a symbolic space for human fulfilment. Elsewhere, Freud spoke of the regulatory social function of religion as a collective parental voice, an internalized parent or super-ego, who one seeks to please, who provides comfort and chastisement, rewards, punishments, and ideals.

In *Civilization and Its Discontents* and *Moses and Monotheism* Freud (1949; 1989, 722–71) interprets the stories of Moses through an oedipus myth: the murder of the father by the son and the repression of the son's desire to murder

---

8. See "Screen Memories" and "On Dreams" in Freud 1989, 117–26, 142.

him. Moses murders all that his adopted father Pharaoh stands for when he murders an Egyptian overseer. By seeking a new order, he replaces Pharaoh's paternal order with the God of the Hebrews. In turn, the Hebrew people symbolically murder Moses by the rebellion of making a golden calf to worship, rather than waiting for Moses' law. After they repent, their covenant to keep Moses' law internalizes the paternal authority they had previously rejected. Freud associates this oedipal dynamic with the symbolic order of religion: the symbolic order is formed by repression of basic instincts rechanneled into socially acceptable utilitarian purposes.

In Freud's use of myth to explain this primordial, internalized oedipus dynamic, the son finds his identity as a man through a mimetic (both idealized imitative and competitive aggressive) relationship with the father. The son's struggle against the dominance of the father stirs him to metaphorically kill the father. Then he feels remorse over this unacceptable aggression against the one who loved him, and effectively recreates the father internally, by willingly binding himself to enact and keep the law of the father. As a consequence, the absent (and metaphorically murdered) father functions as the internalized conscience or superego of the son. Thus, for Freud, culture is the product of repression of desire; culture rechannels desire into guilt and remorse, which in turn transform it into conformity to laws designed to restrain expression of aggressive and erotic desire. Desire is reprogrammed through the oedipus drama. The law of the father is acted out spatially in adult appropriation of the symbolic order that shapes daily practice. Desire cannot seek fulfilment directly, for this would result in another murder. It is rechanneled in order to fulfil the father's law. The paradox persists psycho-dynamically. The oedipus drama is resolved by means of civilization, but civilization is built upon repression of desire. People are not satisfied when they are separated from their instinctual feelings. They become dead to themselves, though they may live out their lives going through the motions of legal and socially acceptable expression.

Lefebvre's Threefold Spatiality Compared With Winnicott's Spaces of the Self

Freud's oedipus complex speaks to the spatial relation between myth and the internal dynamics of childhood. Adult behaviors are acted out socially in identification with particular roles that embody an aspect of the symbolic order. In the effort to theorize a link between formative relationships and spatiality, I compare the twentieth-century theorist of space Henri Lefebvre's threefold spatiality with psychoanalytic thinker, Donald Winnicott's understanding of distinct "spaces" in the formation of the self (see my other contribution to the present volume). To join this spatial theory to language at the limit of experience, I juxtapose my synthesis of Winnicott and Lefebvre with Lacan's thought about language as a compensation for absence.

Lefebvre's sense that space is "first of all my body" is congruent with psychoanalytic thinker Donald Winnicott's developmental spaces. Winnicott's clinical observations of pediatric and psychoanalytic practice led him to hypothesize that the child, initially fused the mother, gradually develops a distinct sense of self through relationship with a facilitating maternal environment.

Winnicott identified three developmental spaces in the formation of the self:[9]

1. A holding space, or holding environment, provides for the infant within the womb and in total dependence after birth. The nursing child us in a place of trust, in total dependence on the mother.

2. A bounded space, like a play pen or baby-proofed house, is a space created by parents to allow for the safety of the child. In the bounded environment, the infant is free to play, freely as if "alone," while securely in the presence of her/his mother. The child begins to establish a sense of separateness from the mother through this process of play. Mother and child mirror back recognition in the play of nearness and distance between them.

3. A transitional space enables the child to move between feelings associated with attachment to the parents and the desire to play at different roles and identities, strategies and choices, associated with the larger social order. It is a liminal space between the world of society and the child's inner family circle. Winnicott saw the child's ownership of a possession, like a blanket or teddy bear, with the consent of the parents but not under the control of the parents, as a sign of transference of feelings into imagination, or transitional space. The child projects reality onto the blanket, creating new spatial identities. According to Winnicott, art and science, religion and culture, are born in this transitional space of the imagination.

Spatial awareness is a process of regression backwards and progression forwards: regression back to earlier dependency feelings associated with the holding environment, progression forwards to seek mirroring or recognition associated with the task of identity formation in relationship to a significant other, and the process of reconfiguring these movements symbolically through creative use of transitional objects in which one imagines new roles and identities. As in Lefebvre's spatial trialectic, spatial consciousness is a movement in tension between all of these aspects of spatiality, all the time. One is dependent on the physical environment (holding space), has a perception of what is outside one's body (bounded space), and at the same time may be using "objects" spatially to project or reconfigure one's sense of self in relation to the external reality (transitional space). All of these continue to blend and re-integrate in the process of developing a sense of self.[10]

If Winnicott is correct that these "spaces" are formed through the transference of feelings in relationship to significant others, this helps to explain the cathartic relationship between mythic or religious language and the archaeology of the

9. My description of Winnicott's spaces is derived from "Maturational Processes and the Facilitating Environment" in his *Collected Papers* (1975, 97–98, 183, 230–39).

10. Compare the discussion of innovative thought patterns based on synopsis, identity, integration, and imagination in Fauconnier and Turner 2002.

self. Both Freud and Winnicott locate the development of religious and cultural myths in between engagement with the symbolic order of the external world and the need to work out tensions originating in primary relationships in childhood. The spatial phenomenology of religious feeling is based not simply in the symbolic order but also and more foundationally in the tensions associated with the earliest relationships.

Winnicott's spaces can serve as a lens for interpretation of Lefebvre's threefold spatiality.[11] Lefebvre's physical space, or space of everyday life, can be linked to the space of holding within the womb and at the breast of the mother. Spatial differentiation, correlative to Lefebvre's lived space, occurs through the child's beginning to perceive her/his separateness from what is outside her/his body through a process of mirroring and bounded free play. Lefebvre's notion of conceived space, designed by architects and planners, is oppressive; these powerful constructs dominate the space of nature and everyday life in a neo-capitalist society. Ironically, it is comparable in microcosm to the potential space created by the imaginative child imposing her will on the teddy bear or blanket.

Winnicott's awareness of the developmental spatiality of the self supports Lefebvre's emphasis on the body as the basis for spatial awareness. Lefebvre sees the production of space as an appropriation of (or an ability to effectively use) desire. His spatial perspective is consistent with assumptions made by Winnicott. The child imposing his will on the teddy bear feels very powerful; he sees himself as autonomous, as does the architect or planner. But in fact the ability of the individual to create space at all, the ability to differentiate self from other, remains grounded in the body. The body is spatially dependent upon its environment. This dependence originates from a spatial feeling of primal dependence on the facilitating maternal environment.[12] Bodily awareness facilitates regression back to feelings of dependence. Reconnecting with the body and its connection with one's environment renews this primary connection, healing parts of the self that were inadequately formed in childhood. Both Winnicott and Lefebvre see this regressive fusion back to the facilitating environment as a healing step backwards that enables renewal of vital connection within one's habitat (Lefebvre 2003, 27; Winnicott 1975, 97–98).

The Polarity of Language and Spatiality: Lacan's Challenge to Winnicott

Though Winnicott did not overtly study spatiality, his perspective (informing the psychoanalytic school of Object Relations) is inherently spatial. Winnicott thought of the mother–child dyad as a "nursing couple," and saw the infant as

---

11.   My discussion of the thought of Lefebvre and Winnicott on spatiality and regression is a summary from a comparison of their thought in my other essay in this volume.

12.   This mystical and romantic inspiration is clearer in Lefebvre's shorter, early works, e.g., *Key Writings* (2003). In contrast, his major work, *The Production of Space*, a scathing denunciation of modern industrial capitalism, laments the imposition of its conceived space upon the fragile and relatively passive space of nature and ordinary life.

inseparable from a facilitating maternal environment. In contrast, following Freud's emphasis on the infant's task of individuation and separation from primary feelings of attachment, Lacan opposed Object Relations, charging that focus on the original fusion and dependence between infant and mother lacks transcendence (Lacan 1988, 213). Whereas Winnicott understood the object of desire as a two-person relationship, Lacan understood the object of desire as one person based on the fantasies of the other (Mitchell 1982, 4). Unlike Lefebvre and Winnicott, Lacan positioned the formation of the human self not within the body in relationship within a facilitating environment, but within language. Language forms the human subject in abstraction from the body. For Lacan, language emerges not because of the bodily presence of the mother, but as a cry in response to her absence. Thus language, for Lacan, is like zero; it emerges from nothingness, or empty space; the symbolic order that language constructs is formed out of desire to compensate for gaps in relationship, to compensate for absence (Lacan 1982, 165).

I disagree with Lacan's account of language as a "cry," in that it fails to take the relationality of language into account. Children learn to speak from the cooing of their mothers more than from their cries of abandonment.[13] Yet his poignant image of speech is striking. Even in the pre-oedipal stage of dependence, Lacan sees speech as a cry, born out of absence (Lacan 1977, 22–23, 214). I pursue it here as a clue to language at the limit of experience, as speech uttered out of need. For Lacan, desire itself only exists by its alienation; he speaks of a "lost object," insatiable desire that never gets over the pain of losing its mother's breast. Desire only appears in the absence of the object, as in Oedipus' desire for what he could not have. In contrast, Winnicott begins with original fusion as the subject.[14]

In Lacan's interpretation of Freud, language frees the mind from the body, eluding the gendered determinisms of "nature." Lacan maintains that the whole symbolic order is a space holder that is empty, like zero, born out of nothing. Feminist critic Juliet Mitchell defends this unembodied, abstract bent in Lacan

---

13.   Ludwig Wittgenstein's account of how language is learned by context is much more satisfactory (Wittgenstein 1997).

14.   So Julliette Mitchell (1982, 4, 6, 25, 31), a feminist critic who exposes the patriarchal bias within the classical Freudian elaborations of the oedipus complex: it leans toward biological determinism; the normative drama is a male competition between father and son. Nevertheless, Mitchell values Lacan's reading of Freud specifically because of its potential for transcendence of culturally coded gender roles. In the oedipus complex, the intrusion of a difference, which upsets the original fusion between mother and child, is symbolized by the appearance of the father. Mitchell rejects the identification of woman with the female body or, in the cultural symbolic order, with the earth, for to speak thus promotes biological determinism. Though Mitchell accepts cultural coding of the symbolic order, even including penis envy as male control of the construction of the symbolic order, she considers Lacan's privileging of language as opposed to body as a strategy that is potentially liberating of women. Lacan describes the libido as a "lamella," like an amoeba that moves wherever its energy floats. It is not necessarily heterosexual, nor is it driven to uphold patriarchy. She questions biological determinism in association with the oedipus dynamic, maintaining that love for the preferred parent, not necessarily the parent of the opposite sex, is crucial.

by arguing that this negation of bodily connection allows space for a women's identity that is transcendent. A woman becomes a speaking subject, free from imprisonment in the body, through language. For Lacan, speech is the cry that needs to be uttered only because of the absence of the mother; speech born of absence is the origin of consciousness, not bodily presence spatially contained in relationship with the mother.

This contrasts sharply with Winnicott, who presupposes a continuity of being between infant and mother, and presupposes that link even after the child achieves maturity and independence. The individual develops by a process of transference of these feelings of primary love and attachment onto other love objects in later stages of life (Winnicott 1975, 97–98, 297). In contrast, for Lacan the lack of a clear break or separation generates an unhealthy fusion and denies the possibility of freedom from the maternal relationship. The self is formed as a free subject, says Lacan, not because of any physical connection with the mother, but on the basis of her absence (Lacan 1977, 23, 29, 77; Mitchell 1982, 40–46).

Storied Maps in Everyday Life

In response to Lacan's view that language transcends the spatiality of the body, I will reflect on how the spatiality of language can be construed. Language is characteristically spatial when it is an extension of bodily feeling or desire. By this I mean it seeks to satisfy or resolve primary needs and conflicts; it attempts to satisfy these in the living of everyday life. In this sense, spatial consciousness, awareness of living in the present, conscious of the feelings in one's body in one's environment, is like religious feeling; it is connected with desire. Similarly, the feeling of identification with a character in a story emerges when one senses a common motive or desire, and this shared feeling enables connection between the symbolic world of the narrative and desires tracing back to primary relationships.

People make sense of these tensions in language at the limit of experience. The appropriation of particular types of religious language appears to evoke distinct spatialities. For example, the narrative of pre-creation in 1 John 1:1 evokes the intimacy of dependency and sensory touch reminiscent of the holding environment.

> What was from the beginning, what we heard, what we saw with our eyes, what we admired and felt with our hands, even the word of life has appeared, and we saw and testified and announced to you the eternal life which was alongside the father and has appeared to you. (my translation)

Experiential bodily reality, "what we touched," is juxtaposed with a particular kind of language: "the word of life." The beginning and the telos, the eternal, are held together in this place too. These relate back to early feelings of dependency. People contextualize stories and myths and images to bridge this edge of experience, to allow their own feelings to come to speech. People use storied language to move through the currents of inner feeling, to acknowledge feelings of dependence and gratitude, to gain courage to make choices, or to regret them in remorse.

In psychoanalytic theory, memory and unconscious patterns of emotional and somatic response from early childhood are twisted together, forming the wordless archaeological dig of inner emotional life. Desire and dread are the threads leading into the labyrinth of one's own life story. Feelings of dread lead like threads connecting conscious motivations to the threshold of unconscious desires. Like a blanket or teddy bear they take on different identities; like characters in a fairytale they act out the representative challenges of a myth. In encountering feelings hidden deep within, one eventually faces choices. One has to choose. What will I do? How will I respond? The spatial question is existential.

Imagine playing a computer game with multiple choices in each turn of the dungeon. You chose your own adventure at each step of the journey. For example, you have come face to face with the minotaur, or in another language, Satan the adversary. In the face of this threat, you can choose: to recoil in horror, make a fearful retreat, to pass by in sleuth, to challenge the beast head on. Will it crunch your bones to powder or will you act out your infantile wish: find a secret passage to the throne room of the castle? The computer game is like the myth; the myth is like the existential journey. The myth, like dreams, clothes feelings of fear and desire, placing them within the structure of storied spaces. Language that enables the extension of desire into purposeful action in everyday life is spatial, by virtue of the connection it makes between bodily feelings and actions in the real world of society.

Myths, fairytales, stories of ancestors, and popular songs and movies function like sacred scripture. They are storied spaces in which one can choose to play out parts of one's own life journey. Language that is lived out in practice becomes spatial. Word becomes flesh when it shapes the everyday lives of real people. People use stories as transitional objects, choosing to embody imaginatively now one verse, now another character, or a piece of one matched to the other. They are worn like clothes chosen to fit one's body, to fit the needs of the occasion.

What is irreducible is not an effect of language, says Lacan; the effect of language is the patheme or passion of the body; language is an adorning, it is all rhetoric and can only be conceived through use, the subject is determined by being, that is to say, by desire (Lacan 1982, 165).

To move into unknown territory is frightening. One does not go naked to the elements; the stories, like clothes, protect the body from exposure and excessive vulnerability. As we wrap the body of the newborn and the dead, language at the limit of experience protects and names connections desired between bodies.

Language is needed by the bodily experience of spatiality because entering a space in which one does not know how to be requires more than raw feeling. To live with the feelings in one's body, navigating the currents of desire, requires restraint and is fraught with danger. It requires someone having been there before to know how to act in courage, how to carve out the capacity to love. Storied language, like a star that guides the compass, directs feeling into known paths, already plotted within the symbolic order.

Oedipus Myths: The Spatiality of Language and Transcendence of Desire

The oedipus dynamic bridges between infantile desire and adult production of social space. Such transference of feeling is spatial in that it presupposes a holding space (primary love), a perceived space of one's own identity (idealized and mirrored), and a transitional space of the reappropriation of primary feelings through symbolic language in order to transform old feelings to create a new relationship.

Freud analyzed the selection and appropriation of symbolic language from cultural myths and religious ideas to reveal the center of gravity in a culture as well as in the individual's personal experience of themselves.[15] In *Civilization and Its Discontents* and in *Moses and Monotheism* he uses the oedipus complex exegetically to interpret particular religious ideas in relation to "coming of age" scenarios within individuals' experience.

Patterns of relating from one's family of origin imprint upon one's inner emotional constitution. These create internalized tensions. The dynamic re-emerges in relational dynamics in adult life. The levels in the computer game acknowledge the need for skill and wisdom, the challenge to maturity beyond one's capability. The myth is like the developmental journey. It functions as a storied map. It tells about the journey, the choices faced, and their consequences in the conventional wisdom of the symbolic order. It represents guidance from people who have felt these feelings before, who have faced comparable choices and lived to tell the tale. The popular language of songs, movies, hymns, prayers, stories of heroes and ancestors gives linguistic expression to a public symbolic order. People mix and match the stories to suit the occasion. Storied language provides a container for the transfer of feelings from earliest child-hood. Images of self emerge from the tension of identifying the particularity of oneself within this range of choices. Like stone jars, they are filled with water, but the story transforms the feelings into wine to meet the occasion, changing ordinary life into the pattern of a drama. The symbolic language of myth becomes spatial when it clothes the desires acted out in everyday life. Freud's analysis of love helps to explain this transition in which the oedipus dynamic acts as a bridge from the current of feeling to its search for satisfaction in purposeful social action.

Freud understood the bodily feelings that flow like currents of a river or electricity to be the grounding of love, but his interest in sexual drive is but one aspect of his understanding of love.[16] It stands in tension with love's other face, its self-transcendence. This is the will to hold out for what is desirable for the

---

15. See "The Case of Schreiber" in Freud 1958.
16. See Julia Kristeva (1987) on the complexity of Freud's analysis of love.

well-being of the loved one, to reach toward what is beyond oneself, to relate fully to one who is other than oneself. Self-giving love embodies ethical practice.

When feelings of gratitude and affection, the sacred legacy that one receives in childhood from parents, are transferred to a significant other in adulthood, the beloved becomes the receptacle for one's deepest and highest affection. In romantic love, when the values associated with the example of parents are projected on to the object of erotic desire, both sensual and affectionate currents of feeling flow together.[17] And yet, the intensity of such feelings demands distance. Language allows for such transcendence. The language of love songs makes cosmic claims—"Fly me to the moon and let me sing among those stars... In other words, please be true, in other words I love you"[18]—clothing feelings at the limit of comprehension or control. These feelings return a person to an experience of primary love, as old as infancy, projected into the heart of an adult relationship. The oedipus dynamic acts as a bridge between desire and the production of social space.

Similar to Lefebvre's three-fold spatiality, language operates in a dynamic process in relation to a physical context, to the making of meaning, and to a modeling of meanings tested in relation to context (conceptual blending) (Fauconnier and Turner 2002, 138, 195, 208, 217–48). People choose the words that resonate with the internal dynamics felt in social situations they face (Freud 1959, 309). They select the spatiality they choose to embody from the symbolic order of meanings associated with images and symbols chosen from within their culture. The oedipus complex is a way of explaining this blend of body and symbol that produces cultural space. It allows for movement through the emotions in a growth towards maturity in society. The sequence of the story chosen to facilitate that movement provides cognitive structure. The structure holds desire for return to a primal maternal relationship in tension with the distance necessary to avoid an unhealthy fusion or return to dependency. The connection of these intense feelings with symbolic language transcends enmeshment in feelings that can be paralyzing.

Identification with the storyline of a movie or love song or religious ritual functions as an oedipus drama. People use the symbolic order to find a path through the labyrinth of primary emotions. Thus feelings employ symbolic language to become spatial in order to extend desire into daily life. The oedipus drama holds regressive primary feelings in tension through the medium of a story or language.

Freud's oedipus complex presupposes transitional space. To be faced with an oedipus-like complexity in one's emotional life, an individual must already be capable of imaginative role reversal. To work toward resolution of that dilemma requires movement in and out of transitional, bounded, and holding space. An internalized oedipal myth provides an individual with a structure for thinking

17. See Freud's writings on the affectionate and sexual currents of libido in Freud 1989, 274, 279, 395–96, 397–98.
18. Lyrics by Frank Sinatra.

through inner conflicts; oedipal plots are constructed to meet the situation by cobbling together symbolic language selected from society at large. They bridge the inner struggle to overcome difficulties. Language becomes embodied in the act of attaching it to one's own feelings, like covering your body with clothes.

The symbolic order of language lacks a spatiality of its own; it only actually becomes spatial when people attach its meanings to their bodies. For this reason, language is flexible. Lefebvre's conceived space of architects and planners imposes structure on the relatively passive everyday life of people in urban environments. Unlike conceived space, language has not been irresistibly imposed. It becomes spatial only when people project their experience into it and use it as a transitional object. Then, through language, feelings can be transferred and meanings reconfigured. The symbolic order structures conventions and expectations, but there is a degree of freedom. People chose how to frame their responses. The symbolic order is not irresistibly imposed upon society by language.

Language at the limit of human expression is socially meaningful when it gives structure to feelings that were inarticulate, thus enabling them to be communicated and appropriated in actions in the real world. The oedipus complex functions like a religious passion within the psychodynamic structure of the individual. It enables people to connect the internalized mythic drama of their inner life within larger culturally agreed upon narratives. An individual uses it hermeneutically (transitionally) to reconfigure both the symbolic order and their own understanding of their struggle within it. Ordinarily, as one matures, the outworking of feelings toward mothers and fathers is transferred onto other significant relationships in adulthood; ordinarily one does not kill one's actual father or marry one's biological mother or father. The incest taboo signals the necessity of familial boundaries. Instead, healthy development sublimates and transcends regressive desire.

Freud saw cultural activity as an acting out of unresolved inner tensions (which he called the "family romance") in the public and social realm. It is significant that he explains this process, which in Lefebvre's language is a production of space, through the lens of myth (Freud 1989, 5, 167). His appropriation of the oedipus dynamic, replete with repression and idealization, overlapping sensual and ideal love, resonates with Hebraic biblical themes (Kristeva 1987). The mythic structures of inner development of the self focus around tensions of religious magnitude, at the limit of experience, such as:

- love lost through separation;
- appearance of a third person who excitingly represents the external world;
- acting on desire in a disobedience to rule;
- responding to remorse by remaking oneself as a sacrifice in accordance to a rule;
- gratitude for recovery of a sense of connection with a force that gives life.[19]

---

19. I derived these themes from James Fentress and Chris Wickham's 1992 discussion of narrative plots in fairytales.

The inner emotional structures choose to clothe themselves in the storied language of plots in order to bring transformation into everyday life. The bodily feelings underneath the language produce social space.

If we use Lacan's image of language as a cry, an utterance born out of absence, then it is possible to think of language as an imprint from the missed body of a mother; it is language formed by neediness for a bodily presence which it lacks (Lacan 1988, 157). The language at the limit of experience, like myth, is an abstraction that somehow uses distance, absence, to help to resolve primary tensions. It is shaped by consciousness of the need "to seek out desire," to reconnect with a primal sense of belonging (Lacan 1988, 170). Feelings generated in ordinary life reach out to clothe themselves spatially in something that is missing; they learn to recognize desire through symbolic language (Lacan 1988, 170). Feelings that cannot be resolved in the body are met through the medium of absence in language, in the same way that Ted Hughes' translation of "Alcestis" breathes his own struggle with the ghost of his dead wife.

Feelings are linked to the spatiality of the body, and myth to perceptions of the symbolic order. Language becomes spatial when feelings resonate in it. Feelings are changed when an engagement with a myth processes and reconfigures one's actions in society. Accordingly, the myth becomes spatial or is recontextualized through transformation of the everyday experience of the person who wears it. A person who revisits his or her own inner struggle in enacting the journey of Jesus has invested "The Passion" with their own passion, causing its language to become spatial, to again take on flesh as they walk stations of the cross within the structures of that society.

Language has a quality of communicating feeling. Language at the limit of experience is spatial in that it becomes the expression of desire, the abstract and yet near compensation for absence. This spatial dimension of language holds "abstract" mythic concepts within a physical container, the body in everyday life. Spatial awareness acknowledges bodily dependence upon a facilitating environment. Dependence upon what is outside one's body, a feeling at the limit of human ability to comprehend or control, is in itself a religious feeling. Language, attached to this feeling, can facilitate a return, full circle, in the full exercise of one's powers, to desire a primary connection that has the power to restore and to heal.

Works Cited

Benjamin, Jessica. 1988. *The Bonds of Love: Psychoanalysis, Feminism and the Problem of Domination*. New York: Pantheon.

Bultmann, Rudolf. 1958. *Jesus Christ and Mythology*. New York: Scribner.

Chodorow, Nancy J. 1994. *Femininities, Masculinities, Sexualities: Freud and Beyond*. Lexington: University of Kentucky Press.

Fentress, James, and Chris Wickham. 1992. *Social Memory: New Perspectives on the Past*. Oxford: Blackwell.

Fauconnier, Giles, and Mark Turner. 2002. *The Way We Think: Conceptual Blending and the Mind's Hidden Complexities*. New York: Basic Books.

Freud, Sigmund. 1949. *Moses and Monotheism*. Translated by Katherine Jones. New York: Knopf.

_____. 1958. The Case of Schreiber. Pages 39–79 in *The Case of Schreiber: Papers on Technique and Other Works*, vol. 12. [1911–13]. Translated by James Strachey. London: Hogarth.

_____. 1959. *Collected Papers*, vol. 1. Translated by J. Riviere. New York: Basic Books.

_____. 1989. *The Freud Reader*. Edited by Peter Gay. New York: W.W. Norton.

Irigaray, Luce. 2001. *To Be Two*. Translated by M. M. Rhodes and M. F. Cocito-Monor. New York: Routledge.

Kristeva, Julia. 1987. *Tales of Love*. Translated by Leon S. Rondiez. New York: Columbia University Press.

Lacan, Jacques. 1977. *The Four Fundamental Concepts of Psychoanalysis*. Translated by A. Sheridan. New York: Penguin.

_____. 1982. *Feminine Sexuality: Jacques Lacan and the Ecole Freudiene*. Edited by Juliet Mitchell and Jacqueline Rose. Translated by Jacqueline Rose. New York: Macmillan.

_____. 1988. *The Seminar of Jacques Lacan: Freud's Papers on Technique 1953–54*. Edited by Jacques-Alain Millel. Translated by John Forrester. Cambridge: Cambridge University Press.

Lefebvre, Henri. 1991. *The Production of Space*. Translated by Donald Nicholson-Smith. Oxford: Blackwell.

_____. 2003. *Henri Lefebvre: Key Writings*. Edited by Stuart Elden, Elisabeth Lebas, and Eleonore Kofman. New York: Continuum.

Mitchell, Juliet. 1982. *Introduction to Feminine Sexuality: Jacques Lacan and the Ecole Freudiene*. Edited by Juliet Mitchell and Jacqueline Rose. Translated by Jacqueline Rose. New York: Macmillan.

Rizzuto, Ana-Maria. 1979. *The Birth of the Living God: A Psychoanalytic Study*. Chicago: University of Chicago Press.

Tracy, David. 1986. *The Analogical Imagination: Christian Theology and the Culture of Pluralism*. New York: Crossroad.

Winnicott, Donald W. 1975. *Through Paediatrics to Psychoanalysis: Collected Papers*. London: Karnac.

Wittgenstein, Ludwig. 1997. *Philosophical Investigations*. Translated by G. E. M. Anscombe. 2d ed. Oxford: Blackwell.

Part II

Mapping the Bible

BIBLICAL GEOGRAPHY AND CRITICAL SPATIAL STUDIES

Thomas B. Dozeman

Biblical geography represents a complex genre, which has yet to receive thorough literary-critical investigation. The historical-critical study of the Bible in the modern period has tended to focus on time and chronology, not on the spatial and geographical dimension of the literature. The history of the modern interpretation of the Bible has uncovered a complex system of chronology, dating, and the sequencing of events. Contemporary interpreters of the Bible have become accustomed to the debates surrounding the time of the exodus, the date of the United Monarchy, or the sequence of the missions of Ezra and Nehemiah. All biblical interpreters are aware of the nuanced ideology in the construction of events and chronology in biblical literature. The same spatial-critical methodology has not yet been applied to the presentation of geography in biblical literature. The consequence, according to D. Newman, is that "the concrete manifestations of places and locations have not been subject to the level of critical enquiry that has been characteristic of the events that were supposed to have occurred within these same places" (Newman 1998, 157). The result is that most debates about geography in biblical studies focus on historical problems, such as the specific location of a city or a region, and not on ideological construction.

The focus on history and time is not restricted to biblical studies, but has also characterized many disciplines of research in the modern period. Contemporary theorists, such as Y.-F. Tuan, J. Berger, and H. Lefebvre, are beginning the critical task of reassessing the role of space in critical social theory, after its subordination to time and history in the modern period. E. W. Soja gives voice to this new methodological orientation, when he writes in *Postmodern Geographies* that, in the contemporary geopolitical world, "it may be space more than time that hides consequences from us, the 'making of geography' more than the 'making of history' that provides the most revealing tactical and theoretical world" (Soja 1989, 1). Soja's insight about contemporary social theory raises a similar methodological question for biblical interpreters, which is the focus of my study: Does the "making of geography" in biblical literature also reveal a hidden "tactical and theoretical world"? I will explore the theoretical use of biblical geography by reviewing its important role in the field of Geography and Religion as background for interpreting two distinctive geographical texts in the Pentateuch, The Four Rivers of Paradise and the Wilderness Journey from Kadesh through the Transjordan.

Biblical Geography and Geography and Religion

The field of Geography and Religion investigates the multiple ways in which religious beliefs and practices interact with their environment, forming a cultural landscape. The discipline is divided into phases, representing two broad historical periods (Park 1994, 1–30). The first phase encompasses the pre-modern period. A defining characteristic of the pre-modern period is that all geographical representations were made to conform to religious presuppositions. Geographers of religion characterize this phase of their discipline as the period of "Religious Geography." A second phase, "Geography of Religion," arises in the modern period, when social scientific methodologies changed the study of geography to a more rationalistic and historical orientation.

Geographers of religion note the important role of biblical geography in both phases of their discipline. Biblical geography provided the resource for a theological and cosmological representation of the world in the pre-modern period, while also providing the catalyst for a more historically oriented discipline in the modern period. The following overview of the role of biblical geography in the distinct phases of Geography and Religion will underscore the complex character of the genre.

Religious Geography

Geographers of religion agree that most early forms of geography, whether text or map, fall under the rubric of Religious Geography. The essential characteristic of Religious Geography is religion (Isaac 1965, 2). All geographical representations of the land or of the broader world are made to conform to religious presuppositions. The focus of Religious Geography is on religion's role in shaping human perceptions of the world and of humanity's place within it (Stump 1986). Theological imagination and religious cosmology play an active role in representing geographical space, since the aim of Religious Geography is to "point out the working of God in the world" and to clarify acts of salvation from a geographical perspective (Büttner 1974, 164). L. Kong (1990, 356) writes: The "concerns linking geography and cosmology in the mind of the religious person lay at the heart of early geography, and in that sense a geography that incorporated religious ideas was evident from the earliest times." This is true for the geographical representations in the ancient Near East, for the early Greeks, and, as we shall see, for biblical geography as well. Y.-F. Tuan (1976) captures the dynamic and subjective role of Religious Geography with the term "geopiety," which covers a range of emotional bonds between humans, God, and nature.[1]

---

1. See also J. K. Wright (1947, 12), who would define religious geography as "geosophy," meaning the study of geographical knowledge, which presents "subjective conceptions" of the world. He defines geosophy more broadly than religion as "the geographical ideas, both true and false, of all manner of people—not only geographers, but farmers and fishermen, business executives and poets, novelists and painters, Bedouins and Hottentots—and for this reason it necessarily has to do in large degree with subjective conceptions."

The Egyptian cosmological maps found in tombs and on sarcophagi provide ancient illustrations of religious geography, reflecting the worldview of the Egyptians (Fig. 1). The maps are representations of the Egyptian gods, especially the cosmology associated with the Ennead, the nine deities of the Heliopolitan Theology: Atum, Shu and Tefnut, Geb and Nut, Osiris, Isis, Seth, and Nephthys. The cosmological map of the Heliopolitan Theology usually highlights the god, Shu, who represents the void between the sky, the goddess Nut, and the earth, the god Geb. The cosmological map is pictorial. It shows Shu separating the sky goddess from the earth god. The feet of Shu are on the earth, while his arms support the sky. Geb and Nut represent the boundary of the created world (Shore 1987, esp. 120).

Figure 1. *The Egyptian Cosmological Map of the Creation of the World from the Book of the Dead of Nesitanebtashru*

The Babylonian Map of the World interweaves geometrical design and cosmic Ocean. It is more abstract than the Egyptian cosmological map. The map presents an overview of the surface of the earth. The earliest possible date of the map is the ninth century B.C.E., but is more likely a product of the sixth century B.C.E. (Millard 1987, 113–14). Two concentric circles define the area of the map. The inner circle marks the border of Babylon. Geometric shapes indicate significant topographical locations, including mountains, swamps, channels, and cities (i.e. Babylon, Urartu, Susa). The outer ring indicates the border of Ocean, while the triangles that protrude from Ocean represent unexplored lands. The map represents the religious worldview of the Babylonians. It is accompanied by commentary on the role of Marduk in creation as well as heroic humans, such as Utnapistim, the hero of the flood, and the legendary kings Sargon and

Nur-Dagan. W. Horowitz concludes that the purpose of the map may have been
to locate and describe distant regions. Much of the commentary describes the
strange animals that are assumed to populate the lands across the sea (Horowitz
1998, 20–42).[2]

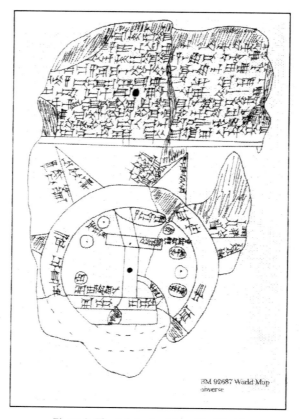

Figure 2. *The Babylonian Map of the World*

The writing of the Greek philosopher, Anaximander of Miletus (611–546
B.C.E.), provides insight into the Greek tradition of geography. He is credited
with representing land and sea (Ocean) in a description of the known world. He
influences later authors, such as Hecataeus of Miletus, whose *Periodos Ges*
("journey around the world") written around 500 B.C.E., may have included a
circular map with the Ocean surrounding a land-mass. O. A. W. Dilke (1985, 56
fig. 7) provides the following conjectural reconstruction of Hecataeus' map of
the inhabited world (Fig. 3).

2.   R. North (1979, 13–17) notes two additional maps, one from Nuzi and another from Nippur.

Figure 3. *Hecataeus' Map of the Inhabited World Surrounded by Ocean*

The map indicates the significant role of Ocean in Anaximander and for other early Greek geographical writers. And, unlike the Babylonian representation, Ocean appears to be endless in size. E. Isaac (1965, 2–3) concluded that the representation of Ocean in the Greek tradition is a manifestation of the religious principle of boundless space (*apeiron*).[3] He concluded that the geographical representation of Ocean is an attempt to demonstrate graphically the bounds set to things by the boundless. J. S. Romm agrees. He writes, in the Greek tradition of geography, the location of such borders (*peirata*) are "purely an imaginative construct" (Romm 1992, 11). Herodotus (*Hist.* 2.23, 4.36) adds support to the conclusion, criticizing the early Greek representations of the Ocean as originating with the poets, such as Homer, and thus deriving from tales, which cannot be disproved.[4]

The representations of the Egyptian cosmology, the Babylonian map of the world, and the Ocean in the Greek tradition are best categorized as Religious Geography, aimed at supporting traditional legend and mythology.[5] And it is against this background that we must interpret biblical geography in general, including the realistic geography in the historical writings. The pre-modern history of interpretation would certainly support this conclusion. The earliest interpretations of biblical geography are firmly anchored within the world of Religious Geography, emphasizing its symbolic and religious significance over

3. See also Romm 1992, 8–11.
4. See the discussion in von Fritz 1936, esp. 327–28.
5. On the role of imagination in exploration and its influence on geographical knowledge, see the discussion by Allen 1976.

historical geography. Examples of Religious Geography include *Jubilees* 8–9 (Alexander 1999), the Qumran literature (1QM), and early Christian writing, such as Luke–Acts (Bechard 2000), the Pseudo-Clementine *Recognitions* (*Rec.* 1.27–71), and the *Diamerismos* of Hippolytus (Scott 2002). It also continues in the medieval *mappaemundi* tradition, as evidenced by the Ebstorf map (Fig. 4), which represents the world as the body of Christ, with Jerusalem as the navel (Woodward 1987, 310 fig. 18.19).

Figure 4. *The Ebstorf Map*

The more abstract T-O maps (Fig. 5), with the inhabited world divided between three continents (the "T") encircled by Ocean (the "O"), accompanied manuscripts of biblical books, providing commentary on texts such as the table of nations (Gen 10).[6]

---

6.   See Woodward 1987, 291, 310–11, 328–30).

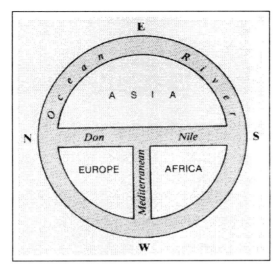

Figure 5. *A T-O Map*

The medieval *mappaemundi* in general were also tied to texts, if not directly, then by content. A.-D. von den Brincken (1968) interprets the maps as pictorial analogies to biblical texts. Cities, regions, and place names were often guided by a narrative, which was intended to teach about significant events, locations, or salvation history. And, although the medieval *mappaemundi* often provided detailed information on historical geography and topography, they represent, in the end, Religious Geography. D. Woodward (1987, 290) writes: "In medieval religious life, a *mappamundi* might stand as a representation of the world, for the transitoriness of earthly life, the divine, wisdom of God, the body of Christ, or even God."

The Madaba Map in St. George's church illustrates the religious use of real-istic biblical geography (Fig. 6). Its composition in the sixth century C.E. makes it a precursor to the medieval *mappaemundi* tradition and one of the oldest maps of Palestine. In his study, M. Piccirillo concluded that the map is intended to be a document of biblical geography, which had "the *Onomasticon* of Eusebius as its primary source."[7] The map is rich in historical detail. H. Donner (1992, 18) notes the details of the mountains east of the Dead Sea, the flow of the Jordan River, as well as the position of deserts, plains, valleys, and the Nile Delta. Yet, with all of its geographical realism, the Madaba map remains firmly anchored in the world of Religious Geography. "The Bible," writes Donner (1992, 21), "is the main prerequisite for its cartographical representation." He clarifies: "The Bible is not so much the source of the details as it is of the general idea" of salvation history. The entire map is oriented to the east, like Christian churches. Jerusalem is central to the map, while its general details derive from the story of

---

7. Piccirillo (1992) attributes the map as part of the renewed classicism of the Justinian era.

salvation. The influential role of salvation history is particularly evident with the representation of the Nile River, which flows from the east on the map, rather than from the south, illustrated in the portion of the Madaba map represented in Figure 6.

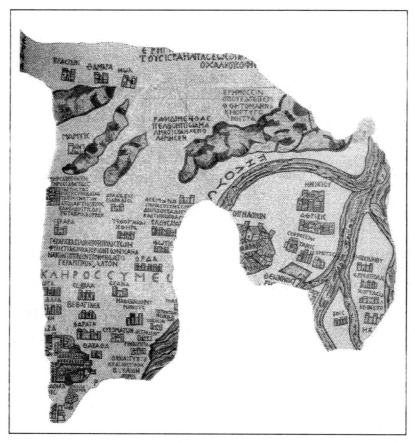

Figure 6. *Portion of the Madaba Map.*
Reproduced from Donner 1992, Appendix C.

This section of the map represents the Negeb desert on the left and the Nile Delta on the right. The Nile River flows from the east into the Mediterranean Sea, rather than from the south, a clear and blatant misrepresentation of historical geography. The reason for the presentation of the Nile River is not ignorance of topography by the map-maker, but conflict between "real geography" and "religious geography," writes Donner. He explains: "In ancient Christian tradition the Nile was one of the rivers of Paradise, and the Paradise was situated in the east according to Gen. 2: therefore the Nile had to run from the east to the west without any regard for the geographical facts, even though people may have known them" (Donner 1992, 19, 67). The Madaba map illustrates the active role of biblical geography in fashioning a symbolic representation of Religious Geography, one in which "geopiety" takes precedence over historical geography.

Geography of Religion

The field of Geography and Religion undergoes a transformation in perspective and in methodology in the modern era, prompting geographers to divide their discipline between Religious Geography and Geography of Religion. Central to the change in perspective is the separation of geography from theology (Büttner 1974, 165), along with the re-evaluation of religion as a human institution (Park 1994, 18). The result is that Geography of Religion is "concerned less with religion *per se* than with its social, cultural, and environmental associations and effects" (Stump 1986, 1).[8] The goal of Geography of Religion is to explore the impact of religion on physical, cultural, and political landscapes, or the reverse, the influence of environment on the formation of religion.[9]

Geography of Religion emerges with the renaissance.[10] The term first appears in the writing of G. H. Kasche in the late eighteenth century.[11] But the new orientation receives clarity with the philosophical and geographical writing of I. Kant and with the rise of the social sciences in the late nineteenth century, when a more rationalistic perspective replaced the previous religious orientation.[12] The transition from Religious Geography to Geography of Religion signals the rise of modern historical geography. E. Isaac has argued that biblical geography was a catalyst in the reorientation of the field of Geography in the late nineteenth and early twentieth centuries. The realism of biblical geography provided a resource for restraining the role of symbolic geography, which had dominated not only the study of biblical geography, but the entire tradition of map-making in medieval Europe. The emphasis on realism in biblical geography over symbol resulted in the "secularizing of the landscape," according to Isaac, both in the study of the Bible and in the larger presentation of world geography, which he describes as "historical geography of biblical times" (Isaac 1965, 8–9). The goal of the new enterprise was "to identify places and names in the Bible and to determine their locations" (Kong 1990, 357).

---

8. See also Fickeler 1962; Isaac 1960; Kong 1990; Cooper 1992; and Tuan 1976b.

9. The field of Geography of Religion branches out into many different areas of concern, including sacred space, architecture, settlement patterns, land use, environment, etc. See the overview in Park 1994.

10. Smith (1987) detects this turn to "geographical realism" already with the early reformers. Luther and Calvin used biblical maps of the exodus, the Holy Land, and the Garden of Eden "as vehicles for the propagation of their religious views."

11. Kasche 1795. See Büttner 1987.

12. Geographers note two works of I. Kant in particular, *Religion Within the Boundaries of Pure Reason* (1793) and *Anthropology from a Pragmatic Point of View* (1798).

Geographers of religion note a variety of influences for the turn to realism in biblical geography. The emergence of ecclesiastical geography shifted the focus of spatial representation from symbolism to realism as the church sought to map the spread of the Christian religion, often relating historical geography and religious colonialism. The rise of the humanistic tradition, with its rationalistic presuppositions, brought advances in Semitics, philology, and exegetical method in the study of Bible. At the same time, the development of critical-biblical studies was accompanied by a mystical hermeneutic, in which a corrupted textual tradition was evaluated as a shell or form, which contained an original revelation with clear historical content (Isaac 1965, 7–10). The goal of the new historical-critical methodology was to reclaim the original text, which would provide reliable historical and geopolitical information about past tradition. The result was a growing interest in geographical research within biblical commentaries as represented by Andrea Masius and Jacque Bonfrere, and the development of a special field of biblical geography inaugurated by J. D. Michaelis (Isaac 1965, 7–10; North 1979, 115–19 and passim).

The shift from Religious Geography to Geography of Religion resulted in the narrowing of biblical geography to historical geography, especially in the study of the historical literature of the Pentateuch and the Former Prophets.[13] The symbolic interpretation of biblical geography retained some influence in the study of sacred space, temple architecture, and even in more geographically oriented topics like the cosmic mountain.[14] But interpreters increasingly sought topographical and geopolitical interpretations of the geography within the historical literature. And, as a result, the study of geography was split between sacred space (cosmic mountains, temple architecture, etc.) and historical geography (itinerary lists, boundary lists, etc.). The dichotomy is evident even within the study of the cosmic mountain tradition in ancient Israel. The symbolic significance of Mount Zion remained a topic of study, especially in the Psalms and in prophetic eschatology, while the interpretation of Sinai and Horeb tended to focus on their location in the desert, where the two symbols were often merged into a single entity with one location.[15]

The prominent role of nature in nineteenth-century social scientific methodology fueled the study of historical geography even further as a means for understanding the environmental forces shaping biblical religion.[16] It was assumed that a realistic interpretation of biblical geography would provide insight into the natural environment that shaped Israelite religion. The emphasis on etiological legends in the research of A. Alt and M. Noth is a direct outgrowth of the new prominence given to the natural environment. Central to their hermeneutical perspective was the assumption that biblical legends "could only have grown

---

13. See the discussion of Scheffler 1996.
14. See, for example, Eliade 1959.
15. For interpretation and bibliography on Mount Zion, see Ollenburger 1987; for Sinai/Horeb see Dozeman 1988.
16. For an overview of the literature on religion and environmental determinism, see Cloke, Philo, and Sadler 1991.

out of specific localities, since they are an attempt to give meaning to natural phenomena found there" (Isaac 1960, 14). The Nomadic Ideal advanced by K. Budde provides another example, in which the natural environment provides a key for interpreting Yahwistic religion. Budde (1895, 235–79) argued that the austerity of the desert and the nomadic lifestyle were important catalysts in the rise of monotheism in ancient Israel.[17] The turn to realism received still further momentum with increasing travel to Palestine and, in its wake, the emergence of archaeology, for which biblical literature often provided the template for research.

The result of the changing perspective in the eighteenth and nineteenth centuries was that historical geography came to dominate the study of biblical geography. And, over time, it also carried religious and hermeneutical significance, since the truth of Scripture was no longer in its symbolic meaning, as was the case in the medieval *mappamundi* tradition, but in the historical reliability of its geographical data. The changing hermeneutical perspective is evident in H. Fischer's appraisal of U. Seetzen (1767–1811): "in Palestine, Seetzen was the first to roam the land of the Bible with the Bible in hand and...he did a lot to prove the enduring truth of Scripture even in its geographical data."[18] The effect of the historically oriented hermeneutic of Geography of Religion is evident in the language of "minimalist "and "maximalist" in contemporary biblical studies. The criterion that separates these two terms is the historical reliability of the geographical and geopolitical representations in the biblical literature. A broader and more nuanced contrast between Religious Geography and Geography of Religion in the study of the genre of biblical geography is excluded in the debate.

Biblical Geography in the Pentateuch

The summary of biblical geography in the field of Geography and Religion has clarified the contrasting hermeneutical perspectives of Religious Geography and Geography of Religion. The distinct orientations for interpreting biblical geography are summarized in the following chart.

	Religious Geography	*Geography of Religion*
Time-Period	Pre-Modern	Modern
Worldview	Religious Presupposition	Rationalistic Presupposition
Geographical Representation	Theological, Cosmological, and Symbolic Representations of Geographical Space	Sociological and Historical Representations of Geographical Space
The Aim	To Clarify the Working of God in the World To Support Legend and Mythology	To Identify Places in the Bible To Produce an Historical Geography of Biblical Times

17. See also Flight 1923.
18. For the quotation, see North 1979.

The changing role of biblical geography in Geography and Religion, from the unqualified "geopiety" of Religious Geography to the quest for history within Geography of Religion provides two initial conclusions for interpreting specific geographical texts in the Pentateuch. The first is the multivalent character of biblical geography. The genre of biblical geography yields both symbolic and realistic interpretations. The second conclusion is the insight that biblical geography functions at the crossroads of Religious Geography and Geography of Religion. And, as a consequence, it is able to provide a resource for both symbolic and historical representations of the world at the same time, which argues against a clear dichotomy between the two approaches. Two distinctive texts will underscore the unique challenges that biblical geography poses for interpreters of the Pentateuch—the mythological Four Rivers of Paradise in Gen 2 and the more realistic presentation of the Wilderness March from Kadesh through the Transjordan.

The Four Rivers of Paradise
The Four Rivers of Paradise in Gen 2 will be interpreted from both the perspective of Religious Geography and Geography of Religion. The focus of interpretation will be on representing the four rivers visually as a map. The comparison of the distinct interpretations will underscore the multivalent character of biblical geography, as well as the methodological challenges that arise with a text that is able to convey both realistic and symbolic representations of the world at the same time.

Creation in Gen 2 occurs when God waters dry ground, as compared to the opposite process in Gen 1, where the deity must control chaotic sea in order to bring forth dry ground. The result of watering the ground in Gen 2 is a perfectly irrigated garden, Eden, located in the east. The river which irrigates the Garden of Eden branches into four parts: the Pishon flows to the land of Havilah, a land of pure gold and precious stones; the Gihon flows around the land of Cush; the Tigris flows east of Assyria; and the fourth, the Euphrates, receives no further description. The four rivers progress from fantastic locations (the Pishon) to a river so well known to the author that it requires no description (the Euphrates). The mixing of geographical references from the fantastic to the mundane creates a problem for interpreters, which is reflected in the representations of the Four Rivers of Paradise in Gen 2:10–14 in Figures 7 and 8.

The map on the left is a rendition of the Four Rivers of Paradise from *The Macmillan Bible Atlas* (Yohanan et al. 1993, 21 fig. 14). The geographers have approached the biblical narrative from the perspective of Geography of Religion. The interpretation begins with the Tigris and Euphrates rivers in Mesopotamia, since they can be clearly located on the map. The representation is realistic, conforming to the standards of modern map making. The map includes precise renditions of the bodies of water in the region (now known as the Mediterranean Sea, the Red Sea, and the Persian Gulf), along with the exact flow of the rivers over the topography of the land. Once the region has been realistically reproduced, the authors address the problem of locating the Pishon and Gihon rivers, which they concede may represent symbolic geography. Yet they conclude, "since Havilah (the land associated with the Pishon river) is one of the regions of Cush (Gen 10:7), it would seem that the two major branches of the Nile (the Blue and the White) are intended." The result is a very realistic rendition of Gen 2:10–14 as an example of historical geography. The Four Rivers of Paradise provide fresh water for Mesopotamia and North Africa. There is no place in such a realistic map for a mythological garden, even though the Garden of Eden is the main geographical topic of the story.

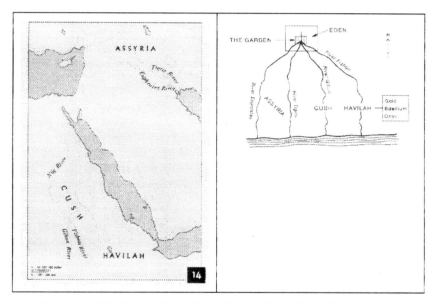

Figures 7 and 8. *The Four Rivers of Paradise in the* Macmillan Bible Atlas *and in the* Anchor Bible Dictionary

The map on the right is a drawing of the Four Rivers of Paradise by P. S. Alexander from the *Anchor Bible Dictionary* (1992, esp. 979). Alexander is approaching the text from the perspective of Religious Geography. The map lacks all realistic topography. Instead he seeks to provide an abstract drawing of the text without recognizable details. The central focus of the map is the mytho-logical Garden of Eden. In representing the four rivers, Alexander begins with the more obscure rivers, the Pishon and the Gihon, since they are described first in the text. He notes that the rivers are arranged from east to west. Thus, the Tigris and the Euphrates rivers are located on the west side of the Pishon and the Gihon rivers, just the opposite from their position in the *Macmillan Bible Atlas*. The Four Rivers of Paradise represent cognitive mapping, according to Alexan-der, in which the author does not write geography based on experience, but, instead, seeks to impose order on space. Yet, Alexander is quick to add that the geography in Gen 2:10–14 is not fiction. Rather the biblical author is seeking to anchor the Garden of Eden in real geographical space, where it is located at the headwaters of four great rivers, which flow from north to south.

The two maps are strikingly different in their representations of the Four Rivers of Paradise. They reflect the contrasting hermeneutical perspectives of Geography of Religion and Religious Geography in the interpretation of biblical geography. And they produce very distinct reactions in the reader. Yet it is difficult to evaluate which map represents the stronger interpretation, since each underscores different aspects of the text. The *Macmillan Bible Atlas* translates the Four Rivers of Paradise into Geography of Religion by locating the rivers firmly within historical geography. The map begins with the Tigris and Euphrates and only then brings the Pishon and the Gihon rivers into conformity with them. The article by Alexander in the *Anchor Bible Dictionary* emphasizes, instead, the role of the text within the world of Religious Geography. And, as a consequence, his map avoids all realistic topography, especially with regard to the Tigris and Euphrates rivers.

The two maps underscore important aspects of the description of the Four Rivers of Paradise, while also falsifying the text. They "lie" in different ways, to use a phrase from I. Cornelius (1998).[19] The hyperrealism of the *Macmillan Bible Atlas* masks the cosmological implications of the Four Rivers of Paradise, while the rendition in the *Anchor Bible Dictionary* suppresses the realism of the reference to the Tigris and Euphrates rivers. Placing the two maps side by side provides a strong visual illustration of the way in which biblical geography functions at the crossroads of Religious Geography and Geography of Religion, intermingling the genre of the fantastic, as described by T. Todorov (1980), and the historical. A simple dichotomy between fact and fiction will not capture the dynamic role of geography in the writing of biblical history. Rather the two perspectives must be related in a geographical interpretation of the Four Rivers of Paradise.

The Journey from Kadesh through the Transjordan

The modern interpretation of the wilderness journey from Kadesh through the Transjordan illustrates the problems of interpreting more realistic biblical geography when the methodology of Geography of Religion is used to reconstruct geopolitical history. The journey is recorded multiple times in the historical literature of the Hebrew Bible (Num 20–21, 33; Deut 1–3; and Judg 11). The biblical writers provide exact locations, specific roadways, and carefully placed borders to define the extent of the Israelite march and its relationship to the neighboring ethnic groups, Edom, Moab, and Ammon. And, although each account is characterized by geographical realism, the stories diverge significantly in tracing the Israelite journey. Most notably, the Israelites are confronted by a hostile Edomite nation in Num 20, prompting their journey around Edom and Moab in Num 20–21, while Deut 1–3 presents a story of hospitality, in which the Israelites journey through the territory of Edom and Moab (Dozeman 2002).

19.　See the discussion of modern map making by Monmonier 1996.

J. Wellhausen (1899, 109–11, 341–46, and passim) establishes the paradigm for the modern interpretation of the journey from Kadesh through the Transjordan. The conflicting presentations of geography prompted him to reject the historical claims of the text. The literature could not have arisen from the late Bronze Age, according to Wellhausen, because an historical interpretation demanded firmly established nations in the Transjordan, which did not exist in that time period. Yet, Wellhausen continued to interpret biblical geography as historical geography, only of a later geopolitical period. Wellhausen interpreted the geography of the journey as the political circumstances of a later (anonymous) J author, writing during the monarchical period, when conflicts with Edom (Num 20:14–21), Arad (21:1–3), Sihon (21:21–31), and Og of Bashan (21:32–35) were a political reality. The divergent accounts in Deuteronomy and Judges represent literary adaptations of the original story based, in part, on the changing geopolitical circumstances of subsequent writers. Thus, although the placement of the story in the Bronze Age is fiction, according to Wellhausen, its presentation of geography is not symbolic Religious Geography. Rather, once decoded as political geography, the journey from Kadesh through the Transjordan becomes firmly anchored in the world of Geography of Religion, as a reliable source for tracing the social and geopolitical rise of Yahwism under the Israelite monarchy.

H. Gressmann (1913, 300–310) builds on the interpretation of Wellhausen, agreeing that the Israelite possession of the Transjordan represents the geopolitical world of the monarchy. But he also expands the historical interpretation of biblical geography. The journey around Edom and Moab in Num 20–21 cannot simply be interpreted as a geopolitical allegory of the monarchical period, according to Gressmann, because monarchical authors would have presented the Israelites in a better light than their round-about journey to avoid the Edomites and Moabites. The awkward journey indicates an historical tradition behind the literary accounts, which influenced the later writers. Thus, for Gressmann, biblical geography is historical geography even from the late Bronze Age.

The methodological problems of reducing biblical geography to historical geography become evident in the work of M. Noth (1940, 1944; 1968, 148–66). He begins by following the lead of Wellhausen and Gressmann, noting that the geography of the wilderness journey presupposes geopolitical experiences of a later time. But Noth's interest in historical geography goes well beyond either Wellhausen or Gressmann. For Noth, historical traditions must be interpreted in the context of the physical geography of the land. And his increased knowledge of historical topography and geography introduced a new problem in the modern interpretation of biblical geography. It became clear to Noth that the Israelites could not pass the northern end of the Gulf of Aqabah without coming into conflict with the Edomites as Num 20–21 stated. Other problems also emerged for Noth. The authors supplied no reason for the Israelite journey south around Edom, and there is no intrinsic connection between Kadesh and Edom. Thus, Noth concluded that the authors of the journey through the Transjordan have only a "vague idea of the geographical relationships involved" in the monarchical period (Noth 1968, 151–52). His solution to these problems was to judge the wilderness journey into the Transjordan a literary invention to relate two independent traditions (the wilderness journey and the conquest), rather than an account of historical geography. And, according to Noth, it is this creative literary activity that gives rise to the "vagueness" of the geographical representation. But Noth's literary solution to the scriptural map of the journey into the Transjordan also reopened the door of symbolic, Religious Geography, as a means for interpreting the realistic presentation of the journey from Kadesh to the Transjordan.

The more recent research on the historical geography of the Transjordan by J. M. Miller (1987, 1989) reinforces the initial conclusion of Noth. After comparing the different accounts of the journey from Kadesh through the Transjordan he cautions against using biblical geography to deal with problems of toponymy in the region. He judged the geographical presentations in Deut 2 and Judg 11 to be loose and misleading, while Num 20–21 is "incomprehensible in terms of geographical realities of southern Transjordan" (Miller 1989, 582–87). As a result, Miller doubts that biblical writers were familiar with Moabite geography, especially south of the Arnon. Miller's research reinforces the conclusion of Noth, that the journey from Kadesh through the Transjordan is not historical geography. The work of Miller also raises a more fundamental question, namely whether biblical geography was ever intended to be translated into maps, representing historical geography, since even where precise information is provided, it has become "garbled as a result of the blending of traditions and redactional activity" (1989, 588).

The interpretation of the Israelite journey through the Transjordan illustrates the dominant role of historical geography in the modern period of interpretation, and the drawbacks of such a limited approach to biblical geography. The insights of Noth and Miller, in which both researchers are working within the perspective of Geography of Religion, bring the study of biblical geography full circle. Their increased knowledge of historical geography has once again forced interpreters to reevaluate biblical geography as Religious Geography. Paradoxically, it is their knowledge of Geography of Religion that has led them to this hermeneutical insight about the biblical literature.

Conclusion

The overview of biblical geography in the field of Geography and Religion allows for several conclusions that may influence future research.

1. Biblical geography is multivalent, requiring a comprehensive approach that incorporates both the symbolic representations of Religious Geography and the more historically oriented interpretation arising from Geography of Religion. The summary of biblical geography in the discipline of Geography and Religion has underscored the narrow focus in the modern period to the investigation of historical geography. The symbolic interpretation of biblical geography has retained some influence in the study of sacred space, temple architecture, and even in more geographically oriented topics like the cosmic mountain. Yet,

interpreters have increasingly evaluated the more realistic geography of biblical history writing against the geopolitical conditions in Palestine from the early Iron Age of the monarchical period into the Second Temple period. The result is a one-sided approach to biblical geography in contemporary study, which lacks a critical exploration of the ideological role of setting in creating a cultural and religious landscape in the writing of biblical history.

2. The multivalence of biblical geography requires that the distinctive approaches of Religious Geography and Geography of Religion be clearly separated.[20] The absence of a comprehensive approach to biblical geography, which identifies the different hermeneutical claims of the distinct approaches, has created methodological confusion in contemporary study. Y. Aharoni (1979, ix) illustrates the problem when he writes: "Historical geography of the Holy Land is a reflection of the mutual relation between God and Israel as understood and interpreted by Israel's national faith." Aharoni's research goals are within the field of Geography of Religion; he wishes to describe historical geography. Yet, his remarks are squarely in the field of Religious Geography, a spatial commentary on a theological text that is intended to describe the presence of God on earth, a divinely chosen people, and their holy land.[21] Both the historical and the theological inquiry are legitimate areas of study. But the two orientations must be distinguished in order to discern their creative relationship in the construction of ancient history writing. If a distinction is not maintained, the author's tactical and theoretical world of geography is simply rendered as the recording of historical facts. And, as Soja rightly notes, a study limited to historical geography cannot be "substituted for an explanation of the social production of space" (Soja 1989, 123). Newman (1998) illustrates the political implications of such methodological confusion, tracing the intricate relationship between biblical geography, conceived as historical geography, and political theories of territory among certain religious groups in Israel. He concludes that homeland discourse, interwoven with imagined geographies from "geo-theological narratives" has influenced concrete landscape formation and reconstruction (1998, 159).[22] The lack of a clear understanding of the genre of biblical geography has also fueled dialectical debate among researchers, often structured around the absolute language of myth vs. history, fact vs. fiction, or, more recently, the maximalist vs. minimalist interpretation of biblical geography and history. Such debate may clarify the presuppositions of different interpreters, but not the genre of biblical geography.

---

20.   See C. Nicolet (1991, 2, 3–5, 9), who introduced the important distinction between "historical geography" and "the history of geography" for studying ancient history. "Historical geography" investigates geographical realities, including vegetation, cultivation, roads, land possession, population, settlements, and boundaries. The "history of geography" explores the awareness of territory and its representation in the literature, uncovering "the mentality and ideology" of the writers.

21.   See the geopolitical study of these topics in Grosby 2002.

22.   For a broader application of the same phenomena beyond land transformation in Israel, see Tuan 1991. For discussion of territoriality, see Sack 1986.

3. The ability of biblical geography to function at the crossroads of Religious Geography and Geography of Religion requires that, once the distinct representations of geographical space are described, they must also be related in a broad methodology of critical spatial study. New insights into the complex genre of biblical geography are emerging in a variety of related fields, which hold promise for future research.

First, Z. Kallai has initiated a study of the genre of biblical geography through a series of articles on scribal practice in the composition and transmission of territorial texts.[23] He has demonstrated that geography serves both descriptive and intellectual purposes in Israelite historiography.[24]

Second, J. Van Seters (1983, 8–18, 23, and passim) has demonstrated that geography, along with genealogy, are central concerns in the development of antiquarian historiography both in the Assyrian Annals (the Sargon Geography) and in the Greek tradition of history writing. Van Seters notes that the forerunners of Herodotus were geographers (Anaximander and Hecataeus). J. S. Romm (1992) reinforces the conclusion of Van Seters with his study of geography in the Greek literary tradition. He documents the changing role of geography from the epic tradition of Homer, in which mythical topography dominated, to the historiographical writing of Herodotus, which provides promising comparison for interpreting biblical geography as well. Comparison to ancient Near Eastern, and, more importantly, Greek historiography promises a broad context for relating the descriptive and intellectual function of geography in the writing of biblical history.

Third, the growing body of research on critical spatial theory is also providing the framework for relating the distinct aspects of biblical geography into a comprehensive methodology. Lefebvre (1991) and Soja (1989) offer a three-part model for interpreting spatial representation in contemporary society, not ancient historiography. Yet, their categories of space (perceived, conceived, and lived) may provide methodological focus for relating the different functions of biblical geography.

The first category is perceived space (also called by Lefebvre "spatial practice"): it is the concrete, physical geography of our world (Lefebvre 1991, 33 and passim; Soja 1989, 74–79). Perceived space in biblical geography is the

---

23. For a collection of his work, see Kallai 1998; see in particular the essay "Territorial Patterns, Biblical Historiography and Scribal Tradition—A Programmatic Survey" (1998, 157–64).

24. Kallai (1982, 184) states the conclusion in the following manner, "historiographical and historiosophical considerations exert a profound influence on the formation of Biblical narrative." The different boundary texts provide an example. Kallai notes the diverse conceptions of the boundaries of the land in the Hebrew Bible, with distinct titles (i.e. promise to the patriarchs, land of Canaan, and land of Israel). He concludes that they are constructed within a scribal tradition of historiography to address larger themes like covenant, the relationship of Israel to its neighbors, or the divine right to land. The use of geography as both realistic and patterned language provides an important starting point for defining the genre of biblical geography. Kallai's research on patterns of composition within scribal schools on such topics as topographical lists, territorial delimitations, and regional structures invites comparison to similar form-critical research on genealogy, where the focus is also sociological and theological, not historical.

representation of topography and geography, grounded in the physical terrain and open to testing and modification, as is illustrated in the research of Miller on the topography of the Transjordan.

The second category, conceived space, includes the social order that is interwoven and imposed on physical geography (Lefebvre 1991, 33, 245; Soja 1996, 66–67). Conceived space is a self-conscious construction of physical space. It is created or imagined by a society, thus representing public and overt social forms of power and ideology. Conceived space in biblical geography would represent the contrasting accounts of the wilderness journey around and through Edom, where the writers seek to relate physical geography with national, ethnic, and social structures.

The third category, lived space, is the immediate world of experience (Lefebvre 1991, 33; Soja 1996, 31). Lived space embraces physical geography (perceived space) and public social structures (conceived space) within the immediacy of one's inhabited world of emotions, events, and public choices. Both Lefebvre and Soja underscore the overlap between conceived and lived space, and this is especially true in the presentation of biblical geography, since both categories arise from an author's experience. A possible distinction is that lived space is a less self-conscious construction, representing more the immediate and overwhelming influence of a worldview, an historical experience, or perhaps a particular form of Yahwism. The lived experience of an author, moreover, may not always be evident in an ancient text, but function instead as a presupposition for the writing. An example of the effect of lived space on a biblical author may be the impact of the exile, while an example of lived space on Herodotus may be his use of environmental determinism to contrast Persian and Greek customs (*nomoi*). Both are presuppositions and driving forces in the worldview of the ancient writers, while each also shapes the literary design of the different histories.

Lefebvre and Soja stress that the three representations of space must be related, not separated. The application of their model for interpreting biblical geography would reinforce the same point. The power of geographical representation in biblical history arises from the interweaving of physical and historical geography with social and ideological representations, which are shaped further by the immediacy of lived experience. The goal of a critical spatial interpretation of biblical geography is to describe the interrelationship of these distinct categories of space in the production of the text and in the ongoing history of interpretation.

Works Cited

Aharoni, Y. 1979. *The Land of the Bible: A Historical Geography*. 2d ed. Philadelphia: Westminster.

Alexander, P. S. 1992. Early Jewish Geography. In *ABD* 2:977–88.

_____. 1999. Jerusalem as the *Omphalos* of the World: On the History of a Geographical Concept. Pages 104–19 in *Jerusalem: Its Sanctity and Centrality to Judaism, Christianity, and Islam*. Edited by L. I. Levine. New York: Continuum.

Allen, J. L. 1976. Lands of Myth, Waters of Wonder: The Place of Imagination in the History of Geographical Exploration. In Lowenthal and Bowden 1976, 41–61.

Bechard, D. P. 2000. *Paul Outside the Walls: A Study of Luke's Socio-Geographical Universalism in Acts 14:8–20*. Analecta Biblica 143. Rome: Pontifical Biblical Institute.

Ben-Arieh, Y. 1989. Nineteenth-Century Historical Geographies of the Holy Land. *Journal of Historical Geography* 15:69–79.

Brincken, A.-D. von den. 1968. *Mappa mundi* und Chronographia. *Deutsches Archiv für die Erforschung des Mittelalters* 24:118–86.

Budde, K. 1895. The Nomadic Ideal in the Old Testament. *The New World* 4:235–79.

Büttner, M. 1974. Religion and Geography. *Numen* 21:163–96.

_____. 1985. On the History and Philosophy of the Geography of Religion. *Geographia Religionum* 1:13–121.

_____. 1987. Kasche and Kant on the Physicotheological Approach to the Geography of Religion. *The National Geographical Journal of India* 33:218–28.

Cloke, P., C. Philo, and D. Sadler. 1991. *Approaching Human Geography: An Introduction to Contemporary Theoretical Debates*. New York: Guilford.

Cooper, A. 1992. New Directions in the Geography of Religion. *Area* 24:123–29.

Cornelius, I. 1998. How Maps "Lie"—Some Remarks on the Ideology of Ancient Near Eastern and "Scriptural" Maps. *JNSL* 24:217–30.

Dilke, O. A. W. 1985. *Greek and Roman Maps*. Baltimore: Johns Hopkins University Press.

Donner, H. 1992. *The Mosaic Map of Madaba: An Introductory Guide*. Kampen: Kok Pharos.

Dozeman, T. 1988. *God on the Mountain*. Atlanta: Scholars.

_____. 2002. Geography and Ideology in the Wilderness Journey from Kadesh through the Transjordan. Pages 173–89 in *Abschied vom Jahwisten: Die Komposition des Hexateuch in der jüngsten Discussion*. Edited by J. C. Gertz, K. Schmid, and M. Witte. Berlin: de Gruyter.

Eliade, M. 1959. *The Sacred and the Profane: The Nature of Religion*. New York: Harcourt, Brace.

Fickeler, P. 1962. Fundamental Questions in the Geography of Religions. Pages 94–117 in *Readings in Cultural Geography*. Edited by P. L. Wagner. Chicago: University of Chicago Press.

Flight, J. W. 1923. The Nomadic Idea and the Ideal of the Old Testament. *JBL* 42:158–226.

Fritz, K. von. 1936. Herodotus and the Growth of Greek Historiography. *Transactions of the American Philological Association* 7:315–40.

Gressmann, H. 1913. *Mose und seine Zeit: Ein Kommentar zu den Mose-Sagen*. FRLANT 1. Göttingen: Vandenhoeck & Ruprecht.

Grosby, S. 2002. *Biblical Ideas of Nationality: Ancient and Modern*. Winona Lake: Eisenbrauns.

Harley, J. B., and D. Woodward, eds. 1987. *The History of Cartography: Cartography in Prehistoric, Ancient, and Medieval Europe and the Mediterranean*. Vol. 1 of *The History of Cartography*. Chicago: University of Chicago Press.

Horowitz, W. 1998. *Mesopotamian Cosmic Geography*. Winona Lake: Eisenbrauns.

Isaac, E. 1960. Religion, Landscape and Space. *The Landscape* 9:14–18.

_____. 1965. Religious Geography and the Geography of Religion. Pages 1–14 in *Man and Earth*. University of Colorado Studies, Series in Earth Sciences 3. Boulder: University of Colorado Press.

Kallai, Z. 1982. The Wandering-Traditions from Kadesh-Barnea to Canaan: A Study in Biblical Historiography. *JJS* 33:175–84.

_____. 1998. *Biblical Historiography and Historical Geography: Collection of Studies*. Frankfurt am Main: Peter Land.

Kasche, G. H. 1795. *Ideen über religiose Geographie*. Lübeck.
Kong, L. 1990. Geography and Religion: Trends and Prospects. *Progress in Human Geography* 14:355–71.
Lefebvre, H. 1991. *The Production of Space*. Translated by D. Nicholson-Smith. Oxford: Blackwell.
Lowenthal, D., and M. J. Bowden, eds. 1976. *Geographies of the Mind: Essays in Historical Geosophy in Honor of John Kirtland Wright*. New York: Oxford University Press.
Millard, A. R. 1987. Cartography in the Ancient Near East. In Harley and Woodward 1987, 106–16.
Miller, J. M. 1987. Biblical Maps: How Reliable are They? *BR* 3:32–41.
_____. 1989. The Israelite Journey Through (Around) Moab and Moabite Toponymy. *JBL* 108:577–95.
Monmonier, M. 1996. *How to Lie with Maps*. Chicago: University of Chicago Press.
Newman, D. 1998. Metaphysical and Concrete Landscapes: The Geopiety of Homeland Socialization in the "Land of Israel." Pages 153–82 in *Land and Community: Geography in Jewish Studies*. Edited by H. Brodsky. Studies and Texts in Jewish History and Culture: The Joseph and Rebecca Meyerhoff Center for Jewish Studies University of Maryland 3. College Park: University of Maryland Press.
Nicolet, C. 1991. *Space, Geography, and Politics in the Early Roman Empire*. Jerome Lectures 19. Ann Arbor: University of Michigan Press.
North, R. 1979. *A History of Biblical Map Making*. Beihefte zum Tübinger Atlas des Vorderen Orients 32. Wiesbaden: Dr. Ludwig Reichert.
Noth, M. 1940. Numbers 21 als Glied der "Hexateuch"-Erzählung. *ZAW* 58:161–89.
_____. 1944. Israelitische Stämme zwischen Ammon und Moab. *ZAW* 60:11–57.
_____. 1968. *Numbers: A Commentary*. OTL. Translated by J. D. Martin. Philadelphia: Westminster.
_____. 1981. *A History of Pentateuchal Traditions*. Translated by B. W. Anderson. Chico, Calif.: Scholars Press.
Ollenburger, B. 1987. *Zion, the City of the Great King: A Theological Symbol for the Jerusalem Cult*. JSOTSup 41. Sheffield: JSOT Press.
Park, P. C. C. 1994. *Sacred Worlds: An Introduction to Geography and Religion*. London: Routledge.
Piccirillo, M. 1992. Medeba. In *ABD* 4:658.
Romm, J. S. 1992. *The Edges of the Earth in Ancient Thought: Geography, Exploration, and Fiction*. Princeton: Princeton University Press.
Sack, R. D. 1986. *Human Territoriality: Its Theory and History*. Cambridge Studies in Historical Geography. Cambridge: Cambridge University Press.
Scheffler, E. H. 1996. The Interface Between Historical Geography and the Holistic History of Ancient Israel. *Old Testament Essays* 9:294–307.
Scott, J. M. 2002. *Geography in Early Judaism and Christianity: The Book of Jubilees*. SNTSMS 113. Cambridge: Cambridge University Press.
Shore, A. F. 1987. Egyptian Cartography. In Harley and Woodward 1987, 117–29.
Smith, C. D. 1987. Maps in Bibles in the Sixteenth Century. *The Map Collector* 39:2–14.
Soja, E. W. 1989. *Postmodern Geographies: The Reassertion of Space in Critical Social Theory*. London: Verso.
_____. 1996. *Thirdspace: Journeys to Los Angeles and Other Real-and-Imagined Places*. Malden, Mass.: Blackwell.
Stump, R. W. 1986. The Geography of Religion—Introduction. *Journal of Cultural Geography* 7:1–3.

Todorov, T. 1980. *The Fantastic: A Structural Approach to a Literary Genre*. Ithaca: Cornell University Press.

Tuan, Y.-F. 1976a. Geopiety: A Theme in Man's Attachment to Nature and to Place. In Lowenthal and Bowden 1976, 11–39.

_____. 1976b. Humanistic Geography. *Annals of the Association of American Geographers* 66:266–76.

_____. 1991. Language and the Making of Place: A Narrative-Descriptive Approach. *Annals of the Association of American Geographers* 81:19–35.

Van Seters, J. 1983. *In Search of History: Historiography in the Ancient World and the Origins of Biblical History*. New Haven: Yale University Press.

Wellhausen, J. 1899. *Die Komposition des Hexateuchs und der Historischen Bücher des Alten Testaments*. 3d ed. Berlin: Georg Reimer.

Woodward, D. 1987. Medieval *Mappaemundi*. In Harley and Woodward 1987, 286–370.

Wright, J. K. 1947. *Terrai Incognitae*: The Place of the Imagination in Geography. *Annals of the Association of American Geographers* 37:1–15.

Yohanan, A., M. Avi-Yonah, A. F. Rainey, and Z. Safrai, eds. *MacMillan Bible Atlas*. 3d ed. New York: Simon & Schuster Macmillan, 1993.

BIBLE MAPS AND AMERICA'S NATIONALIST NARRATIVES

Burke O. Long

In a recent essay, Zur Shalev succinctly summarized a perspective on maps and map making that for some time has been moving toward the center of cartographic scholarship. Although long recognized as sources for historical geography, Shalev wrote, "old maps…are essential also for navigating the often-troubled cultural landscapes into which they were born, and which, in turn, they helped to mold." Maps illuminate the "concerns and assumptions of their authors and readers" and suggest how their creators "conceptualized and enacted space and territoriality." In short, Shalev concluded, maps do not simply depict geography, that is, the surface features of the earth, its climate, natural resources, and human activity. Maps are also "primary documents for cultural and intellectual history" (Shalev 2002, 1).

As geographer and historian of cartography J. B. Harley put the matter more than a decade ago, "Maps are never value-free images, and except in the narrowest Euclidean sense they are not in themselves true or false." In selectivity of content and manipulation of symbols, Harley continued, maps are purposeful articulations of reality. They are a kind of controlled fiction, a way of "structuring the human world which is biased toward, promoted by, and exerts influence upon particular sets of social relations" (Harley 1988, 278). Accepting the premise that knowledge is a form of power (Foucault 1980), Harley added that maps not only represent reality in some neutral sense, but they also articulate, and often disguise, vested interests. Each constructs a version of the world that follows the territorial imperatives of a particular political system (Harley 1988, 279; 2001). Or as James Flanagan argued, maps "disguise social contexts and impose their own hegemonies of power and privilege" (Flanagan 2001, 2). In this post-colonialist perspective, salient interrogations of cartography seek to discover cultural, historical, political, and ideological entanglements which lie beneath a map's epidermis of settled factuality.

Of course, nothing can diminish the elegant imagination, care, art, and meticulous, even scientific scholarship which individuals have lavished upon their maps. Furthermore, if not obviously propagandistic, maps enjoy a presumption of authority that is encouraged by "cartohypnosis" (Boggs 1947), a willingness to accept maps and mapmakers, like science and scientists, as authoritative and neutral avenues toward truth.

Maps as Socio-Spatial Practice

However, it is useful to recognize the limits of such a conviction about carto-graphy. Two-dimensional images of geophysical reality embody disciplinary definitions of objectivity as well as layers of material, social, and individual experience. A map of the Holy Land, for example, represents *material* place. It is artful work that delimits infinite possibility, all places, into a representation of one place, a defined geographic area. Yet, more fundamentally, this particular bringing to consciousness of objective reality is like all human constructions of experience. A sense of definable world, of self apart from world "out there," arises in the relational experience of interacting with the flux of inchoate nature (Mead 1934, 1938; Hodder 1989; Richardson 1989).[1] Moreover, as the designa-tion "Holy Land" already indicates, a mapmaker represents and perpetuates other complex social relations, which make that "somewhere" a place of cultur-ally specific history and significance. Cartographers and users of Holy Land maps variously engage and valorize that cartographic space. They endow it with religious feeling, define it with religious concepts, enliven it through personal and social relations, and enshrine its cultural reality in both memory and action.

Such participatory engagement means that while any modern map is an instrument of Euclidean measurement, it is also an artifact of, and occasion for, socio-spatial practices. As Edward Soja argues, this idea of constructed and enacted space belies a common assumption that space is inert emptiness, a mere stage where events happen. Space is better thought of as human invention, socially constructed like history and society. Symbols, structures of intellectual mapping, human interactions, architecture, for example, all arise in processes that construct and constitute multiple realities of any given space. In short, the places that count in human affairs are not simply "out there." They have been imagined and enacted in practices that, in relating to place, vest it with eco-nomical and political value, ideological commitment, and social relations (Soja 1996).

Yet such practices are always partial, and the truths they proclaim about the world partisan. In cartography, mapmakers and readers collaborate in creating a purportedly real or true image of place, say the Holy Land, while obscuring many alternative spatial practices that enact different holy lands.

For Soja, participating in the dominant ethos of a socially constructed space is one aspect of spatial practice. But so is resisting that dominance. And Soja sees both as potentialities within any given realization of space. Thus a particu-lar urban design, a modern skyscraper, or a map of the Holy Land, all reflect what has been and what can be. They are socially constituted spaces in which potentially "all histories and geographies, all times and places, are immanently presented and represented, a strategic space of power and domination, empower-ment, and resistance" (Soja 1996, 311).

1.   Harold Remus, Professor Emeritus at Wilfred Laurier University, very kindly put me on to some of the recent social interpretations of material culture. I am also much indebted to James Flanagan and David Penchansky, who read portions of this essay and generously offered critiques.

For my purposes, it is most important to regard cartography and maps as belonging to the evolving vocabularies of contested socio-spatial practices. Material place (which has to be imagined in some fashion), concepts (which impart significance and value), and multiple perspectives (which allow for competing constructions and actions)—all these aspects of socio-spatial practice overlap in the simultaneity of spatial experience. Cartography effaces these complexities, while a critical approach to spatiality seeks to uncover them. There are many spaces, so to speak, or rather many localized practices that may be at work in any realization of material place.

As Denis Wood put the matter, maps bespeak actively realized social space, the "milieu we simultaneously live in and collaborate on bringing into being." Maps connect what individuals or participants in social groups have done with what they want to do. If maps have one use, for example as a road survey or sub-division plan, they nonetheless represent these "many livings" (Wood 1992, 1, 16).

I take these "livings" to include the socio-spatial practices of individuals, networks of individuals and larger communities, impersonal bureaucracies and nations, all of which enliven cartographic space with specific cultural, eco-nomic, historical, and political interests. But never impartially. Maps encode hegemonic scenarios of memory and identity that regularly suppress dissent, obscure contested plays of power that shape social experience, and exclude alternative histories of that experience.

To situate maps in the complicated richness of their social and historical contexts, to see them as both product of, and occasion for, competing construc-tions of space, is what I have tried to do in studying *The March of Civilization*, published by C. S. Hammond & Company. This atlas graphically illustrated European and United States history for post-World War II, primarily American readers. Cartographers and editors integrated their maps into a biography of Western cultural advancement and triumphant post-war nationalism. At the imagined point of beginnings lay the Holy Land, a space of primal impulse in the march from primitive chaos to higher order civilization.

A Treasury of Historical and Racial Facts

First published in 1949 and last revised in 1965, the Hammond atlas achieved modest commercial success by today's trade book standards, selling about 10,000 copies. Nonetheless, it went through multiple editions and revisions, and for some fifteen years was unrivaled as a text for use in homes and secondary schools.

The publisher's current sales and marketing director recalls that the atlas was meant to portray the geographical settings of "world history, Bible history, American history, and the races of mankind" (Koch 2002, personal communica-tion). This "treasury of historical and racial facts," as one editor wrote, offered a "lucid presentation of the political, social, racial and economic progress of man" (Hammond 1950, Introduction, n.p.).

Along with this notion of cultural advancement, the atlas propagated a capacious idea of American civilization which, as Charles and Mary Beard wrote, had by 1940 become an "ultimate construct of values for countless Americans." In this form, civilization embraced a moralistic conception of history as "a struggle of human beings in the world for individual and social perfection... against ignorance, disease, the harshness of physical nature, the forces of barbarism in individuals and in society. It assigns to history in the United States, so conceived, unique features in origins, substance, and development" (Beard and Beard 1942, 672).

A primary text in the very history it documents, the Beards' lengthy study summed up America's long preoccupation with defining what "civilization" was coming to be, and why in the early 1940s it again required defense. The Hammond atlas participated in that same history, voicing a post-war conviction that Western (American) civilization had survived through military victory and was continuing its trek, as the Beards had written, "amid divagations, defeats, and storms, toward its distant, ever enlarging vision" (Beard and Beard 1942, 674).

Figure 1a and 1b. Line Drawing from the end papers of Hammond, *March of Civilization*. Courtesy of Hammond World Atlas Corporation, NJ. Release #12613

Alluding to Arnold Toynbee, the Hammond editors likened the history of civilization to individuals ascending a mountain, each attempting the feat by different means, and each intent on reaching the summit. Many if not most civilizations have expired. And of those remaining? "One particular civilization, as a result of its dynamic vitality and vast geographical range, exhibits the greatest chance for survival. This civilization is our own and its story is the one that most concerns us" (Hammond 1950, "Foreword" to Part II, H-2).

If the title of the atlas reinforced this theme, a line drawing on the end papers visually realized its ethnocentric and Darwinian assumptions (see Fig. 1).

From left to right, one's eye moves from stone-age primitiveness to Christianity (note the Jesus/shepherd figure, the lamb, and the monk). Medieval (European) warriors come along next, yielding eventually to icons of the American revolution. Then, Edwardian figures lead to a man attired in a two-button, wide-lapel jacket and amply cut trousers of 1940s America.

The U.S. history section of the atlas extended this narrative with maps of discovery, settlement, and territorial expansion. As was typical of public school instruction, the story was presented simplistically, graphically, and with moralistic overtones. To the editors, historical change entailed positive ethical achievement and cultural advance, at least for those readers who were included within the symbol-rich narrative of the imagined community (Anderson 1983; Zelinsky 1988).

The American revolution, readers were told in one graphic illustration, was a simple matter of economic justice and freedom. Success led to the democratizing of land ownership and westward expansion (Hammond 1950, Part III, 10). Other charts projected a wide eyed wonder at the increase in economic value (Part III, 13, 30), growth of population (Part III, 17) and advances in transportation technology (Part III, 36), all of which characterized U.S. history. One half-page chart visualized "The Growth of Democracy in America," and myopically announced that by 1944 the United States had at last achieved "universal suffrage" (Part III, 28). Another map commemorated the Monroe Doctrine, illustrating both the heft and reach of the United States' claim to dominance over the Western hemisphere. Sitting astride North and South America, a youthful Uncle Sam pronounced his purportedly selfless "No"! to further colonialism on these two continents and forswore any meddling in Western Europe's "strictly internal affairs" (Part III, 15).

Other maps and commentary tended to absorb European history into this American myth of innocence. The march of civilization embodied a destiny of territorial expansion (Hammond 1950, Part III, 16–20), benevolent enterprises (Part III, 10, 17, 24–25), and defense of the good, notably against Hitler's barbarous "empire (built on) a cornerstone of blood and terror" (inset to map "High Spots of World War II," Part II, H-40). America's success was an "amazing chapter in history," wrote one editor.

A wilderness has been tamed, and a powerful nation has arisen to take its place among the foremost countries of the world. A land populated by every race, creed and color, and a haven of refuge for the oppressed, its phenomenal growth has never been

equaled. Far removed from the traditions and hampering fetters of the Old World, it has
chartered a new course of government. Its freedom loving peoples have devoted their
energies to developing the riches that Nature has so lavishly supplied (Hammond 1950,
Part III, 32).

This self-congratulatory narrative, which in many respects extended an established tradition of uncritical nationalist historiography (Bancroft 1883–85;
Zelinsky 1988, 144–52; Plumb 1970; Rossiter 1971), reached its apogee in the
colonialist space of "American Overseas Expansion" (see Fig. 2).

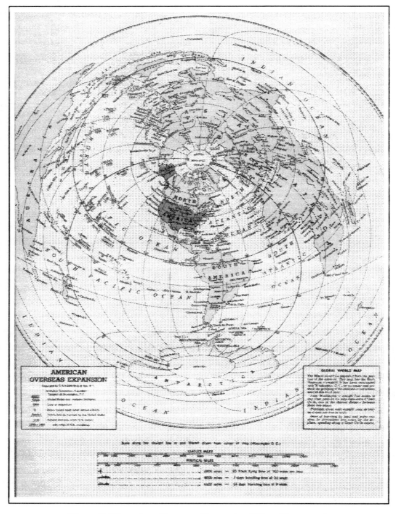

Figure 2. "American Overseas Expansion," from Hammond,
March of Civilization. Map courtesy of Hammond World Atlas Corporation, NJ.
Release #12613

Adopting "the North American viewpoint," a cartographer put Washington, D.C. at the center of an azimuthal equidistant projection that marked out in color U.S. possessions and territories (Part III, 34). Nothing of the far-flung network of European colonies was shown. In effect, the imperial mantle had passed to the United States in the aftermath of World War II, even though not much real estate was involved. From Dwight D. Eisenhower's White House, as it were, one might imagine "American overseas expansion" as a space of benign hegemony denoted by a few cartographic symbols—mostly islands in the western Pacific. Obscured, however, was the projection of U.S. economic and military dominance which constituted an empire less about territory than about, as the Cold Warriors claimed, defense of democracy and containment of Soviet expansionism.

And about the superiority of United States technology. On this map, one could draw a straight line from Washington D.C. to any point on the globe and measure the shortest distance by air between the two points. Thus, to visualize "overseas expansion" was also to celebrate the wonder of post-war air travel. Following the "Great Circle Route," airplanes could now abandon the coast-hugging routes of the pre-war past and deliver people and goods—and military ordnance—anywhere, and more quickly than ever before.

To these texts and images of civilization's march to post-war America, the Hammond editors added "The Races of Mankind," a photographic portfolio of bronze sculptures by Melvina Hoffman that were first exhibited nearly two decades earlier at the Chicago Natural History Museum (Field 1933a, 1933b). Published separately in 1934, this catalogue of "racial types" went through several printings, the last of which found its way into the *March of Civilization* where it remained until the atlas went out of print in 1965 (Field 1934; Field and Hambly 1946).

For her 1933 exhibition, Melvina Hoffman created a monumental sculpture of three figures, "Mongoloid" (West Asian), White (Nordic) and Negro (African)" (see Fig. 3). While depicting what most anthropologists at the time accepted as a fundamental taxonomy, her heroic figures, which were said to symbolize "the unity of Mankind," also strode forth into the heated climate of racial politics.

Hoffman assumed that the unity of mankind was an immutable truth despite superficial physical differences among human beings that anthropologists might document, or that racist regimes might exploit.

Anthropologist Henry Field agreed. He added historical dimension to the essentialist claim of unity and, intervening in another ideologically charged debate of the day, adroitly trod the line between evolutionism and biblical literalism. "Whether we accept the Biblical account of man's creation or his emergence by evolutionary means, we have to believe in the original unity of mankind" (Field 1933a, 10). Moreover, Field wrote elsewhere, artist Hoffman had shown something greater than calipers and camera could disclose. She had

immortalized in bronze the spirit and character as well as the bodily form of each of her subjects. Not a single type has been idealized or subjected to racial prejudice; each model is portrayed in a natural pose, with sympathy and appreciation of his individuality. (Field 1933b, 146)

Indeed, asserted Berthold Laufer in another introduction to the exhibit, although anthropologists may classify racial types, they offer no comfort to racist ideologues. "There is…no such thing as an Aryan race," Laufer wrote. "Race" was to be understood in a biological, not cultural sense. It means "breed and refers to the physical traits acquired by heredity, in contrast with experience and the total complex of habits and thoughts acquired from the group to which we belong" (Field 1933a, 6).

Figure 3. "The Unity of Mankind." Sculpture by Malvina Hoffman. Photograph ©
The Field Museum, #MH89, Chicago.
Used by permission

When adding the "Races of Mankind" to the Hammond atlas in 1949, the publishers dropped all direct allusions to Nazi ideology, which of course was still a fresh memory. However, they retained Hoffman's gently politicized homage to the "unity of mankind." They also let stand the physiognomic defini-tion of "race," thus reasserting the claim that racial classification was free of the cultural entanglements and demagogy of racism (Hammond 1950, Part IV, preface to "Description of Races," n.p.).

Try as they might, however, the Hammond editors could not banish the ambivalence about race that lay in the heart of America's idea of civilization, or what the Beards had called the "ultimate construct of values" (Beard and Beard 1942, 672). Illustrators and writers acknowledged the role of slavery in U.S.

history (Hammond 1950, Part III, 21–22), but their story of civilization's advance had no place for the debilitating legacy of slavery or the laws that excluded Asians from the full rights of citizenship. The catalogue of "racial types" confronted racism, but not at home, preferring to associate it with Nazi ideology and misguided non-scientific attitudes.

Moreover, despite her statement about the "unity of mankind," Hoffman's idealized sculptures both perpetuated and avoided the divisive complications of racial politics in America. Although the figures are dignified, their nobility seems stylized, mannerist, and imposed. The "racial types" are aesthetic types, exemplars of robust, muscular, and quietly resolute physical beauty (see Fig. 4).

Figure 4. "Sara Girl, Sara Tribe, French Equatorial Africa."
Photograph © The Field Museum, #MH2, Chicago.
Used by permission.

The people seem content with their work or play, and completely submissive to Hoffman's privileged gaze. They are models of physical perfection, without much hint of cultural differences, deprivations, discontents, or political exclusions that marked the social realities of race in the United States. Many of Hoffman's sculpted figures seem akin to the "children of the jungle and desert," which she romanticized in a short preface to the catalogue ("While Head Hunting for Sculpture," Hammond 1950, Part IV, n.p.).

These figures inhabited a visual space cleared for colonial and racial fantasy. They yielded themselves to the socio-spatial practices of Anglo-European aesthetics and anthropology. While adhering to high standards of art and science, such practices effaced the unequal allocations of status and economic reward that had been characteristic of the United States but ignored in typical narratives of American national identity.

Hoffman's sculptures, and later the photographic images of her work, offered a world that had been carefully constructed and populated with dark-skinned people who contentedly went about their lives. In this respect, they were similar in social function to many photographs in the *National Geographic* that depicted idealized settings in which "race was not an issue and where white people did not have to reevaluate the sources of their privilege" (Lutz and Collins 1993, 159). Readers of the Hammond atlas did not have to confront the links between geographical science and colonialist constructions of race (Livingstone 1992, 216–59) or, closer to home, deal with the fires of racial conflict that had been temporarily dampened by the urgencies of World War II.

At the root of this racialized project of nationalist history stood the Bible and the Holy Land. Like a *dramatis persona*, the "Atlas of Bible Lands" (Hammond 1950, Part I, B1–B32) took its place on stage, occupying the primal space of generative impulse toward civilization's rise, and its march toward America's achievements.

Fantasy and Historical Rectitude

The Bible atlas followed longstanding vernacular and scholarly conventions of illustrating a Bible that had been woven into the fabric of Holy Land attachments. Maps, commentary, and photographs encouraged readers to enter spaces where desire enabled fantasies of "real" biblical history suffused with nostalgic longing (Long 2002). Contemporary issues—the politics of Zionism and post-World War II Israel, for example—did not intrude on the romanticized landscapes which were meant only to evoke biblical memory and the triumphs of Christianity. The title page is entirely typical in this regard (see Fig. 5).

Rose-toned desert crags and distant vistas dwarf conventionally stylized desert dwellers and invite readers to enter idealized antiquity. Effacing that dreamy fantasy, a caption writer summoned up instead the solid ground of history, the "rose-red rock city of Petra" and its "once wealthy Nabatean kingdom...in the time of Jesus."

HAMMOND'S
ATLAS OF THE BIBLE LANDS

WADI MUSA ENTRANCE TO THE ROCK CITY OF PETRA

The sandstone cliffs shown here form the waterway or Wadi Musa entrance to the rose-red rock city of Petra. Two hundred feet below lies the once wealthy Nabatean kingdom which in the time of Jesus was a center of caravan trade, commanding as it does the routes to Gaza in the west, Damascus in the north, Elath on the Red Sea and across the desert to the Persian Gulf.

C. S. HAMMOND & CO.
305 East 63rd Street
NEW YORK, N. Y.

Figure 5. Title Page from Hammond's Atlas of the Bible Lands,
March of Civilization, Part 1.

Emphasizing this sort of historical rectitude, and following a long tradition of biblical geography, cartographers located biblical events in the topography and toponomy of ancient Palestine (Butlin 1992, 1993). Maps affirmed that biblical history and the Bible, like scientific cartography itself, were matters of trustworthy, settled facticity. The cartographic spaces, however, were entangled with complex social realities.

Three maps, for example, transmitted the dominant ideological tendencies of Exodus through Judges and reduced the underlying material to a narrative of national origins (Hammond 1950, Part I, B8–9). The Hebrews ("all Israel") left bondage (Map: "Egypt...with the Probable Route of the Exodus"), entered the Promised Land (Map: "Canaan Before the Conquest"), and settled into their assigned tribal regions (Map: "Canaan as Divided Among the Twelve Tribes"). Ignoring scholarly controversies about all these matters, not to mention Middle Eastern politics of the time, cartographers visualized Canaan simply and exclusively as biblical. They cleared the space for an ethnically unified biblical Israel and sign posted it with locations of biblical events. In the broader context of the *March of Civilization*, mapmakers encouraged a view that the advancement of Western culture began in a singular erasure (even destruction) of non-Hebrew "Canaanites." This version of ascending the summit of civilization would eventually include yet another sweeping hegemony, the missionary activities of Saint Paul (Maps: Saint Paul's Journeys, Hammond 1950, Part I, B 28).

Moreover, cartographers encoded modern cultural experience in their rendering of ancient space. For example, in "Canaan as Divided Among the Twelve Tribes" (Hammond 1950, Part I, B9), they followed common practice and rendered color-coded Israelite tribal allotments as distinct regions. By ignoring ambiguities of both biblical text and scholarly research, mapmakers reinforced the presumption that this map (and scientifically produced maps in general) directly reflected settled factuality. Moreover, the map of ancient well-defined tribal spaces enabled a reader to visualize something like modern political entities that exercise sovereignty through bureaucratic and military control of territorial borders.

However, some scholars now question such nationalist assumptions (Rogerson 1999), which lead to an elitist idea of political order. Such socio-spatial practices give ethnic and territorial definition to what was more likely to have been, as Keith Whitelam has argued, "unruly autonomies of the local" (Whitelam 2001, 6). In this way, Hammond's atlas of the Holy Land (and most maps illustrative of biblical history) reinforced Anglo-European national biographies, which in turn frequently presumed a cultural affinity with biblical antiquity (Kuklick 1996, 176–95; Long 2002, 141–63).

Such connections would have hardly seemed credible except for longstanding cultural appropriation of the Bible and with it another assumption, that the Holy Land's present-day condition afforded direct access to the life and times of biblical heroes. In the mode of ancient Christian pilgrims, most nineteenth- and twentieth-century travelers from Europe and America, including many technically trained biblical scholars, assumed that the Holy Land had remained essentially biblical and unchanged through some two millennia. These were centuries, one may add, in which civilization in the West had made great advances. An ancient Land of the Bible so imagined thus inspired fantasies of primal religious origins while confirming attitudes of cultural, even racist superiority over the land's contemporary inhabitants (Said 1978, 2000).

A photograph of the "Watering Well in Jericho" is typical of many such images of a Holy Land held in *stasis* for modern consumption (see Fig. 6).

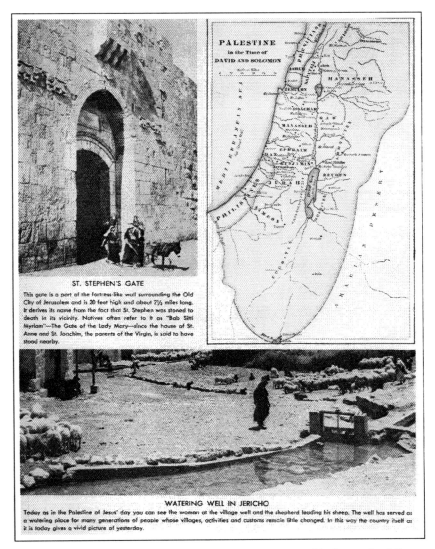

ST. STEPHEN'S GATE

This gate is a part of the fortress-like wall surrounding the Old City of Jerusalem and is 20 feet high and about 2½ miles long. It derives its name from the fact that St. Stephen was stoned to death in its vicinity. Natives often refer to it as "Bab Sitti Myriam"—The Gate of the Lady Mary—since the house of St. Anne and St. Joachim, the parents of the Virgin, is said to have stood nearby.

WATERING WELL IN JERICHO

Today as in the Palestine of Jesus' day you can see the woman at the village well and the shepherd leading his sheep. The well has served as a watering place for many generations of people whose villages, activities and customs remain little changed. In this way the country itself as it is today gives a vivid picture of yesterday.

Figure 6. "Watering Well in Jericho." From Hammond, *March of Civilization*, Part I, B 10. The arrangement of this page reinscribed a notion of Christian scripture. Photographs evoked narratives from Old and New Testaments, and the map "Palestine in the Time of David and Solomon" encoded the canonical version of Israelite history. Map courtesy of Hammond World Atlas Corporation, NJ. Release #12613

Beneath a tranquil scene of herdsmen and grazing sheep, the editors' nostalgic caption reassuringly transported a reader back to the time of Jesus, less a matter of chronology than an imagined space of emotional attachment:

> Today as in the Palestine of Jesus' day you can see the woman of the village well and
> the shepherd leading his sheep. The well has served as a watering place for many
> generations of people whose villages, activities, and customs remain little changed. In
> this way the country itself as it is today gives a vivid picture of yesterday. (Hammond
> 1950, Part I, B 10)

As is evident, the Hammond "Atlas of Bible Lands" had a quality of religious
pilgrimage about it. The assemblage of maps and photographs encouraged
readers to move through a Palestine undisturbed by a troublesome present and
occupy a past in which nostalgic devotion vivified the Bible's eternal story of
religious transformation. Maps of the exodus, conquest, settlement, the Davidic
and Solomonic kingdoms, of Jerusalem, the Palestine of Jesus' Day, and the
world of Paul—all constructed visual spaces of settled history. Yet the journey
imagined a particular version of history, a Christian story from Abraham to
Paul, which of course presupposed the idea of the Old and New Testaments
unified in the perspective of Christian conviction.

Thus the well in Jericho and its "woman of the village" not only evoked the
"time of Jesus," but drew upon a vernacular tradition of representing Old Testament ancestors, especially Rebekah, in dreamy scenes beside watering places
(see Fig. 7).

Figure 7. Rebekah at the well was a popular Victorian image. This advertising card, c.
1890, evoked fantasies of a feminized "Oriental" antiquity: biblical, female, alluring,
slightly decadent.

On the same page (see Fig. 6), a map of Old Testament, "Palestine in the Time of David and Solomon," lay alongside a photo of St. Stephen's gate, a paradigmatic New Testament image that had for many centuries been used to disambiguate Christian history and characterize it as martyr-inspired, universalizing mission.

The atlas not only implied this unified biblical world of Old and New Testaments. It also offered a specifically Protestant journey through that space, and gave special privilege to *sola scriptura* over against dubious Church tradition. Edward Robinson's meticulously scientific and fervently devotional travel accounts set the pattern for nineteenth-century America (Robinson 1841). Hammond's "Atlas of Bible Lands" reinscribed it for yet another generation of Protestants. A scientific voice instructed readers that this gate set into the fortress wall of Jerusalem was "20 feet high and about 2 1/2 miles long." It had acquired its name (here an appeal to authoritative Scripture intrudes) "from the *fact* that St. Stephen was stoned in its vicinity." Moreover, this assured link between locale name and privileged biblical text stands in marked contrast to unsubstantiated folk tradition. For the local "natives," presumably Catholic and Orthodox Christians, speak piously of the "Gate of the Lady Mary," since the house of Mary's parents "is *said* to have stood nearby" (Hammond 1950, Part I, B 10, emphasis added).

This and many other pages of the Bible atlas suggested that a reader could imagine and occupy the spaces of momentous biblical events. One could enter a world that still retained its essential biblical character. Never mind that most of what could be seen of Jerusalem's wall and all its gates were late medieval and Turkish. Gazing upon St. Stephen's Gate, one could recall the days of early Christian expansion, the very root of civilization, and be assured of the Bible's historical trustworthiness. At the same time, one could visualize what was no longer visible: the glorious and God-favored empires of David and Solomon. These were spaces marked by territorial borders with nary a hint that the biblical account might have been exaggerated, or that those kingdoms may have been less like a modern nation-state than usually presumed. Moreover, in 1950, such a construct of cultural affinity with glorified sovereignty would have likely reinforced the idea of righteous empire that so permeated the notion of American civilization and its imagined community of "freedom-loving people…developing the riches that Nature has so lavishly supplied" (Hammond 1950, Part III, 32).

Retrospective

Hammond's *March of Civilization* cast the Bible and the Holy Land within a narrative of civilization's agonistic advance from antiquity to the post-World War II triumphs of the United States. In creating their assemblage, the Hammond editors drew upon vernacular and scholarly conventions of representing the Holy Land as a space of nostalgia, desire, and history. Commentary, maps, and photographic illustrations worked in tandem to enable fantasies of "real" places of

primal origin. This was a story of Holy Land attachments and triumphant
Christianity folded into the paradigm of evolution. And it was a story that had
been valorized as cultural progress.

Among other things, these socio-spatial practices served the interests of a
racialized, political ethos in the United States. Cartographic spaces reiterated a
history of innocence, a narrative of origin, expansion, and righteous empire at
the pinnacle of her success. Moreover, an implicit cultural genealogy suggested
that Western (American) civilization not only had the "greatest chance of
survival" (Hammond 1950, Part II, H-2), but that it was rooted and nourished in
Holy Land soil and the Christian Bible.

Works Cited

Anderson, Benedict. 1983. *Imagined Communities: Reflections on the Origin and Spread of Nationalism*. London: Verso.

Bancroft, George. 1883–85. *The History of the United States of America from the Discovery of the Continent*. 6 vols. New York: D. Appleton & Co.

Beard, Charles A, and Mary R. Beard. 1942. *The American Spirit. A Study of the Idea of Civilization in the United States*. Vol. 4 of *The Rise of American Civilization*. New York: Macmillan.

Boggs, S. W. 1947. Cartohypnosis. *Library Journal* 72:433–35.

Butlin, Robin. 1992. Ideological Contexts and the Reconstruction of Biblical Landscapes in the Seventeenth and Early Eighteenth Centuries: Dr. Edward Wells and the Historical Geography of the Holy Land. Pages 31–62 in *Ideology and Landscape in Historical Perspective: Essays on the Meaning of Some Places in the Past*. Edited by Alan Baker and Gideon Biger. Cambridge: Cambridge University Press.

_____. 1993. *Historical Geography: Through the Gates of Space and Time*. London: Edward Arnold.

Field, Henry. 1933a. *The Races of Mankind: An Introduction to the Chauncey Keep Memorial Hall*. Chicago: Field Museum of Natural History.

_____. 1933b. Special Correspondence. The Races of Mankind. *Science* n.s. 78:146–47.

_____. 1934. *The Races of Mankind*. New York: C. S. Hammond & Company.

Field, Henry, and W. D. Hambly. 1946. *The Races of Mankind*. New York: C. S. Hammond & Company.

Flanagan, James. 2001. Mapping the Biblical World: Perceptions of Space in Ancient Southwestern Asia. Pages 1–18 in *Humanities Group Working Papers* 5. Edited by Jacqueline Murray. Windsor, Ont.: University of Windsor Press. Online: www.case.edu/affil/GAIR/Constructions/xtrapapers2000.html.

Foucault, Michel. 1980. *Power/knowledge: Selected Interviews and Other Writings 1972–1977 of Michel Foucault*. Edited by Colin Gordon. New York: Pantheon.

Hammond, C. S. 1950. *The March of Civilization in Maps and Pictures: A Graphic Reference Book Covering Man's Development and Conquests from 4000 B.C. to the Present Day*. New York: C. S. Hammond & Company.

Harley, J. B. 1988. Maps, Knowledge and Power. Pages 277–312 in *The Iconography of Landscape: Essays on the Symbolic Representation, Design, and Use of Past Environments*. Edited by Denis Cosgrove and Stephen Daniels. Cambridge: Cambridge University Press.

_____. 2001. *The New Nature of Maps: Essays in the History of Cartography*. Baltimore: Johns Hopkins University Press.

Hodder, Ian, ed. 1989. *The Meanings of Things: Material Culture and Symbolic Expression.* London: Unwin Hyman.

Kuklick, Bruce. 1996. *Puritans in Babylon: The Ancient Near East and American Intellectual Life, 1880–1930.* Princeton: Princeton University Press.

Livingstone, David N. 1992. *The Geographical Tradition: Episodes in the History of a Contested Enterprise.* Oxford: Blackwell.

Long, Burke O. 2002. *Imagining the Holy Land: Maps, Models and Fantasy Travels.* Bloomington: Indiana University Press.

Lutz, Catherine, and Jane Collins. 1993. *Reading National Geographic.* Chicago: University of Chicago Press.

Mead, George Herbert. 1934. *Mind, Self, and Society from the Standpoint of a Social Behaviorist.* Chicago: University of Chicago Press.

_____. 1938. *The Philosophy of Act.* Edited by W. C. Morris et al. Chicago: University of Chicago Press.

Plumb, J. H. 1970. *The Death of the Past.* Boston: Houghton Mifflin.

Richardson, Miles. 1989. The Artifact as Abbreviated Act: A Social Interpretation of Material Culture. In Hodder 1989, 172–77.

Robinson, Edward. 1841. *Biblical Researches in Palestine, Mount Sinai and Arabia Petraea.* 3 vols. Boston: Crocker and Brewster.

Rogerson, John. 1999. Frontiers and Borders in the Old Testament. Pages 116–26 in *In Search of True Wisdom: Essays in Old Testament Interpretation in Honour of Ronald E. Clements.* Edited by Edward Ball. JSOTSup 300. Sheffield: Sheffield Academic Press.

Rossiter, Clinton. 1971. *The American Quest, 1790–1860: An Emerging Nation in Search of Identity, Unity, and Modernity.* New York: Harcourt & Brace.

Said, Edward W. 1978. *Orientalism.* New York: Vintage.

_____. 2000. Invention, Memory, and Place. *Critical Inquiry* 26:175–92.

Shalev, Zur. 2002. Mapping the Holy Land, Mapping Sacred Scholarship. *Religious Studies News/SBL Edition* 3:1–3.

Soja, Edward W. 1996. *Thirdspace: Journeys to Los Angeles and Other Real-and-Imagined Places.* Oxford: Blackwell.

Whitelam, Keith. 2001. Transcending the Boundaries: Expanding the Limit. Paper presented at the annual meeting of the SBL, Denver, Co. November 17–20. Pages 1–10. Online: http://www.cwru.edu/affil/GAIR/Constructions/Constructions.html (accessed April 2004).

Wood, Denis. 1992. *The Power of Maps.* New York: Guilford.

Zelinsky, Wilbur. 1988. *Nation into State: The Shifting Symbolic Foundations of American Nationalism.* Chapel Hill: University of North Carolina Press.

Part III

SPACE IN BIBLICAL NARRATIVE

A BAKHTINIAN READING OF NARRATIVE SPACE AND ITS RELATIONSHIP TO SOCIAL SPACE

William R. Millar

I shall divide them [Simeon and Levi] in Jacob,
And shall scatter them in Israel. (Gen 49:7 NRSV)

They [Levi] teach Jacob your ordinances,
    And Israel your law;
They place incense before you,
And whole burnt offerings on your altar. (Deut 33:10 NRSV)

Scholars widely agree that old songs like those we now know as the Blessing, or Testament, of Jacob in Gen 49 and the Blessing of Moses in Deut 33 were early ways to talk about the origin and development of Israel. The names of gathered eponymous tribal ancestors formed the collective social unit of Israel at some point in its history. Using text-critical study grounded in the history of the Hebrew language, along with a study of literary patterns within Hebrew poetry, a number of old songs have been identified: Blessing/Testament of Jacob (Gen 49), Song of Miriam (Exod 15), Blessing of Moses (Deut 33), Song of Deborah (Judg 5), Song of Hannah (1 Sam 2), an old Divine Warrior hymn (Hab 3). On linguistic grounds, these old songs are usually dated earlier than the surrounding prose in which they are currently found; that is, the songs were embedded in some subsequent prose narrative producing layers of text for the contemporary reader, not unlike strata one would find in an archaeological mound.

It becomes immediately apparent to the reader that the presentation of Levi in the two ancient songs quoted above is quite different, even though they share the same genre as a collection of eponymous tribal ancestors commented upon by an epic hero: in one case by Jacob/Israel, and in the other by Moses.

In 1973, Frank Moore Cross published a programmatic essay on the "Priestly Houses of Early Israel" (Cross 1973). In it he argued that the conflict narratives reflecting a tension between Moses and Aaron have their source in a corresponding tension between priestly houses in early Israel, each claiming either Moses or Aaron as their eponymous ancestor. In 1980, Robert Wilson expanded on this insight to present an overview of prophecy within its social world, contrasting tensions between northern Ephraimite prophetic tradition and southern Judahite prophetic tradition (Wilson 1980). Richard Elliott Friedman (1997) has applied Cross's insight to argue that the conflict narratives contribute to our understanding of how the Bible came to be, as understood in his reading of the documentary hypothesis. I have linked this insight of competing priestly houses to an exploration of the theological systems affirmed by the Mushite Levites reflected in the Deuteronomistic History and the Aaronid Zadokite Levites reflected in the Chronicler's work (Millar 2001). Recently, Cross's essay has been reprinted in a *Festschrift* for S. Dean McBride entitled *Constituting the Community: Studies on the Polity of Ancient Israel* (Strong and Tuell 2005). Once again, the tenor of the collected essays reflects the observation that the Hebrew Bible, "rather than being a monolithic voice, contains a dialogue among opposing groups vying for power and influence, each trying to hone the definition of Israel according to its own perspective" (Strong and Tuell 2005, 7).

The discussion thus far has largely been dominated by diachronic readings, that is, readings that have presented the argument in categories of time. The archaeological metaphor of literary strata used above is a case in point. Without dismissing the important historical work that has been done on these biblical texts, recent theorizing on space is beginning to give biblical scholars a vocabulary and tools to invest as much energy on reading texts synchronically. This shift in paradigm allows the biblical interpreter to highlight the multivoiced nature of the biblical canon as received as well as to lift to the surface issues of power and social location.

In this endeavor, the literary-critical work of Mikhail Bakhtin has recently captured the attention of biblical scholars (Green 2000). Among Bakhtin's many important insights are his comments on the importance of synchronic connections and boundaries: "In our enthusiasm for specification we have ignored questions of the interconnections and interdependence of various areas of culture... [T]he most intense and productive life of culture takes place on the boundaries of its individual areas and not in places where these areas have become enclosed in their own specificity" (Bakhtin 1986, 2).

For the purposes of this study, drawing from his work on Dostoevsky, it is Bakhtin's claim that Dostoevsky saw and conceived his world in terms of space, not time, that is of special interest: "This stubborn urge to see everything as coexisting, to perceive and show all things side by side and simultaneous, as if they existed in space and not in time, leads Dostoevsky to dramatize, in space, even internal contradictions and internal stages in the development of a single person" (Bakhtin 1984, 19). Bakhtin could claim that Dostoevsky's "perception in the cross-section of a given moment...permitted him to see many and varied things where others saw one and the same thing" (1984, 30). This insight gives us a point of entry to understand why Levi and Levite could mean different things in different parts of the Bible, as in the case of Gen 49 and Deut 33.

Defining Space

Narrative space is relatively easy to understand. Narrative space is one of the tools available to an author in the construction of a rhetorical strategy designed to persuade an audience toward a particular idea. Using as an illustration the body of literature making up the nineteenth-century British novel, Wesley Kort

(2004) argues that narrative space is a construct—along with character development, plot, and interpretation of historical events—that weaves together to form the author's presentation. Kort further characterizes the kinds of narrative space his authors used to organize the place-relations of their characters and argument. His list includes *cosmic* or *comprehensive space* as in Thomas Hardy's heath, or Herman Melville's sea. "This is a sense of placement within a space that precedes, outstrips, and includes humans and their constructions" (Kort 2004, 19). One can see a biblical parallel in the use of the wilderness in the Elijah narratives.

A second kind of place-relation is *social* or political space. Kort argues that a particular problem his authors often expose is "that human place-relations are swamped by the power and pervasiveness of social, political space" (Kort 2004, 20). Not only can it occlude a reader's access to comprehensive space, but it can invade a third kind of place-relation he identifies as *personal* or intimate space. Here the author invites the reader into the personal space of a character. A biblical example that illustrates the invasive power of social, political space is the author of Kings' invitation to the reader to enter the private space of David's bedroom in his elder years to witness David's inability to keep warm, but also to observe the behind-the-scenes maneuvering of Nathan and Bathsheba to ensure that Solomon be David's royal successor. What Kort calls *social space* would normally be the locus of narrative action taking place in a constructed public, social setting. What is being argued is that space is not a neutral category in which things are and happen; narrative space is part of a constructed rhetorical strategy to persuade.

Social space outside of narrative is more difficult to grasp. Bakhtin has some helpful insights for us. An author's ability to visualize an event and recreate it artistically is born and shaped by the author's consciousness rooted in his own space-time. And yet, the artistic representation is still a product of the author's creativity, separate from the environment of the author's consciousness. In Bakhtin's words, "The represented world, however realistic and truthful, can never be chronotopically [his word for an author's constructed time-space] identical with the real world it represents, where the author and creator of the literary work is to be found" (Bakhtin 1981, 256). He also states:

> As long as the organism lives, it resists a fusion with the environment, but if it is torn out of its environment, it dies. The [created] work and the world represented in it enter the real world and enrich it, and the real world enters the [created] work and its world as part of the process of its creation as well as part of its subsequent life, in a continual renewing of the work through the creative perception of listeners and readers. (1981, 254)

There is thus data relevant to the historian and the sociologist in a narrative text; but those data do not fuse with their historical or sociological ground. The chronotope makes the artistic visualization possible. The lack of a one-to-one fusion of narrative and external social space, however, requires that the reader be disciplined in the reading of a text. In Bakhtin's words, we must never confuse—as has been done up to now and as is still often done—the *represented* world with the world outside the text (naïve realism), nor must we confuse the author-creator of a work with the author as a human being (naïve biographism), nor confuse the listener or reader of multiple and varied periods, recreating and renewing the text, with the passive listener or reader of one's own time (which leads to dogmatism in interpretation and evaluation). (Bakhtin 1981, 253)

Social Space

To explore further the complicated nexus between a constructed social space in narrative and the external social space of the author, the work of Henri Lefebvre (1991) and Edward Soja (1996) has offered us more refined categories with which to understand the dynamics of space. Lefebvre's *lived space* (Soja's Thirdspace) is the space within which we live, filled with all the turbulence of having to negotiate from moment to moment the multitude of relationships that make up our lives. Michel de Certeau (1984) uses the metaphor of "walking in the city." At the "street-level" of our lived space we are so close to the daily demands of living that we frequently do not have the psychic distance to see the "big picture." And yet it is out of the turbulence of lived space that we construct what Lefebvre calls our *perceptions* (Soja's Firstspace) and *conceptions* (Soja's Secondspace). Our perceptions are those experiences of our physical world that gain meaning as they collapse almost immediately into our Secondspace conceptions.

Given the lists of eponymous ancestors that make up the old songs being investigated, we see a connection between a perceived tribal space and an ancestor's name. In this regard, James Flanagan's insight on the organization and perception of space in segmented social systems is helpful: "in such societies, people move through people, not through space. Spatiality and people are organically linked" (Flanagan 2001, 13; cf. Camp 2002, 77). Claudia Camp adds an important insight from her study of postexilic Ben Sira: "people also apparently read through people, not through books (or scrolls). Textuality and people are organically linked" (Camp 2002, 77).

The task suggested by these definitions of space, linked to a self-conscious attempt to read synchronically across the Bible's literary canon, is to see if a *lived space* context can be discerned that could generate the apparent conflicting *Secondspace* conceptual presentations of Levi in Gen 49 and Deut 33.

Genesis 49:5–7

The work of Stanley Gevirtz (1981) has opened up the possibility of offering a synchronic reading of the Genesis text in its relationship with the material on Levi in Deut 33. A reading for Gen 49:5–7 often proposed is to connect it with the material in Gen 34, which presents the story of Dinah and Shechem. Since there is nothing in Gen 34 that suggests Levi held a priestly status, it has led to the proposal that Levi was once a secular tribe that was "scattered" and at some subsequent point in Israel's history became a priestly tribe. Much of the discourse has been directed toward identifying that period of transformation.

But can we assume that the Simeon and Levi mentioned in Gen 34 provides the context for the reading about Simeon and Levi in Gen 49:5–7? Could it be the other way around? Has the poetry of Gen 49:5–7 shaped the prose narrative of Gen 34? On the assumption that normally the old songs were earlier and offered data upon which later prose narrative was based, it is worth pursuing the proposal that Gen 49:5–7 has shaped the telling of Gen 34. Gevirtz has explored this latter proposal and illustrates for us how narrative space and textual/literary criticism work together as methodological tools for interpretation.

To explore this proposal, we first must set aside reading Gen 49:5–7 in the light of events recorded in Gen 34 and raise the prior question: Is it possible to reconstruct a narrative space for Gen 49 in its own right, one that makes historical sense? Drawing on principles of the history of Hebrew language and poetic parallelism, Gevirtz offers the following translation of Gen 49:5–7. Placed in the mouth of Jacob are the following words:

> Simeon and Levi are spent owls,
> Cashiered hawks are they.
> Into their council I will not enter,
> In their assembly I do not rejoice.
> For in their anger they kill(ed) men,
> And in their caprice tore out a bull.
> Cursed be their anger so potent,
> And their vehemence so callous!
> I shall divide them in Jacob,
> And shall scatter them in Israel. (Gevirtz 1981, 93)

Notice that there are no references to Shechem, Hamor, or Dinah. There is no mention of Canaanites or Perizzites. There is a condemnation of the anger of Simeon and Levi expressed as a violent killing of men and the tearing out of a bull. The closing couplet clearly refers to Jacob-Israel as a social unit, suggesting that Simeon and Levi are also being conceived in this instance as tribal entities expelled from some sort of social status in the collective that was Israel.

In dealing with the word *ʾaḥîm* of v. 5, Gevirtz suggests that the usual translation "brothers," while an option, does not really fit the context of Gen 49:5. Since all the sons of Jacob are mentioned in the poem, why designate just these two as brothers? They are all brothers. Nor is the negative assessment applied only to Simeon and Levi. Reuben and Issachar are criticized as well. This led Gevirtz to explore whether there were other options for translating *aḥîm*.

In Isa 13:21, the word *ʾaḥîm* also appears where the translation "brothers" does not fit, as part of a list of animals that inhabit desolate places. When given an o-vowel, rather than the a-vowel for the word brother, Gevirtz suggests that the word can also mean "owl." Pointing to possible parallels in cognate languages, he proposes that the word in Gen 49:5 means an eagle-owl, a predator if you happen to be a small creature in a desert place.

The final *mem* is explained as an "enclitic *mem*" or older ending often placed in the construct position, a practice that eventually fell out of the language. Gevirtz reads the next word from the verbal root *klh* ("to be finished, spent, exhausted"). He notes: "The reconstructed phrase, then, would signify 'spent (or: exhausted) owls,' literally, 'eagle-owls of exhaustion'" (Gevirtz 1981, 97). Using a similar procedure, Gevirtz reconstructed the parallel phrase "cashiered hawks are they."

His reading of Simeon and Levi as predatory birds is further supported by the fact that "six others of the sons of Jacob in this Blessing of Jacob find characterization as animals—Judah 'a lion's whelp,' Issachar 'a donkey,' Dan 'a serpent,' Naphtali 'a hind,' Joseph 'a wild ass' foal,' and Benjamin 'a wolf'" (Gevirtz 1981, 96). This removes the question of why only these two were referred to as brothers. "Characterizing Simeon and Levi as perishing birds of prey, he [the poet through Jacob] dissociates himself from them, censures their actions, and condemns them to dispersion" (1981, 93).

But what have they done that elicits this negative assessment of their behavior? In what manner is the poet reading through people whose names carry spatial implications? Gevirtz finds the solution within the poem itself. Envisioning the state of Israel as the collective household of Jacob normally would symbolize its union; that is, it would be a literary means of conceiving the coming together of tribes to form a united Israel. If so, Gevirtz argues, "then the figure of the dying Jacob-Israel will have served to symbolize the 'dying' nation, i.e., the dissolution or disintegration of political Israel" (Gevirtz 1981, 115). Gevirtz argues that this persona of Jacob-Israel was a deliberate choice, the literary device through which the author/poet "comments upon and responds to the geopolitical situation that is current in his own day, describes and passes positive and negative judgment on those separate groups which, collectively, formed the body politic" (1981, 115). What do we know about the tribes of Simeon and Levi, apart from Gen 34, that would fit into that kind of narrative space?

Focusing on the couplet "For in their anger they kill(ed) men / And in their caprice tore out a bull," Gevirtz argues there is nothing intrinsically improbable—indeed, it fits into the normal practice of poetic parallelism—in seeing the first line as a reference to Simeon, and the second line as a reference to Levi. If we are thinking of Simeon in this instance as a tribe, the first line can easily be interpreted as a military action, but it would be an action not favored by the author of the poem.

Gevirtz sees this military action involving Simeon recorded in Judg 1:3-8, wherein Simeon joined Judah to conquer Judah's allotted territories, an action that included the capture of Jerusalem. Judah's emergence as a dominant tribe under the leadership of David—particularly from a non-Judahite, northern perspective—was a breach of an earlier pre-Davidic federation. That earlier ideal vision of a united Israel was "seriously disrupted by the forceful emergence of Judah as a political entity" (Gevirtz 1981, 116). Even in the passages of the Bible that celebrate the successes of David, there are people mentioned who were not supportive of his rule. Note that, at one point, David's own son Absalom led an open rebellion, forcing David to flee Jerusalem.

Subsequent disaffection by some of the tribes with policies emanating from Jerusalem under rulers like Solomon and Rehoboam would eventually create in the northern territories "the establishment of a House of Joseph in opposition to the House of Judah/David" (Gevirtz 1981, 116). While the south would perceive the creation of the House of Joseph as an illegitimate secession from the union centered in Jerusalem, northern groups would see it as "an attempt at a resurrection of the pre-Davidic federation" (1981, 117). If Gen 49, in the persona of a dying Jacob-Israel, reflects a northern view wherein an earlier vision of the union of Jacob-Israel was seen to be under threat, then Simeon's alliance with Judah would have contributed to the disintegration of Israel, a "dying" Jacob-Israel, and a source of the author's negative assessment of Simeon.

With regard to Levi, Gevirtz proposes that "the act of violence perpetrated by Levi was one probably of despoliation, and was directed specifically against a 'bull'" (Gevirtz 1981, 121). This is where we begin to see the advantage of regarding Gen 49 as earlier than Gen 34. There is no bull in the story of Dinah. With the lack of any indication in Gen 34 of Levi's priestly connections, and then reading Gen 49 in the light of Gen 34, scholars have been led down a path of exploring Levi's presumed one-time secular status as a tribe. That raises the subsequent problem of why that secular tribe was scattered, only later to reappear in biblical tradition as a priestly tribe.

Reading Gen 49 as prior to Gen 34 resolves those problems. The words of a dying Jacob-Israel can be read as the assessment by the author of events moving toward the dissolution of the United Monarchy, toward the division into two competing kingdoms. The dispersion of Levi in Gen 49:7 can be linked, historically, to Jeroboam I's expulsion of Levites from northern territories when he came to power in that region, along with his setting up of the golden calf/bull at the northern sanctuary of Bethel. This brings Gen 49:5–7 into discourse with other passages—passages like 1 Kgs 12 and Exod 32—shaped by that same collection of events, which begin to give us *chronotopic* windows for the reconstruction of a *lived space* setting.

Spatial realignments are being read through people. The dispersion alluded to in Gen 49 would be a reference to the expulsion of Levites by Jeroboam I when he came to power in the northern territories (see 2 Chr 11:13–17). David's earlier strategies to establish control over the northern territories included the designation of certain cities as Levitical cities in recognition of their service to the king. Gevirtz draws on Benjamin Mazar's assessment of David's formation of Levitical cities:

> [Mazar] has proposed that the cities in which the Levites were granted rights of habitation, and on whose outskirts they were granted grazing privileges, served as provincial administrative centers of the government in Jerusalem; that the grants constituted a form of compensation to the Levites for their service to the state; ...and that in the period of the United Monarchy the Levites were agents specifically of the Davidic dynasty centered in Jerusalem. (Gevirtz 1981, 118)

Acting either as agents of the Jerusalem government before Jeroboam came to full power, or in response to their expulsion and replacement by non-Levitical priests (1 Kgs 12:31), Gevirtz argues, "Levites did something to the bull-calf, which 'something' the poet particularizes as, …literally, 'and in their caprice they tore out a bull.' This will have had reference to what, in the poet's eyes, was a gratuitously forcible removal of the sacred bull-calf image at Bethel by Levites acting as agents of the central government in Jerusalem" (1981, 127).

The story is going to be complicated further when we take into account that there was more than one Levitical family reading this series of events. In one account, a certain Ahijah of Shiloh would approach Jeroboam in support of Jeroboam being the agent through whom God would remove support from the regime of Solomon. In this view, Shiloh Levites could have been in support of Jeroboam's reopening old sanctuaries like Bethel and Dan in the northern territories, expecting that they would receive appointments as priests. Another Levitical family, claiming legitimacy in Jerusalem and exercising its authority from Jerusalem, could have forcibly removed early efforts to establish a bull icon at Bethel. The Chronicler mentions that Abijah, Rehoboam's successor in Jerusalem, captured Bethel in a battle against Jeroboam (2 Chr 13:19). When Jeroboam came to power, possibly not distinguishing among Levitical families, he evicted Levites indiscriminately from the north, hiring non-Levitical priests for his sanctuaries.

To sum up, Gevirtz reads Gen 49:6 as reflecting a northern, negative assessment of a Jerusalem attack on the Bethel cult.

> Calculated to do so or not, this act of spoliation will have offended the religious sensi-
> bilities of the cult's adherents, and will have provided what religious motivation may
> have been deemed necessary for Jeroboam's eviction of the Levites upon his assump-
> tion of power. In literary terms the seizure of the sacred image will have constituted an
> unconscionable affront to the persona of the poem. (Gevirtz 1981, 127)

Deuteronomy 33:8–11

Like Gen 49, parts of Deut 33 show all the markings of an ancient poem that predates the prose material that surrounds it. Albright has argued that when an author or editor moves poetry into a prose context, the tendency is for the poetic forms to break down under the pressure of the literary flow that is characteristic of prose. He observes that what we have been calling repetitive parallelism becomes less defined. Instead it is replaced by such things as assonance, that is, the repetition of sounds but in nonrhyming stressed syllables; or paranomasia, that is, a play on words, as in a pun. Definite articles and relative pronouns that are characteristic of prose style begin to move into the text. For Albright, this becomes evidence for the relative dating of material arranged in a sequence (Albright 1968).

Moses' Blessing of Levi can be discussed in three units: v. 8, vv. 9–10, and v. 11. The first and third units, I shall argue, create a frame that is "broken" by the middle unit.

Deuteronomy 33:8

> Give to Levi your Thummim,
> Your Urim to your faithful one [Moses],
> Whom you tested at Massah,
> Whom you tried at Meribah.

Frank Cross restores the opening line of v. 8 as "Give to Levi," following the reading of this line found in the Dead Sea manuscript, 4QDt[h], and in the Greek. Cross proposed that "Give to Levi," not in the received Masoretic Hebrew text, had dropped out. As one would expect in repetitive parallelism, this places the name of Levi in parallel with "your faithful one." The reference to Massah and Meribah which follows would suggest that the faithful one was Moses, who was a Levite. Cross follows Wellhausen, who argued on the grounds of repetitive parallelism that each stands for the other—Levi and "faithful one" (Moses).

In Exod 17:2–7, we read of the Israelites quarreling with Moses over their lack of water. By complaining to Moses, they were testing his leadership in bringing them into the wilderness. Moses approached God who instructed him to bring some elders to a rock at Horeb, the name consistently applied to God's mountain throughout Deuteronomy. Moses did so, and they were supplied with water: "He called the place Massah and Meribah, because the Israelites quarreled and tested the Lord, saying, 'Is the Lord among us or not?'" (Exod 17:7). In Deut 33, Moses and his tribe Levi were authorized to receive the Thummim and Urim, priestly tools of the trade used to interpret God's words to the people.

Deuteronomy 33:11

> Bless, Yahweh, his [Levi's] might;
> The works of his hands, accept thou!
> Smite the loins of his foes,
> His enemies, whoever attacks him.

Verse 11 constitutes the other half of the frame. Cross and Freedman, in their *Studies in Ancient Yahwistic Poetry*, suggest that it is "swarming with archaisms and may well have been the original blessing of Levi" (Cross and Freedman 1950, 220). Levi is praised for his strength and God is asked to accept the works of Levi's hands. The second bicolon of this unit suggests there is tension in the air. Levi has foes; enemies who attack. Once again we find Levi presented to the reader as one engaged in hostile activity. The section itself does not immediately identify the nature of the hostility.

Deuteronomy 33:9–10 as a "Frame-Break"

> 9:　who said of his father and mother,
> 　　　"I regard them not";
> 　he ignored his kin,
> 　　　and did not acknowledge his children.
> 　For they observed your word,
> 　and your covenant, they kept.

10:    They teach your ordinances to Jacob,
       and your law to Israel;
       they place incense before you,
       and whole burnt offerings on your altar.

It is the intervening vv. 9–10 that lend themselves to a discussion of syn-chronic connectedness. Robert Polzin has applied many of the insights of Bakhtin to his extended reading of Deuteronomy and the Deuteronomist. By paying close attention to the compositional strategies of Deuteronomy, Polzin makes the following observation:

> One of the immediate results of this exceedingly complex network of utterances within utterances is the deliberate representation in Deuteronomy of a vast number of inter-secting statements, sometimes in agreement with one another, sometimes interfering with one another. This enables the book to be the repository of a plurality of view-points, all working together to achieve an effect on the reader that is multidimensional. (Polzin 1980, 26)

One of the strategies that Polzin observes in Deuteronomy is the Deuterono-mist's use of the frame-break as a means for the Deuteronomist to construct meaning. Though Polzin does not discuss Deut 33:9–10, the principle of a frame-break does offer an explanation for the observation Cross and Freedman make regarding these verses:

> In vss. 9–10 there is a complete break in style, meter and content with the rest of the poem. The relative pronoun, …the sign of the definite accusative, …and the article, all suspicious in ancient poetry, occur in these lines. The poetic structure is dubious, and vs. 9 at least seems to be largely prose. Significant from the point of view of the writers is the absence of tenth-century spellings and archaic forms in this passage, while the surrounding verses abound in both. How much, if any, of vss. 9–10 belong to the origi-nal blessing must remain a question. The passage is rejected *in toto* as a late addition by some scholars. (Cross 1950, 220)

Looking at the content of vv. 9–10, there is a shift away from the Massah/Meribah story mentioned in v. 8. Instead, the focus in vv. 9–10 shifts to events recorded in Exod 32, the golden calf story and the apostasy of Aaron. In that setting, Levites are presented as being faithful to God in response to Moses' call for action even against one's own kin, followers of Aaron. Deuteronomy 33:9 has rather odd praise for Levi when he regards not his father and mother and ignores his kin.

Exodus 32:26–28 gets close to that same sentiment when Moses sees the people dancing before a golden calf they created at the foot of God's mountain:

> Moses stood in the gate of the camp and said, "Who is on the Lord's side? Come to me!" And all the sons of Levi gathered around him. He said to them, "Thus says the Lord, the God of Israel, 'Put your sword on your side, each of you! Go back and forth from gate to gate throughout the camp, and each of you kill your brother, your friend, and your neighbor.'" The sons of Levi did as Moses commanded, and about three thousand of the people fell on that day.

That event is also referred to in the book of Deuteronomy itself at Deut 9:20: "The Lord was so angry with Aaron that he was ready to destroy him."

Faced with the reference to Levi's might in Deut 33:11 and Levi's capacity to defeat his foes, I would propose that the Deuteronomist utilized again his compositional strategy of the frame-break in evidence in Moses' earlier addresses. The proposed frame-break (vv. 9–10) expands on Levi's singular commitment to Yahweh. This would account for the prosaizing elements introduced in vv. 9–10. The claim being made was that it was the Mushite Levites who were the true servants of God, past and present. The Deuteronomist here is claiming that even kinship connections will not distract the true Levite from his appointed duty.

Toward a Reconstruction of a Lived Space*:*
Generating Genesis 49:5–7 and Deuteronomy 33:8–11

With Solomon's rise to power, the firing of Abiathar, and Ahijah of Shiloh's subsequent contact with Jeroboam I, we begin to see the unraveling of the Davidic regime. That unraveling produced the *lived space*/Thirdspace context that generated the Secondspace claims of different parties in the debate as they struggled for control of the sacred stories. Spatial realignments of power relationships were being read through people and constructed as pieces of Secondspace narrative.

As noted above, the words of a dying Jacob-Israel in Gen 49 can be read as the assessment by a northern author of events moving toward the dissolution of the United Monarchy into two competing kingdoms. The dispersion of Levi in Gen 49:7 can be linked to Jeroboam I's expulsion of Levites from northern territories when he came to power in that region, along with his setting up of the golden calf/bull at the northern sanctuary of Bethel.

Levites tracing their lineage to Levi through Zadok and Aaron, who were given jurisdiction over the Jerusalem temple in the south from Solomon on, could have been responsible for an attack on Bethel, though Exod 32 would suggest that Shiloh Levites resented as well the calf image placed there by Jeroboam I and Jeroboam's non-hiring of Shiloh Levites. These texts provide *chronotopic windows* for a lived space rationale for David's creation of Levitical cities which, among other things, was a strategy to establish control over the northern territories by designating certain cities Levitical cities in recognition of their service to the king.

The Deut 33:8–11 passage would have emerged from northern Levitical tradition grounded in the stories of Moses, whose agenda was to claim full-fledged status for northern Levitical priests in spite of practices at the Jerusalem temple at the time of Solomon and after. Subsequently, Jeroboam I exacerbated the problems for northern Levites at places like Bethel.

Approaching these texts synchronically, reading across the received biblical canon with a conscious focus on spatial categories, it begins to become clear that the assessment of Levi in Gen 49:5-7 and Deut 33:8-11 are not as unrelated as they first appear to be.

Works Cited

Albright, William F. 1968. *Yahweh and the Gods of Canaan*. Winona Lake: Eisenbrauns.

Bakhtin, Mikhail. 1981. *The Dialogic Imagination: Four Essays*. Translated by Caryl Emerson and Michael Holquist. Edited by Michael Holquist. University of Texas Press Slavic Series 1. Austin, Tex.: University of Texas Press.

_____. 1984. *Problems of Dostoevsky's Poetics*. Translated by Caryl Emerson. Edited by Wlad Godzich and Jochen Schulte-Sasse. Theory and History of Literature 8. Minneapolis: University of Minnesota Press.

_____. 1986. *Speech Genres and Other Late Essays*. Translated by Vern W. McGee. Edited by Michael Holquist and Caryl Emerson. University of Texas Press Slavic Series 8. Austin: University of Texas Press.

Certeau, Michel de. 1984. *The Practice of Everyday Life*. Translated by S. Rendall. Berkeley: University of California Press.

Camp, Claudia V. 2002. Storied Space, or, Ben Sira "Tells" a Temple. Pages 64–80 in *"Imagining" Biblical Worlds: Studies in Spatial, Social and Historical Constructs in Honor of James W. Flanagan*. Edited by Paula M. McNutt and David M. Gunn. JSOTSup 359. London: Sheffield Academic Press.

Cross, Frank Moore, and David Noel Freedman. 1950. *Studies in Ancient Yahwistic Poetry*. Baltimore: John Hopkins University Press.

_____. 1973. The Priestly Houses of Early Israel. Pages 195–215 in *Canaanite Myth and Hebrew Epic*. Cambridge: Harvard University Press.

Flanagan, James W. 2001. Mapping the Biblical World: Perceptions of Space in Ancient Southwestern Asia. Pages 1–18 in *Humanities Group Working Papers* 5. Edited by Jacqueline Murrray. Windsor, Ont.: University of Windsor Press.

Friedman, Richard Elliott. 1997. *Who Wrote the Bible?* San Francisco: HarperSanFrancisco.

Gevirtz, Stanley. 1981. Simeon and Levi in "The Blessing of Jacob" (Gen. 49:5–7). *Hebrew Union College Annual* 52:93–128.

Green, Barbara. 2000. *Mikhail Bakhtin and Biblical Scholarship: An Introduction*. Society of Biblical Literature Semeia Studies 38. Atlanta: Society of Biblical Literature.

Kort, Wesley A. 2004. *Place and Space in Modern Fiction*. Gainesville: University of Florida Press.

Lefebvre, Henri. 1991. *The Production of Space*. Translated by D. Nicholson-Smith. Oxford: Blackwell.

Millar, William R. 2001. *Priesthood in Ancient Israel*. St. Louis: Chalice.

Polzin, Robert. 1980. *Moses and the Deuteronomist*. Bloomington: Indiana University Press.

Soja, Edward W. 1996. *Thirdspace: Journeys to Los Angeles and Other Real-and-Imagined Places*. Malden, Mass.: Blackwell.

Strong, John T., and Steven S. Tuell, eds. 2005. *Constituting the Community: Studies in the Polity of Ancient Israel in Honor of S. Dean McBride Jr*. Winona Lake: Eisenbrauns.

Wilson, Robert R. 1980. *Prophecy and Society in Ancient Israel*. Philadelphia: Fortress.

EXPLORING THE UTOPIAN SPACE OF CHRONICLES: SOME SPATIAL ANOMALIES

Steven James Schweitzer

Introduction

This exploration of the book of Chronicles using spatial theory is not intended to be exhaustive, but rather suggestive of future research. That Chronicles contains or consists of "Utopian Space" is not entirely self-evident and will be defended (if somewhat briefly) below. I will examine inconsistencies in the presentation of space in Chronicles, and offer speculation on their significance for interpreting Chronicles.

Utopianism in Chronicles

I employ two theories that enhance each other's explanatory power: utopian literary theory and critical spatial theory. Roland Boer has initiated and advanced a utopian understanding of Chronicles (1997, 1999). I begin with an account of the pertinent aspects of his method and arguments.[1]

Boer's methodology (1997, 15) follows the influential works on utopian literature by Louis Marin (1984, 1993) and on the related genre of science fiction by Darko Suvin (1974, 1979). Suvin defines utopia as a literary genre or verbal construction whose necessary and sufficient conditions are the presence of a particular quasi-human community where sociopolitical institutions, norms, and individual relationships are organized on a more perfect principle than in the author's community, this construction being based on estrangement arising out of an alternative historical hypothesis (1974, 110).

Suvin's definition reflects three central concerns of recent literary criticism on utopia: (1) comparison between the present society and the "more perfect" literary presentation; (2) the principle of estrangement or defamiliarization as an interpretative key; and (3) provision of a different series of events leading to the present or to the future as depicted explicitly or implicitly by the text. These

---

1. My recent book (Schweitzer 2007), which is based on my dissertation completed at the University of Notre Dame (Schweitzer 2005), explores the utopian dimension of Chronicles by incorporating additional utopian theory and providing a more thorough and systematic reading of the entire book than has been done previously. It consists of three main chapters, each examining one aspect of the utopia constructed in Chronicles: a genealogical utopia, a political utopia, and a cultic utopia, and provides a more extensive bibliography on utopian literary theory and Chronicles scholarship.

three tenets both derive from the content and form of utopias and reflect the fact that utopian theory is related, at least in its present form, to deconstructionist and postmodern literary methodologies.

Boer utilizes these three tenets to structure his own reading of Chronicles as if it were utopian literature. He concludes that Chronicles provides a narrative history largely based on the related ideas of "neutralization" and "plurality" (from Jameson 1988), in an effort to construct an alternative world that calls the present order into question at every turn.[2]

Both Marin and Suvin emphasize the importance of social critique in utopian literature as a means of reading such works *not as blueprints* for ideal societies, but rather as *revolutionary texts* designed to challenge the status quo and question the way things presently are being done. Thus, utopias depict the world "as it should be" *not* "why it is the way it is." In other words, utopias are not works of legitimation (providing a grounding for the present reality), but works of innovation (suggesting a reality that *could* be, if its parameters were accepted). Yet, by presenting ideals that avoid simple implementation, utopia is held out as the goal to be continually striven after but never completely reached. This interpretation of utopian literature produces a significant by-product: the utopian construct does not necessarily reflect the historical situation of the author; that is, the author does not legitimize his present, but criticizes it by depicting the literary reality in terms *not* to be found in the author's society. This makes historical reconstruction derived primarily from a utopian text extremely difficult. The utopian text does not reflect historical reality, but future possibilities. For example, attempting to find the structures of society in More's *Utopia* in his contemporary England would produce a distorted view of England during this time period (Jones 2001). However, to take More's portrayal as the opposite or another view of constructing society, the *problems* of his contemporary English society (at least in More's own view) would become accessible to the reader.

Boer depends on the Russian formalist category of *ostranenie* (commonly translated as "defamiliarization") in analyzing the utopian dimensions of Chronicles (1997, 109). He intentionally looks for inconsistencies, impossibilities, and perceived "surprises" throughout the text, focusing on two main issues: "world reduction" with its accompanying "large numbers," and the "inclusive/exclusive" society with its boundary definitions.[3] First, he notes that geography and the borders of the land are compressed throughout the book while the numbers

---

2.   Defending his "reading as" method, Boer rightly observes that "the arrival of a new genre—More's *Utopia* is my example—is not without its cultural precursors. More importantly, the opening of one's eyes to the various contours of the radically new also opens one's eyes to examples and generic forms that provide a foretaste of what is to come" (1997, 122).

3.   Boer notes that "World reduction is a feature of Utopian writing" (1999, 375); in addition, the utopia must not be a completely closed society (a common misconception of utopias), since outsiders must enter, learn, and return to the larger world in order to bring its wonders to light. This second point is true of More's *Utopia* as well as the ancient voyage of Iambulus (in Diodorus Siculus 2.55.1–60.3). In both cases, the utopians warmly receive the outsider and explicitly participate in trade relations with other nations.

utilized for the population and invading armies are greatly inflated in comparison with the accounts in Samuel–Kings. Second, he agrees with recent scholarship that affirms the Chronicler's hope for individuals, whether from the North or foreigners, to join with "all Israel" to worship the LORD in Jerusalem without imposing additional stipulations that would serve as markers of their identification with that group. He concludes that these common utopian concepts manifest themselves in Chronicles as part of the Chronicler's overall arguments about the nature of "Israel" and its relationship to the land. So, for example, by leaving a geographical opening in Rehoboam's defenses in 2 Chr 10–13 (immediately following the division of the kingdom), the Chronicler provides a means for the Northerners to join Judah at the temple (1999, 374–81).[4] Boer next suggests that such an openness indicates that "Israel" is incomplete without the North; that is, the Chronicler awaited the day of full reconciliation between North and South under the auspices of the one temple cult located at Jerusalem.

Boer's use of geography as an indicator of utopianism is similar to Marin's spatial analysis of Thomas More's *Utopia*. Marin contends that "Utopia" is not "no-place" in the sense of being non-existent, but rather "the 'other' of any place" which does exist (1993, 11). Marin especially notes that utopias tend to resist easy representation on a map or straightforward depiction of their detailed societal structures; they are thus victories over the powers that would attempt to contain and control their ideas. Power is indefinitely critiqued and never fully accepted as sufficient or satisfactory in its present form(s) and structure(s). Thus, Marin concludes that "Utopia is an ideological critique of ideology" (1984, 195), especially the dominant ideology which it seeks to undermine or subvert through its own displacement of structures and projection of reality.

In contrast to Marin, Suvin emphasizes that utopia is always located on a map, even if removed from the author's/reader's society by a great distance or temporal displacement (1979, 42). Suvin thereby explains the relationship between science fiction and utopian literature, especially in its modern manifestations. Klaus Geus (2000) points to the same spatial relationship in Hellenistic utopian literature in stressing the importance of locating utopia on the map of the ancient Greek world. Geus's conclusions demonstrate that the spatiality of utopia plays a significant role in its depiction and in its relationship to the cultural ideals of the day. The notion that "utopia" has "space" draws more on its etymology as "good place" rather than its other connotation of "no place," that is, without space. While utopias have long been marginalized as "pie-in-the-sky," unrealistic portrayals of society without reference to the "real world," more recent literary theorists have openly rejected the negative associations of the word "utopia" and have argued for a more sympathetic reading of these lengthy and often-considered "boring" texts (Grey and Garsten 2002).

---

4. Drawing on Marin's comments (see below), Boer notes that the inclusion of Philistine Gath in the list of Judean cities in 2 Chr 11:6–10 neutralizes the perception of a drastically reduced Judah. Thus, this "quirk" enters the system and disrupts the spatial representation, causing the reader to rethink the reality of the system, that is, a small Judah contemporary with the Chronicler (1997, 145).

Yet the location of utopia in relationship to the "outside world" is not the full extent of spatial concerns in the description of utopia. Analysis of utopia's relationship to the outside world is accompanied by an even more intense fixation on its internal structure, organization, planning, system, and hierarchy. Suvin (1979, 50) notes that utopias come in a variety of models and proposals, but *all* of them are *organized*, following intentional rules and patterns, and work themselves out as a literary reality.

Utopian theorists, however, no longer hold the common wisdom that "change is the enemy of utopia." Innovation is not excluded within the utopian system, and utopia does not exist apart from history. Time and space continue to impact the happenings of the utopian society. Utopia exists in a specific place and has, at least, a historical beginning if not a history of its own since the time of origin.[5]

To conclude this section, a very brief point about utopia and science fiction should be made. As stated above, utopia and science fiction are generically related, though which one is the macro-genre is disputed. Either way, a large number of critical observations about science fiction are directly applicable to utopian literature, as noted not only by Boer, but also by literary critics working in one of these two areas, or in both. While science fiction tends to utilize time displacement as a narrative device more often than utopia does, sci-fi also employs a significant amount of space transformation or spatial displacement in its plot structure. Starships move across the universe, through space, with either the Earth or some other world as origin or destination. This "final frontier" is not an empty container, but is filled with entities, objects, and phenomena of various types. Space is vast, as are the possibilities.

Science fiction thus makes extensive use of "spatial anomalies" to create a means of variation and plot development, allowing the unexpected to occur and problems to arise and to be resolved. These anomalies exist in a closed system (the literary world of the sci-fi work) which allows the system to be broken, challenged, critiqued, and to move the narrative forward. Spatial anomalies attract attention because they do not fit the system; they invoke an explorer's

---

5.   The misconception that utopias cannot change their structures or contain development has produced two side-effects: (1) inconsistencies in utopias have been interpreted as deficiencies on the part of the author, and (2) the label "utopia" has been restricted to very few works, almost all of an "eschatological" nature. This is especially true when the term is used for texts in the biblical tradition—for example, the Garden of Eden, the Priestly legislation, Ezek 40–48, and the New Jerusalem of Rev 21:1–22:5 (and related presentations of the eternal *unchanging* future). For these texts, "utopian" has typically meant unattainable, fanciful, unrealistic, and escapist. The fact that the society of Ezek 40–48 and the laws of P were almost certainly never implemented is the source of their "utopian" associations.

The portrayal of society in Chronicles may not project Second Temple practice back into the pre-exilic period for the sake of legitimation, but may be actually more in line with the desired stipulations of Ezekiel's Temple and P. My research shows that scholars often assume that the Chronicler provides us with a source for such reconstruction without considering the pitfalls involved in such an assumption. If Chronicles is utopian in character, then its cultic practices may reflect desired (but not necessarily implemented) changes and, therefore, not historical realities. Accepting this latter position would then have far-reaching implications in writing a history of the Second Temple period, especially a history of the Jerusalem temple cult.

sense of reality and how new phenomena may challenge it. However, in order to assess such "spatial anomalies," a system of organizing space must be constructed.

Spatial Theory

A relative newcomer to the methodological inventory, both for literary critics and for biblical scholars, spatial theory has been warmly received and its parameters continue to be refined. Claudia Camp's recent essay on space in Sirach (2002) reads this ancient literary work using the theoretical model of two of the major architects of spatial theory: Henri Lefebvre (1991) and Edward Soja (1989, 1996). The model proposed by these two theorists and Camp's use and critique of it serve as the foundation of this analysis and will be briefly outlined below. I will also note the role of utopia in the construction of spatiality by Lefebvre and Soja, as previous summaries or critiques have not addressed this aspect of their work.

Space is a construct, not a given, at least as it is organized, encountered, and assigned meaning (Soja 1989, 79–80). Thus, space is a social product, the result of human interaction with the surrounding world and with other beings. Soja (drawing on the seminal work of Lefebvre) divides such spatial constructs into three categories: Firstspace, Secondspace, and Thirdspace (1996, 10).[6] For both of these scholars, the first concept represents the direct interaction of human beings and space, especially in terms of physicality (Lefebvre 1991, 33; Soja 1996, 66). The second is the arena of imposed codes, signs, maps, and ordering of space, especially in terms of ideology (Lefebvre 1991, 33; Soja 1996, 67). The third term applies to the lived reality, when the concrete spaces of the first and the ideological systems of the second are put into practice (Lefebvre 1991, 33; Soja 1996, 10, 67).

Camp details the importance and attraction of Thirdspace for biblical scholars (2002, 65–69). While Secondspace can be a stronghold of power for the elite imposing an ideological matrix on representations of space and reality, Thirdspace has the potential, especially as presented by Soja, of recombining the first two perceptions of space and thus producing an opportunity for "struggle, liberation, emancipation" (1996, 68). However, lest we rush ahead to the freedom of Thirdspace, ready to ignore the seemingly obvious descriptions of Firstspace or the oppressive nature of Secondspace's ordering of reality, Lefebvre warns us that his triad "loses all force if it is treated as an abstract 'model'" and all three groupings "should be interconnected" (1991, 40).[7] Camp also notes the difficulty of separating Secondspace and Thirdspace and the tendency for each theorist to gravitate towards one of the groupings instead of utilizing all three. She rejects the strict division of Secondspace as power and Thirdspace as

6. Compare Lefebvre's terminology: spatial practice, representations of space, and representational spaces or his variant triad of perceived–conceived–lived space (1991, 33, 40).

7. James Flanagan, largely responsible for the recent interest in spatial theory among biblical scholars, agrees with this methodological caution (2000, 242).

resistance; "the oppressors also have lived spaces" and "life just goes on" for those in the margins of Thirdspace. Soja's idealized "thirding-as-Othering is most often the spatially unrealizable work of intellectuals, while the heterotopias of resistance that make life livable for the oppressed usually do little in the way of actual social transformation" (2002, 68).

Camp's critique of Thirdspace as sometimes idealized by theorists is well-founded. She concludes her introduction with the stated concern to assess the "power-mongering and maintaining potential of Thirdspace" in her analysis of Sirach. For Ben Sira, Thirdspatial lived experiences are enlisted by the powers of Secondspace to reinforce the oppressive center without any hope of liberation for the margins. Her analysis of Sirach thus focuses on "Thirdspace as power" and moves forward on the seemingly continuous line connecting Secondspace and Thirdspace in the text (2002, 68–69).

This reading of spatiality in Chronicles takes a somewhat different approach from Camp's. While it would be easy to relegate Chronicles to the same pile of ideologically oppressive texts as Sirach (2002, 69–70),[8] Boer's reading of Chronicles as utopian literature (see above) and the following comments on utopias in the works of Lefebvre and Soja provide a means of moving from Thirdspace to Secondspace, from power to liberation (using Camp's criticism of Thirdspace while rereading Secondspace at the same time).

Lefebvre specifically calls his own book a project which "straddles the breach between science and utopia, reality and ideality, conceived and lived," and draws an explicit parallel between his attempt to indicate "a different society, a different mode of production, where social practice would be governed by different conceptual determinations" and those of the "great utopians," especially of the Marxist variety (1991, 60, 419, 422–23). That Lefebvre would term his own book, which classifies a spatial system in order to critique it, as being of a utopian nature plays an important role in assessing the comments about utopian space throughout his text.

Lefebvre only incidentally mentions utopia in his analysis, but the concept and its associations are found repeatedly and provide important points to consider in adjusting our spatial theory. First, Lefebvre notes the "grid on the basis of 'topias'" to which places can be assigned. One of these is, of course, utopia, which he further defines as "places of what has no place, or no longer has a place—the absolute, the divine, or the possible" (1991, 163–64). When Lefebvre uses "absolute space" or "divine space" or "possible space," then, he is also speaking of utopian space, and such space for Lefebvre is utilized by authoritative powers, especially religious or political, to establish space and restrict access to it (1991, 236–40). Thus, Lefebvre continues, utopian space is truly

8. Camp notes, for example, the difficulty which Sirach presents for feminist hermeneutics. The same criticism can be applied to Chronicles, which is not as openly misogynistic as Sirach, but is neither liberating; however, one "positive" portrayal of women in Chronicles is the lack of open criticism of the "foreign woman." The Chronicler does not polemicize against intermarriage, and foreign women are not "personified evil" as is the case in several wisdom texts and in Ezra–Nehemiah.

Other-space, located in such physical places as temples, tombs, palaces, memorials. Lefebvre is clearly following his second category of "representations of space," with its imposed order, signs, codes, and conceived nature. However, it seems unlikely that Lefebvre would characterize his own book as such a repressive representation of space. While he may prefer to locate his own analysis in the liberation of "representational spaces" (Soja's Thirdspace), his explicit comments clearly locate it as a utopian text, as an ideological work, but chiefly as a counter-ideology to the dominant one. Thus, we have returned to the major tenets of utopian theory as discussed in the opening section of this study. Utopian literature is an ideological critique of ideology. Lefebvre's spatial system does not completely account for the ability of a writing in Secondspace to work against other writings in Secondspace. In order words, is Lefebvre correct that his representations of space (Soja's Secondspace) is only about ideological oppression by the "priestly castes and political power" (1991, 237) without also possibly being about criticism of the same ideology?

As ideology, utopia is naturally located by Soja in Secondspace. While recognizing with Lefebvre that Secondspace is the "dominating" space of power, he expands Lefebvre's limited view of this category. It is also space for "the purely creative imagination of some artists and poets" (1996, 67, 79).[9] However, as with Lefebvre, Soja continues to promote Thirdspace as "the chosen spaces for struggle, liberation, emancipation" (1996, 68). Secondspace recedes into the ethereal background, being "entirely ideational, made up of projections into the empirical world from conceived or imagined geographies... [where] the imagined geography tends to become the 'real' geography, with the image or representation coming to define and order the reality" (1996, 79). Soja, finally, also does not account for the ability of Secondspace to resist power, to offer a different geography from the one commonly accepted by the "powers" of Secondspace, and to attempt to define a new reality by a different projection of a different space that reorders space against the status quo. Utopianism, from utopian theory, rejects the claims of "hegemonic powers" who would maintain the current space and its accompanying social system. Utopian space is "Other-space" working for spatial change, and thus for the social change required to bring its new order into the lived world of Thirdspace. Just as Thirdspace is not always about liberation (Camp's view of power in Thirdspace), so Secondspace is not entirely about ideological oppression. Secondspace can also be the realm of "struggle, liberation, emancipation," especially when it takes the shape of utopian literature, writing designed to cause a "disconnect" between the world of the text and the world of the reader. Utopian space critiques the status quo and its representations of space, thereby forcing new constructions of reality to be developed along new ideological tenets in the place of the old complexes. Utopian space creates a space of resistance, a space in which a new society can be formed (Jameson 1995, 196–97).

9. Although Soja notes that Lefebvre includes artists in this second category, Lefebvre never seems to make much of this idea in his analysis.

When this definition of utopian space is brought to spatial theory, the theory shifts once again (if Camp's critique is regarded as the first adjustment). Secondspace is the realm of utopia, and utopia is the realm of revolution. In utopian literature, space is employed to critique the spatial, and thus societal, structure of the present. Utopian space becomes a means of presenting new options for the future. However, it must be remembered, utopia *can* be located on a map, but with inconsistencies or with details that defy depiction. And these spatial anomalies make evident the conflict between reality and utopia.[10] In exploring the spatial anomalies of a utopian text, the reader journeys into Secondspace with the hope of encountering "strange new worlds."

The Utopian Space of Chronicles

Among the many issues of spatiality in Chronicles, I have selected the following to investigate, both of which have inconsistent presentations in the text: (1) foreign space and the land of Israel, and (2) the temple and its state of holiness.[11]

Foreign Space and the Land of Israel
The relationship between foreign nations and Israel in Chronicles is not one of simple condemnation or whole-hearted acceptance. The Philistines and other surrounding nations are often at war with Israel, Israel is invaded by foreign armies, and the final result of Israel's unfaithfulness is exile to Assyria (1 Chr 5:25–26; 2 Chr 30:6–9) and to Babylon (1 Chr 9:1; 2 Chr 29:9; 36:11–21). However, beside these obviously negative encounters there are other statements: God "stirs up the spirit" of the kings of Assyria (1 Chr 5:26), sends Judah into Babylonian exile (1 Chr 6:15; 2 Chr 36:17), speaks (prophetically!) through Pharaoh Neco (2 Chr 35:20–22), and finally "stirs up" the spirit of Cyrus to begin the return from exile and restoration of the temple (2 Chr 36:22–23). In Chronicles, the God of Israel clearly controls history and influences world events. These claims, of course, are not unique to the Chronicler, but are expressed elsewhere —especially in Isaiah (7:20; 10:5–19; 19:1–25; 44:24–45:13). By repeatedly noting God's involvement, the Chronicler is able to infuse disaster with hope for the future since there is no chaos but only the plan of God for his people (just as in Isaiah). Even the disasters of exile to Assyria and to Babylon are muted in Chronicles. The Assyrian deportation only affected the Transjordanian tribes in the explicit comments by the Chronicler (1 Chr 5:25–26) and the theological interpretation of exile to Babylon as a sabbath-rest for the land in fulfillment of prophecy (2 Chr 36:20–23) shifts attention away from the destruction to the future of the people in the land after a limited, rather than extended, period of time. Thus, following the lead of Isaiah, Chronicles overcomes spatial displacement and openly accepts the political power of foreign nations as being

10.   As utopian theory draws so heavily on deconstructionist methods, this is not surprising. Such readings focus on "gaps," "seams," "inconsistencies," and other points of conflict in a text.

11.   See also my treatment of the burial notices in Chronicles as an example of utopian space in Schweitzer 2007, 119–25.

appointed by God. Foreign space is not "Other" space to be feared, but "Other" space used by God for the benefit of Israel and its land. With such a perspective on history, it is difficult to conceive of the Chronicler as an advocate of political revolution against foreign governments, whether Persian or Hellenistic.

With such a portrayal of the great empires, it is not surprising to find a certain degree of openness to foreigners in Chronicles. Indeed, Chronicles makes no secret of intermarriage between Israelites and individuals from other nations, and mentions it without open criticism, even with reference to David and Solomon (e.g. 1 Chr 2:3; 3:1–2; 7:14–19; 2 Chr 8:11; see more on Solomon below and also Knoppers 2001a, b). This is in direct contrast to the restrictions against intermarriage with the seven nations in Deut 7:1–6 and to the exclusivity of Ezra–Nehemiah, with its concern over the "holy seed" of Israel and the purity of its lineage (Ezra 9:2). In Chronicles, Israel's space is not contaminated by the presence of foreigners in it.[12]

The land of Israel as Israel's identifying "space" is thus an important issue in Chronicles. The intimate relationship between land and people in Chronicles, with special reference to the sabbath-rest at the book's conclusion, has been much discussed in scholarship. Such treatments, however, have failed to address sufficiently a particular spatial anomaly: the presence of other nations in the land. While many scholars have noted the nearly complete absence of the exodus in Chronicles, and thus Israel's apparent long-standing claim to the land, few have taken seriously the implications of what is said about these foreigners in Israel's space.

First, never is anything said to the effect that "this is Israel's land, always has been and will be." Such a land theology is absent from Chronicles.[13] According to Chronicles, Israel is exiled and removed from the now desolate land, which rested during the seventy-year absence (2 Chr 36:20–21). Whatever the historical reality, the ideological nature of this claim is significant. The people were in another space during this period.[14] Second, on several occasions the Chronicler notes the presence of other nations which lived in the land prior to or contemporaneously with the Israelites. First Chronicles 4:40 adds the statement that the "former inhabitants there belonged to Ham"; 1 Chr 7:21 mentions the "native-born" people of Gath (a statement that is never applied to Israelites);

12. Similarly, while 2 Kgs 17 and Ezra–Nehemiah do not reflect positively on the northern tribes, often treating them as if they were foreigners, Northerners are not viewed as second class or outside the "true" people of Israel in Chronicles. The northern tribes are still a vital part of Israel, so much so that Israel is incomplete without them. Boer has pursued this point in some detail (1999).

13. Contra Japhet (1989, 334–93); see the opposing view of Williamson (1982, 81).

14. This is not to ignore the claim against those remaining in the land by the *golah* who returned to the land (as in Jer 24), but was this the point in Chronicles (especially since associations with the "Samaritan schism" in Chronicles have more frequently been rejected by scholars for some time now)? Instead, this statement may have been directed against the people who were so corrupt that they had to be removed so that the land could be restored (2 Chr 36:14–16; cf. the land's "vomiting you out" in Lev 18:24–30; 20:22). This is hardly praise for those taken into captivity, and who were thus ancestors of those who would return to rebuild the temple following the rise of Persia (2 Chr 36:14–23).

2 Chr 1:17–18 and 8:7–9 note that Solomon counted the "aliens living in the land" and conscripted them for his building projects including the temple.[15] Thus, despite lacking any reference to Abraham's migration and mentioning the sojourn in Egypt or the Exodus only in passing, the reality of other nations living in the land of Israel and the fact that they were there first are *not omitted* by the Chronicler in his portrayal of Israel's history. Whatever the nature of Israel's claim to the land in the Second Temple period, Chronicles does not invoke the idea that they had always possessed it. Rather, these spatial anomalies, foreigners living in their midst, have been the case for all of Israel's history in the land, including, most likely, the Chronicler's own day.

The relationship of Israel and the land is thus not permanent or exclusive. Foreigners lived here, do live here, and will most certainly continue to live here. But what about Israel's presence in the land? According to Chronicles, the exile removed the people completely from the land. In a prayer by David at the conclusion of his reign (found only in Chronicles), the king makes a strange declaration: "For we are aliens and transients before you [God], as were all our ancestors; our days on the earth are like a shadow, and there is no hope" (1 Chr 29:15). In a sweeping statement comparable to Qoheleth, Chronicles renders all claims about land and privileged access to it moot. The shortness of life neutralizes the ideologized space of the land as a source of unique identity and creates a utopian space beyond the control of any individual or group.[16] The land exists independently of the people, and the people are only temporary journeymen ("residents" is even too permanent a term) through it.

This assessment of foreigners is further supported by the Chronicler's depiction of Solomon. While many commentators have contended that the Chronicler's avoidance of Solomon's many foreign wives and his resulting downfall (as portrayed in 1 Kgs 11:1–8) is an indication of his idealization of this king, most fail to note that the only explicit mention of a wife for Solomon is Pharaoh's daughter, clearly pointing to intermarriage with an Egyptian (2 Chr 8:11). Thus, the Chronicler does not omit Solomon's intermarriage practice, simply his excessiveness. Also, the Chronicler makes no indication that this action in any way diminishes Solomon's status. On the contrary, Solomon is presented as taking what is apparently an appropriate action: he relocates his foreign wife to another house and supplies the reason for it, which is lacking in Kings, "for the places to which the ark of the LORD has come are holy" (2 Chr 8:11). The removal of the apparently unholy foreign woman[17] from a location that has been changed by the presence of God as manifest in the ark thus

---

15. Note that Solomon employs Huram (or Huram-abi), whose mother was a Danite and whose father was Tyrian, to fashion the temple vessels and most of its component parts (2 Chr 2:13).

16. The people are also identified as "aliens and tenants" in the Jubilee legislation of Lev 25:23–24 (which also stands behind the sabbath-rest idea in 2 Chr 36:21), which names God as owner of the land, restricts the ability of Israelites to sell it, and requires them to redeem it.

17. Or, is it simply her status as woman without concern for ethnicity? The text is not specific as to why she is unfit to be where the ark has been. Also, the issue is clearly about the residual holiness left by the ark, which is no longer in the house of David but in the temple.

establishes a hierarchy of space. Some individuals are allowed to be with the ark or to be where it has been, and some individuals cannot be in either of these spaces. In Chronicles, foreigners can pray toward the temple (2 Chr 8:41–43 // 1 Kgs 8:41–43), but there is no evidence that they can enter into it. Thus, space for foreigners in Israel is created via marriage, but such individuals are apparently excluded from the holy spaces of the community. The Chronicler—writing after the time or literary production of Ezra–Nehemiah—presents a positive portrayal of foreign empires and foreign marriages, with only the proviso that they not enter the temple (and then only in passing without any explicit proscription), and creates a utopian space for these foreigners within the society of the Second Temple period.[18]

The Temple and Its State of Holiness
"One of the few points about which all commentators on Chronicles are agreed is that the temple was of central significance to its author" (Williamson 1991, 15). This comment by Williamson is certainly true, and the temple is certainly at the heart of Chronicles. The temple functions as the place of reform, of connection with God, and of societal structure. Chronicles presents the "good" kings of Israel as deeply concerned about the temple and its cult, its organization, and proper operation. Even the conclusion of the book calls for those in exile to "go up" to build the house of God in Jerusalem (2 Chr 36:23). Throughout Chronicles, cultic matters are always the chief concern of restoration.

David explicitly calls the temple a "holy house" (1 Chr 29:3), and as such a space it is a place set apart from the rest of "ordinary space." Its vessels (1 Chr 9:29; 22:19; 2 Chr 5:5) and offerings (2 Chr 30:17; 31:14; 35:13) are holy as well as its attendants. Specifically, only priests and Levites are allowed to enter into it, for they are holy (2 Chr 23:6; 31:18; 35:3). However, even between priests and Levites a distinction is made: only priests may enter into the inner part of the temple while the Levites are excluded (1 Chr 24:19; 2 Chr 29:16). The duties performed in these areas can thus only be undertaken by individuals allowed to be present. Priests and Levites have distinct duties in Chronicles, while Levites on occasion are seen to act as priests but not vice versa (Knoppers 1999). The organization of the priestly courses and Levitical divisions also reflects the need for controlling access to the temple and its cult, if only on a logistical level. These groupings take on special significance in the reforming actions of the various kings who repeatedly reestablish the courses and divisions on the basis of their institution by David and their use in the temple by Solomon. Having "the right person in the right place at the right time" is important for the proper operation of the temple cult.[19] Thus far, Lefebvre's description of temples

18.   Contrast this view in Chronicles with the "utopian society" of Ezek 40–48 which explicitly excludes all foreigners from participation in the temple cult in the sanctuary (44:5–9) and with the apparently laudatory claims in Nehemiah's Memoir that he cleansed the rooms of the temple because of the foreigner Tobiah (Neh 13:4–9) and also removed "everything foreign" from the people (13:30).
19.   Paraphrasing the comments of Endres 2001, 164.

as places of power and control, and thus of imposed Secondspatial order that will inevitably create margins, fits extremely well with this depiction of the temple and its cult in Chronicles.

The physical location of the temple itself (its Firstspace) is of particular importance for Chronicles. The physical location of David's temple site is equated with Mount Moriah, without any explanation as to the significance of this specific locale in the text (2 Chr 3:1). The only other reference to Moriah (or, to the land of Moriah, on a mountain) in the Hebrew Bible is the *Akedah* of Gen 22, the location of Abraham's sacrifice of Isaac.[20] As the Chronicler skips over the "Patriarchal Age" by the summary genealogies, this spatial association drawn from the Torah is highly suggestive. Whether the Chronicler creates this spatial assimilation or is giving written expression to a traditional view,[21] the emphasis falls clearly on the selection of this particular Firstspace by God for sacrifice. Often viewed as a means of legitimation for the temple site based on God's provision of a sacrifice in place of Isaac (Japhet 1993, 552), such a view is not sufficient to explain the relationship of these two spaces. There is no additional evidence that the site of the *Akedah* was revered prior to its reference in Chronicles or that the sacrifice provided by God was viewed as the institution of an Abrahamic cult (i.e. not an issue of establishing a direct lineage back to Abrahamic sacrifice).[22] Rather, the decision for this particular site by David (1 Chr 22:1) returns the reader to David's fear of the angel immediately preceding this selection (1 Chr 21:28–30), to Abraham's fear of God (Gen 22:12), and also to David's fear of God in response to the death of Uzzah caused by touching the ark (1 Chr 13:9–13)—the holy object to be the centerpiece of the holy temple (2 Chr 8:11).[23] Such fear and awe (emotions that function in Thirdspace, especially in the performance of ritual) is fitting for the holy temple and its contents (Firstspace) as they represent the "Other"-space of God (Secondspace).

Also, Solomon relocates his Egyptian wife outside the city of David because "the places to which the ark of the LORD has come are holy" (2 Chr 8:11). In this case, the ark leaves "residual holiness" in its wake en route to the temple. The holiness of the ark has changed these spaces; for what period of time is uncertain, although "forever" seems logical. Such a claim would seem to fit well with the earlier comments about the exclusive holiness of the temple and the restrictions on who may enter it. In addition, the contrast between the proud Uzziah's entrance into the temple to offer incense—explicitly noted as only a priestly duty (2 Chr 26:16–21)—with his son Jotham's righteousness to "not invade the temple of the LORD" (2 Chr 27:2) would seem to support such a reading of the absolute holiness of the temple and the precautions necessary so that the rituals be performed following correct procedures.

20. Japhet notes that this allusion is "unmistakable" and that the association of the two sites appears for the first known time in Chronicles (1993, 551).

21. Japhet notes both of these possibilities (1993, 552).

22. Japhet assumes such is the case without providing any additional evidence (1993, 552).

23. It is worth noting that the two instances in Chronicles in which David is portrayed in less-than-flattering terms are the ark incident of 1 Chr 13:1–14 and the census in 1 Chr 21:1–30, which immediately precedes the selection of the temple site in 22:1.

So far, Chronicles appears to serve as a text reinforcing the perspective of the elite who control the spatial matrix (an excellent example of Secondspace in the sense of an oppressive elitist ideology). Even here in the description of the holy temple, however, spatial anomalies arise which shatter any simplistic understanding of the efficacy of the cult and its location as it is presented in Chronicles. Chronicles uses spatial anomalies to contest the claims made by those in control of the temple, and to bring about a criticism even of this holy space.

In Boer's analysis of utopian space and the temple, he focuses on the inflated and disproportional dimensions of the temple and its vestibule (2 Chr 3:3–4). He concludes that the inability to represent this image on a spatial map is an indication of utopian literature (Boer 1997, 146). Yet this is not the only anomalous representation of the temple space. More important than the dimensions of the temple are two instances that challenge the absolute holiness of the temple space and its cult.

The first example: as many scholars have noted, when the boy Joash is hidden in the temple for six years, special notice is made that the one responsible is Jehoshabeath, daughter of King Jehoram and the wife of the priest Jehoiada, who also resides with him (2 Chr 22:11–12). The text of 2 Kgs 11:1–3 mentions only the Davidic side of Jehoshabeath's identity; that she is the wife of the leading priest is the Chronicler's own detail. Thus, many scholars have speculated that this information was necessary to explain the presence of a woman in the temple. This reasoning is then compared with the additional comment in the following verses that only priests and Levites may enter the temple, for they are holy (2 Chr 23:6). Thus, according to these scholars, the Chronicler has preserved the holiness of the temple space by making this woman into the "high priest's" wife (Nelson 1993, 135).

Such a view has significant problems, however. First, in this line of reasoning, Jehoiada, the Chronicler's "ideal high priest" (Williamson 1982, 314) would be in violation of the strict marriage laws for "high priests" ("the priest exalted above his brothers") in Lev 21:10–15. These "holiest" of priests are required to marry a virgin of their own kin, a restriction not imposed on other priests. As Jehoiada, according only to Chronicles, has married the daughter of the Davidic king, he stands in direct violation of this stipulation. Given the paucity of explicit commands in the Torah about "high priests," it would seem unlikely that the Chronicler would so blatantly contradict this command (if it did exist at the time of his composition, which is certainly a logical assumption).[24] Second, scholars arguing that Chronicles protects the sanctity of the temple then fail to discuss the fact that such an interpretative move does not affect the status of the boy Joash, a male but also a Davidide, who lives in the temple. If Uzziah the Davidide is prevented from entering, and his son Jotham is praised for his restraint, then what about this non-priestly and non-Levitical toddler in the holy space? Even further, the text provides no justification for the nurse accompanying him in the temple. This incident is clearly a case of the holy space being

---

24. See the further comments in Schweitzer 2003, 397–99.

occupied by people who should not be there; indeed, even the Chronicler's supposed "solution" to this apparent problem from his source causes his leading priest to be disobedient to Torah stipulations. Turning to utopian theory, a suggestion: the ideology of the holiness of the temple and its personnel are critiqued by placing others in this space and using their presence to undermine the "all-or-nothing" approach to the holiness of sacred space. While the Chronicler will not have a "free-for-all" in the temple (2 Chr 23:6), there is a greater good, a *better alternative reality*, a utopia, toward which to strive. The restoration of proper worship (even at the cost of violating holy space or making its leading personnel blameworthy) supercedes perceptions about the restrictions of holy space.

The second example: the reforms of the temple and the celebration of Passover under Hezekiah (2 Chr 29–30) are another prime source of spatial anomalies. First, Hezekiah orders the priests to offer the people's sacrifices, but a problem soon arises—there are not enough priests to accomplish the task (2 Chr 29:31–36). The solution: Levites, who were "more upright in heart," will act as priests until enough priests are able to be sanctified. So much for "right people in the right place"! And yet, Chronicles concludes this event by stating: "Thus the service of the house of the LORD was restored." What about the holy space of the temple? Has its holiness not been violated by these Levites not in their proper space? Evidently not. Ritual, existing and adapting in the "lived space" of Thirdspace, appears more important than the restricted Secondspatiality of defined "sacred space" alone. But the spatial anomalies during the celebration of Passover are even more astonishing.

Hezekiah celebrates Passover in the second month (not in its "proper time" of the first month) because of the insufficient number of sanctified priests (2 Chr 30:2–3). Just as before, the individuals designated to stand in the holy space cannot be there, so now the sacred time must be adjusted (here, space trumps time). This problem of "unholiness" also extends to the people from Ephraim, Manasseh, Issachar, and Zebulun, who came to the celebration but did not sanctify themselves. However, even these individuals ate the *pesach* "otherwise than as prescribed" (2 Chr 30:18). The response: *not* condemnation for violation of ritual law or additional sacrifice to atone for this sin; instead, Hezekiah prays for God to pardon those "who set their hearts to seek God...even though [this was done] not in accordance with the sanctuary's rules of cleanness [!]" (2 Chr 30:19). And God's response: no fire, brimstone, or booming voice rebuking the people; instead God "healed the people" (v. 20). The narrative then continues with a comparison to the glorious days of Solomon and ultimately notes that blessings for the people by the priests and Levites "came to [God's] holy dwelling in heaven" (2 Chr 30:26–27). Thus, all of these apparent violations of the sacred space of the temple stand in marked contrast to the quality of the people's worship. By such spatial anomalies, the Chronicler creates utopian space in this text for variation in ritual practice, for the priority given to the heart "seeking God," and even for the unclean to participate fully in the festival despite the written proscriptions. This understanding of these spatial anomalies radically challenges the extremely common view that the Chronicler's chief concern was for proper ritual and proper respect of the holiness of the temple.

Thus, combined with the earlier comments on Joash, Chronicles demonstrates a masterful critique of claims concerning the temple's Secondspace and Thirdspace. The temple is still holy in Chronicles, but its significance and accessibility have been drastically altered by spatial anomalies introduced in the narrative. By employing the apparently standard view of the temple's holiness and critiquing it through these spatial anomalies, Chronicles exists as a text (thus, Secondspace) which forces a reconsideration of the temple's own Secondspace.

Conclusion

If these examples of spatial anomalies in Chronicles and the related issue of its reformulation of "utopian space" are accepted, the book of Chronicles may no longer be read as a treatise designed to radically and thoroughly legitimize the present situation of the Second Temple period. Rather, this method suggests that a more subtle (and often open) critique of the power structures present at the time of the Chronicler may be seen in the descriptions of institutions and organizational schemes. Chronicles is thus not a lengthy explanation of "why this is the way it is." Instead of providing a past for the present, Chronicles provides a new past for a different future. Such a rejection of the status quo and the formation of social critique occur—at least in part—after an exploration of the utopian space in Chronicles and an attempt to understand the significance of the anomalies found there.

Works Cited

Boer, Roland T. 1997. *Novel Histories: The Fiction of Biblical Criticism*. Playing the Texts 2. Sheffield: Sheffield Academic Press.

_____. 1999. Utopian Politics in 2 Chronicles 10–13. Pages 360–94 in *The Chronicler as Author: Studies in Text and Texture*. Edited by M. Patrick Graham and Steven L. McKenzie. JSOTSup 263. Sheffield: Sheffield Academic Press.

Camp, Claudia V. 2002. Storied Space, or, Ben Sira "Tells" a Temple. Pages 64–80 in *"Imagining" Biblical Worlds: Studies in Spatial, Social and Historical Construction in Honor of James W. Flanagan*. Edited by David M. Gunn and Paula M. McNutt. JSOTSup 359. Sheffield: Sheffield Academic Press.

Endres, John C. 2001. Joyful Worship in Second Temple Judaism. Pages 155–88 in *Passion, Vitality, and Foment: The Dynamics of Second Temple Judaism*. Edited by Lamontte M. Luker. Harrisburg, Pa.: Trinity Press International.

Flanagan, James W. 2000. Space. Pages 239–44 in *Handbook of Postmodern Biblical Interpretation*. Edited by A. K. M. Adam. St. Louis: Chalice.

Geus, Klaus. 2000. Utopie und Geographie: Zum Weltbild der Griechen in frühhellenisticher Zeit. *Orbis Terrarum* 6:55–90.

Grey, Christopher, and Christiana Garsten. 2002. Organized and Disorganized Utopias: An Essay on Presumption. Pages 9–23 in *Utopia and Organization*. Edited by Martin Parker. Sociological Review Monographs. Oxford: Blackwell.

Jameson, Fredric. 1988. Of Islands and Trenches: Neutralization and the Production of Utopian Discourse. Pages 75–101 in *The Ideologies of Theory: Essays 1971–1986*. Vol. 2, *The Syntax of History*. Theory and History of Literature 49. Minneapolis: University of Minnesota Press, 1988.

———. 1995. Is Space Political? Pages 192–205 in *Anyplace*. Edited by Cynthia C. Davidson. New York: Anyone Corp.

Japhet, Sara. 1989. *The Ideology of the Book of Chronicles and Its Place in Biblical Thought*. Translated by Anna Barber. Beiträge zur Erforschung des Alten Testaments und des antiken Judentum 9. Frankfurt am Main: Peter Lang.

———. 1993. *I & II Chronicles: A Commentary*. Old Testament Library. Louisville: Westminster/John Knox.

Jones, Sarah Rees. 2001. Thomas More's "Utopia" and Medieval London. Pages 117–35 in *Pragmatic Utopias: Ideals and Communities, 1200–1630*. Edited by Rosemary Horrox and Sarah Rees Jones. Cambridge: Cambridge University Press.

Knoppers, Gary N. 1999. Hierodules, Priests, or Janitors? The Levites in Chronicles and the History of the Israelite Priesthood. *JBL* 118:49–72.

———. 2001a. The Davidic Genealogy: Some Contextual Considerations from the Ancient Mediterranean World. *Transeuphratène* 22:35–50.

———. 2001b. Intermarriage, Social Complexity, and Ethnic Diversity in the Genealogy of Judah. *JBL* 120:15–30.

Lefebvre, Henri. 1991. *The Production of Space*. Translated by Donald Nicholson-Smith. Oxford: Blackwell.

Marin, Louis. 1984. *Utopics: Spatial Play*. Translated by Robert A. Vollrath. Contemporary Studies in Philosophy and the Human Sciences. Atlantic Heights, N.J.: Humanities Press.

———. 1993. The Frontiers of Utopia. Pages 7–16 in *Utopias and the Millennium*. Edited by Krishan Kumar and Stephen Bann. Critical Views. London: Reaktion.

Nelson, Richard D. 1993. *Raising Up a Faithful Priest: Community and Priesthood in Biblical Theology*. Louisville: Westminster/John Knox.

Schweitzer, Steven J. 2003. The High Priest in Chronicles: An Anomaly in a Detailed Description of the Temple Cult. *Biblica* 84:388–402.

———. 2005. Reading Utopia in Chronicles. Ph.D. diss., University of Notre Dame.

———. 2007. *Reading Utopia in Chronicles*. LHBOTS 442. London: T&T Clark International.

Soja, Edward W. 1989. *Postmodern Geographies: The Reassertion of Space in Critical Social Theory*. London: Verso.

———. 1996. *Thirdspace: Journeys to Los Angeles and Other Real-and-Imaginary Places*. Cambridge, Mass.: Blackwell.

Suvin, Darko. 1974. The River-Side Trees, or SF & Utopia. *Minnesota Review* 2–3:108–15.

———. 1979. *Metamorphoses of Science Fiction: On the Poetics and History of a Literary Genre*. New Haven: Yale University Press.

Williamson, H. G. M. 1982. *1 and 2 Chronicles*. New Century Bible Commentary. Grand Rapids: Eerdmans.

———. 1991. The Temple in Chronicles. Pages 15–31 in *Templum Amicitiae: Essays on the Second Temple Presented to Ernst Bammel*. Edited by William Horbury. JSNTSup 48. Sheffield: Sheffield Academic Press.

INDEXES

INDEX OF REFERENCES

INDEX OF AUTHORS